Shelby Foote

THE CIVIL WAR

A NARRATIVE

Shelby Foote

THE CIVIL WAR

A NARRATIVE

3

★ ★ ★

YORKTOWN
TO CEDAR MOUNTAIN

40th Anniversary Edition

BY SHELBY FOOTE
AND THE EDITORS OF TIME-LIFE BOOKS,
ALEXANDRIA, VIRGINIA

All these were honoured in their generations,
and were the glory of their times.

There be of them,
that have left a name behind them,
that their praises might be reported.

And some there be, which have no memorial;
who are perished, as though they had never been;
and are become as though they had never been born;
and their children after them.

But these were merciful men,
whose righteousness hath not been forgotten.

With their seed shall continually remain
a good inheritance,
and their children are within the covenant.

Their seed standeth fast,
and their children for their sakes.

Their seed shall remain for ever,
and their glory shall not be blotted out.

Their bodies are buried in peace;
but their name liveth for evermore.

— ECCLESIASTICUS XLIV

Contents

★ ★ ★

★

Prologue

In the few months since the disastrous Confederate defeat of Federal forces at Ball's Bluff in October 1861, the tide had seemingly turned, and Northerners began to have much to celebrate. Combined naval and army operations had taken New Orleans, Baton Rouge, and Natchez, securing much of the Mississippi River from the south, and had also taken Island Ten, Fort Pillow, and Memphis from the north, leaving only a central stretch of the Father of Waters in rebel hands. Confederate fleets, both built and a-building to defend the Mississippi, had been virtually destroyed in the process. All of the five border states, with the exception of Lincoln's beloved eastern Tennessee, were in the Union camp. Grant's capture of Fort Donelson had secured Kentucky, and Curtis's Federal defeat of Van Dorn's Confederates at Pea Ridge, Arkansas, had held Missouri for the Union.

In the bloodiest battle of the war thus far, Federals had absorbed and repelled a staggering Confederate attack around Shiloh Chapel, near Pittsburg Landing in Tennessee. That victory, coupled with a slow advance south and west that forced the Confederates to evacuate their base at Corinth, brought much of western Tennessee and some of northern Mississippi under Federal control. Federal troops had also stymied Confederate designs on New Mexico and the far Transmississippi West.

In addition, although cotton reserves in Europe were rapidly declining, there was no sign that England and France were any closer to supporting the Confederacy than they had been in months past.

In the East, the Union ironclad U.S.S. *Monitor* had arrived in time to neutralize the C.S.S. *Merrimac-Virginia* and the Yankees had wrested more Atlantic coast positions, Roanoke Island and Fort Pulaski among them, from rebel control; thus the Federal "Anaconda" drew its coils ever tighter around the Confederacy. These seizures, coupled with a huge military reorganization and build-up around Washington City under General McClellan, forced the Confederates to withdraw south from the Centreville-Manassas area to better defend the southern capital. And to heighten northern elation, McClellan, with the largest unified force either side had gathered thus far, was moving around the rebels' right flank for a massed drive up the York-James peninsula for an attack on Richmond itself.

But the Federal commanders were about to revert to their cautious form. As the Federals advanced in the West, "Old Brains" Halleck, the Union commander there, long on theory but short on action, grew nervous. Those very successes had lengthened lines of communications, and he held up his offensive to resupply and regroup, dispersing his forces throughout the recently gained areas. The Confederates would take advantage of the delay, launching devastating cavalry raids by Nathan Bedford Forrest and John Hunt Morgan that would shatter Halleck's attempts to consolidate his holdings. In addition, Confederate Braxton Bragg defeated Federal Don Carlos Buell in the race to control Chattanooga, thus leaving eastern Tennessee vulnerable to southern invasion. And one lone ironclad, the C.S.S. *Arkansas*, on a suicidal mission, would split and scatter the Federal fleet on the Mississippi, causing the Yankees to abandon Baton Rouge.

Throughout the build-up and the move to the Peninsula, McClellan had been methodical, plodding. Lincoln had wheedled, cajoled, and finally ordered "Little Mac" into action. Once on the Peninsula, believing he was outmanned by Joe Johnston's Confederates, he hesitated. While McClellan prepared and finally began a slow-moving siege through Yorktown and Williamsburg to the Chickahominy River, Robert E. Lee, President Davis's military adviser, encouraged Stonewall Jackson to engage the Federal forces in the Shenandoah Valley. His presence there would threaten the Union capital while the bulk of U.S. troops were down on the Peninsula. The decoy worked, and worried Federal officials withheld men and supplies from McClellan.

As Jackson harassed, and defeated, three separate Federal forces in the Valley, McClellan's Federals traded blows with Joe Johnston's Confederates at Fair Oaks and Seven Pines along the Chickahominy. In the struggle, Johnston was wounded and Lee was given command of the southern army in the field. For Seven Days Lee, joined by Jackson, would batter and pursue McClellan during a "change of base" southward to the James River. Neither side would perform very well and, after the seventh day's action at Malvern Hill, McClellan went into camp along the James, farther from Richmond than he had been a week before. The Confederate commander looked for options.

With McClellan dormant to the south, Lee sent forces under Jackson north to meet the threat of Federal General Pope's advance on Richmond from that direction. Pope would be stopped at Cedar Mountain to await reinforcements behind the Rapidan.

What had been a great string of successes for the Union was coming to an end. As dark clouds spread over the North, the sun appeared to shine brightly on the South.

★   ★   ★

Shelby Foote

*Federal infantrymen march
by a park of mortars and
siege guns massed at Yorktown
for McClellan's 1862 drive
up the Virginia Peninsula.*

ONE

Davis Frets; Lincoln — McClellan

1862 ★ ★ ★ ★ ★ **D**isaster came in various forms this spring, and it moved to various tempos. In the West it came like fireworks, looming after a noisy rush and casting a lurid glow. Whole states, whole armies fell at once or had large segments broken off by the tread of the invader. Kentucky and Missouri, most of Tennessee, much of Arkansas, North Alabama and North Mississippi were lost in rapid succession, along with 30,000 fighting men, dead or in northern prison camps, and finally New Orleans, Memphis, and the fleets that had been built — or, worse, were being built — to hold the river that ran between them. That was how it reached the West. In the East it came otherwise: not with a gaudy series of eruptions and collapses and attendant pillars of fire, but with a sort of inexorable hover, an inching-forward through mist and gloom, as if it were conserving energy for an even more spectacular climax: the collapse of the national capital, the destruction of the head and front of Government itself. On damp evenings, such as the one that fell on May Day, the grumble of McClellan's guns at Yorktown, faintly audible from Richmond's hills, reached listeners through what seemed to them the twilight of the gods.

Nowhere, east or west, had there been a victory to celebrate since Ball's Bluff in October seven months ago. Foreign intervention, the cure-all for-

★

merly assured by early spring because that was when England's cotton reserves were supposed to be exhausted, now seemed further away than ever. "There are symptoms that the Civil War cannot very long be protracted," the once friendly London *Times* was saying. "Let its last embers burn down to the last spark without being trodden out by our feet." Confederates could tell themselves they had known all along that the English had never made a habit of retrieving other people's chestnuts; but additional, less deniable disappointments loomed much nearer. Although the near-exhaustion of the nation's war supplies, especially powder, was kept secret, other effects of the naval blockade were all too well known. After a disastrous attempt at price control was abandoned, the regulated items having simply disappeared from grocery shelves, prices went up with a leap. Meat was 50¢ a pound, butter 75¢, coffee $1.50, and tea $10: all in contrast

---

There were whispers of secret and mysterious Union meetings, and one morning a black coffin was found suggestively near the Executive Mansion, a noosed rope coiled on its lid.

---

to cotton, which had fallen to 5¢. Salt — "Lot's wife" in the slang of the day — was scarce after the loss of the Kanawha works, and sugar went completely out of sight with the news of the fall of New Orleans. What was more, all this took place in an atmosphere not only of discouragement, but also of suspicion. Treasonable slogans were being chalked on fences and walls: "Union men to the rescue!" "Now is the time to rally round the Old Flag!" "God bless the Stars and Stripes!" There were whispers of secret and mysterious Union meetings, and one morning a black coffin was found suggestively near the Executive Mansion, a noosed rope coiled on its lid.

Few citizens approved of the coffin threat, but many approved of its implication as to where the blame for their present troubles lay, and so did a number of their elected representatives. The permanent Congress was different from the one that had come to Richmond from Montgomery — not so much in composition, however, as in outlook. Though for the most part they were the same men, reëlected, they served under different circumstances, the bright dawn having given way to clouds. A member who had resigned to enter the army, but who kept in touch with his former colleagues, told his wife, "It seems that things are coming to this pass; to be a patriot you must hate Davis." They took their cue from R. B. Rhett, whose Charleston *Mercury* was saying, "Jefferson

★

Davis now treats all men as if they were idiotic insects." One among them who felt that way was Yancey. Back from his fruitless European mission, he was angrily demanding to know why Virginia had twenty-nine generals and Alabama only four. Another was Tom Cobb, who wrote home that he and his fellows were secretly debating the deposition of Davis. "He would be deposed," Cobb declared, "if the Congress had any more confidence in Stephens than in him."

If they could not get rid of him, they could at least try the next best thing by limiting his powers: especially in the conduct of military affairs. This had been the basis for the virulent attack on Benjamin, who administered the War Department under the close supervision of his chief. Reasoning that a professional soldier would be less pliant, they attempted to oust Benjamin by recommending R. E. Lee for the position. When Davis refused to make the change, on grounds that the law required a civilian at the post, Congress retaliated with an act calling for the appointment of a commanding general who would have full authority to take charge of any army in the field whenever he thought best. Davis vetoed the measure as a violation of his rights as Commander in Chief, but at the same time — it was early March by then — ordered Lee "to duty at the seat of government," where he would be charged with the conduct of military operations "under the direction of the President." Thus Davis frustrated his enemies in Congress. He gained a military secretary — "an orderly sergeant," one newspaper sneered — without sacrificing one jot of his constitutional prerogative. Lee saw well enough what it came to. Returning to Richmond from his work on the South Atlantic coastal defenses, he observed: "I cannot see either advantage or pleasure in my duties. But I will not complain, but do the best I can."

His best was better than might have been expected, considering the limitations of his authority and his early failures in the field. Mainly what he accomplished was done through tactful handling of the President, whose admission that "events have cast on our arms and hopes the gloomiest shadows" Lee now saw at first hand was the mildest possible statement of conditions. Not only was there a crippling shortage of weapons, it now appeared probable that there soon would be a lack of men to shoulder the few they had. The so-called "bounty and furlough law" having proved a failure, except as a disruptive influence, few of the volunteers whose Sumter-inspired one-year enlistments would expire in April seemed willing to forego at least a vacation at home before signing up again, and many were saying quite openly that they were through with army life for good. In the heat of their conviction that they had earned a rest, the already badly outnumbered southern armies seemed likely to melt away just as the northern juggernaut was scheduled to gather speed in the East as in the West. Virginia had already met the problem by providing for a general enrollment in the state militia of all citizens between the ages of eighteen and forty-five, to be used as replacements for the men whose army enlistments expired. Under the influence of Lee, Davis proposed more stringent measures on a larger scale. In a late-March message to Congress he recommended outright conscription, within the same age bracket, throughout the Confederacy — to make sure, he said, that the burden of fighting did not fall "exclusively on the most ardent and patriotic."

Congress debated hotly, then on April 16, after lowering the upper age limit to thirty-five, passed the first national conscription law in American history. They passed it because they knew it was necessary, but they blamed Davis for having made it necessary by adopting the "dispersed defensive," which they said had dampened national enthusiasm. His reply — that "without military stores, without the workshops to create them, without the power to import them, necessity not choice has compelled us to occupy strong positions and everywhere to confront the enemy without reserves" — did nothing to assuage the anger of the States Righters, who saw in conscription a repudiation of the principles for which the war was being fought. Georgia's governor Joseph E. Brown flatly declared that no "act of the Government of the United States prior to the secession of Georgia struck a blow at constitutional liberty so fell as has been struck by the conscription act." The fire-eaters, already furious at having been denied high offices, renewed their attacks on Davis as a despot. He replied in a letter to a friend, "When everything is at stake and the united power of the South alone can save us, it is sad to know that men can deal in such paltry complaints and tax their ingenuity to slander because they are offended in not getting office. . . . If we can achieve our independence, the office seekers are welcome to the one I hold."

A Confederate recruiting broadside from Tennessee warns potential draftees to avoid the onus of conscription by volunteering for military service in a neighborhood unit.

However, the critics were in full bay now and were not to be turned aside by scorn or reason. Ominously, they pointed out that Napoleon's rise to absolute power had been accomplished by just such an act of conscription. Nothing Davis said or did was above suspicion. Even his turning to the solace of religion — up till now he had never been a formal member of any church — was seen as a possibly sinister action. "The President is thin and haggard," a War Department clerk observed in mid-April, "and it has been whispered that he will immediately be baptised and confirmed. I hope so, because it may place a great gulf between him and the descendant of those who crucified the Saviour. Nevertheless, some of his enemies allege that professions of Christianity have sometimes been the premeditated accompaniments of usurpation. It was so with Cromwell and Richard III."

The descendant referred to, of course, was the clerk's former department chief, Benjamin, now head of the State Department. He was as skillful an administrator as ever, but the problems here were not the kind that could be solved by rapid pigeon-holing. Europe was reacting to the news of Union successes along the line of the Mississippi, and that reaction worked strongly against Confederate recognition. Slidell was beginning to weary of the French emperor's slippery courtesies, which led to nothing above-board or official, and Mason was suffering from the same feeling of affront that had vanquished Yancey. He wrote that he intended to present his next proposal for recognition "as a demand of *right;* and if refused — as I have little doubt it would be — to follow the refusal by a note, that I did not consider it compatible with the dignity of my government, and perhaps with my own self-respect, to remain longer in England." Benjamin's smile faded, for once, as he replied, imploring Mason not to act rashly. His mere presence in London was of enormous value; he must await eventualities.

Fortunately, the Virginian had not acted on his impulse, but his patience was wearing thin, and this was one more worry that had to be passed along to Davis. He had tried to steel his harrowed nerves against the criticisms flung at him from all sides, telling his wife: "I wish I could learn just to let people alone who snap at me — in forbearance and charity to turn away as well from the cats as the snakes." But it was too much for him. He could approach his work with humility, but not his critics. When they snapped he snapped back. Nor was he highly skilled as an arbitrator; he had too much admiration and sympathy for those who would not yield, whatever their cause, to be effective at reconciling opponents. In fact, this applied to a situation practically in his own back yard. The White House stood on a tall hill, surrounded by other mansions. On the plain below were the houses of the poor, whose sons had formed a gang called the Butcher Cats, sworn to eternal hatred of the Hill Cats, the children of the gentry on the hill. The two gangs had rock fights and occasional gouging

★

matches. After one particularly severe battle, in which his oldest son was in-volved, Davis walked down the hill to try his hand at arbitration. He made them a speech, referring to the Butcher Cats as future leaders of the nation. One of them replied: "President, we like you. We don't want to hurt any of your boys. But we aint *never* going to be friends with them Hill Cats."

Davis came back up the hill.

★ ★ ★   *E*verywhere Lee had been in this war he had arrived to find disaster looming ready-made, and this was no excep-tion. Militarily as well as politically, the mid-March outlook in Virginia was bleak indeed. Federal combinations totaling well over 200,000 men were threatening less than 70,000 Confederates strung out along an arc whose chord extended northwest-southeast through Richmond. At the lower end, Huger held Norfolk with 13,000, threatened from below by Burnside with the same number. Down near the tip of the York-James peninsula, Major Gener-al John B. Magruder's 12,000 were intrenched in front of Fort Monroe and its garrison of the same number. Northward, after retreating to their new position at Fredericksburg and along the near bank of the Rapidan, Johnston's 37,000 had been followed as far as Manassas by McClellan, who had 175,000 effectives in and out of the Washington defenses. Both main armies — the Army of Northern Virginia, as Lee now began to style it, and the Army of the Potomac — had detachments in the Shenandoah Valley, where Jackson with 5000 was falling back before Major General Nathaniel P. Banks with twice as many. Final-ly, at the upper or western end of this long arc, beyond Staunton, a little force of 2800 under Brigadier General Edward Johnson prepared to do what it could to block Frémont's proposed descent of the Alleghenies with McClellan's old army of 12,500, which in time would be doubled, despite McClellan's protests, by ac-cretions from his new one.

Much of this was unknown to Lee — especially enemy strengths, which in general were overestimated; the Confederate spy system was yielding very little information these days — but one thing was quite clear. After leaving a sizeable garrison to hold the Washington intrenchments, McClellan's large main body could slide anywhere along that arc, or rather under cover just be-yond it, then bull straight through for Richmond, outnumbering three-to-one — or for that matter ten-to-one, depending on where it struck — any force that stood in its path. Just now its actions were suspicious. After following Johnston's army as far as Manassas, it turned mysteriously back and reëntered the cordon of forts around the northern capital. This seemed to indicate that it was about to start its slide, but before Lee could even begin to try to second-guess its destina-tion, news arrived from the south that upset his already inadequate dispositions: Burnside had taken New Bern. This was a challenge that had to be met, for he

★

*Confederate planners in central Virginia faced threats
from Federal armies massing in Northern Virginia near
Washington, the Shenandoah Valley, and western Virginia.*

was now within sixty miles of Richmond's only direct rail connection with the South Atlantic states. Lee met it in the only way he could: by weakening what was far too weak already. Detaching several regiments from Huger at Norfolk and two brigades from Johnston's right wing at Fredericksburg, he sent them south into North Carolina under Major General Theophilus Holmes, a native of the threatened area.

The following week, March 23, Stonewall Jackson turned on Banks at Kernstown, intending to "inflict a terrible wound" on what he thought was a small segment, but soon retreated, badly cut up himself, when the segment turned out to be a full division. One more defeat was added to the growing list, though the news was less discouraging than it might have been, arriving as it did on the heels of more disturbing information. Just as Lee returned to giving the main danger — McClellan — his main attention, Huger reported by telegraph that more than twenty transports had come down Chesapeake Bay the night before and were disembarking troops at Old Point Comfort, across the way. Soon afterward, this alarming news was confirmed by a wire from Magruder calling urgently for reinforcements. The force confronting him, he said, had risen to 35,000 overnight. Neither general identified the enemy units, but Lee considered their arrival a probable sign that McClellan had started his slide along the arc.

However, even if Lee had been certain of this, he still could not be certain of their goal. They might be on their way to Burnside for operations in North Carolina. They might be mounting an offensive against Norfolk. They might be intended as a diversion to hold Magruder in position while the main body jumped on Johnston. Or they might be the advance of McClellan's whole army, arriving for an all-out drive up the Peninsula. Until he knew which of these possibilities was (or were) at least probable, he would be taking an enormous risk in strengthening the arc at any point by weakening it at another. To lose Norfolk, for example, would be to lose the *Virginia,* which was all that was keeping the Federal gunboats from wrecking Magruder's right flank on their way up the James to bombard Richmond. Or to weaken Johnston's army, already reduced by more than ten percent as a result of detaching the two brigades for Holmes, might be to expose that mainstay of the Confederate defense to utter destruction.

While awaiting further indications, Lee warned Huger and Magruder to be ready for mutual assistance, one to reinforce the other as soon as events showed which was the Federal objective, Norfolk or Yorktown. Meanwhile, the water batteries along the James were strengthened, particularly the ones at Drewry's Bluff, eight miles below Richmond, and the city's scant reserves — two regiments of infantry and some odd squadrons of cavalry — were dispatched to Magruder, who was told to put on as brave a show as possible in the face of the build-up at Fort Monroe. If it became necessary to give ground, he was told to yield it stubbornly, fighting all the way to the gates of the city, sixty miles in his rear. Magruder answered excitedly that a council of war, held the night before, had voted to evacuate Yorktown unless 10,000 reinforcements were sent to him at once. Lee replied that councils of war were always timid in such situations, then repeated his instructions: keep up a bold front and yield nothing except to absolute pressure. He would send him what he could.

★

Whatever he sent him would have to come from Johnston, who had already expressed his unwillingness to furnish any more troops for other commanders. He would bring his whole army down, if ordered, but he was opposed to piecemeal reinforcement as a violation of sound principles. Concentration, not dispersal, was the answer, he declared. He could spare two more brigades — another ten percent of his original force — but that was all. Lee took them, duly thankful for small favors; sent one to Magruder, salving his anxiety a bit, and one to Holmes, hoping thus to keep Burnside out of the squeeze play; and then proceeded to exercise on the touchy Johnston the same tact and delicacy he was using simultaneously in his dealings with Davis, who was quite as touchy. Lighthorse Harry Lee and Peter Johnston had soldiered together in the First Revolution; now their sons worked together in the Second. During the ten days between March 24, when the arrival of the transports was reported, and April 4, Lee managed by gradual detachment to transfer three of Johnston's six divisions from the Rapidan to the James. By the latter date, the Army of Northern Virginia — exclusive of Jackson, out in the Valley — had been reduced to 23,000, while Magruder had 31,500 troops either with him or on the way.

Brigadier General John B. Magruder led Confederates at Yorktown defending Virginia's Peninsula.

They were in capable hands and well employed. If Magruder was high-strung and overimaginative by ordinary standards, it presently developed that these qualities, so doubtful in a military leader, could be positive advantages in an extraordinary situation, such as the one that involved him now. A fifty-two-year-old Virginian, tall and flamboyantly handsome, with a great shock of dark hair, bushy sideburns, and a large but carefully barbered mustache — "Prince John," he had been called in the old army — he spoke with a lisp except when he sang in a clear tenor, as he often did, songs of his own composition. That had been his greatest spare-time pleasure: staging concerts and amateur theatricals, in which he took a leading role, to relieve the tedium of peacetime garrison duty.

Now he had a chance to exercise his talents on a larger scale and for a more dead-ly purpose. Exploiting to the full Lee's admonition to show a brave front to the heavily reinforced enemy, he staged an extravaganza with a cast of thousands, playing as it were to a packed house. He bristled aggressively whenever he imag-ined a Yankee spyglass trained in his direction, shifting his artillery from point to point along his line and firing noisily at anything in sight. No wheeze was too old for Magruder to employ it. One morning he sent a column along a road that was heavily wooded except for a single gap in plain view of the enemy outposts. All day the gray files swept past in seemingly endless array, an army gathering in thousands among the pines for an offensive. They were no such thing, of course. Like a low-budgeted theatrical director producing the effect with an army of su-pernumeraries, Magruder was marching a single battalion round and around, past the gap, then around under cover, and past the gap again.

He had the men working as well as parading; the buskin was supple-mentary to the spade. Utilizing the old British earthworks around Yorktown, moldering since the days of the Revolution, they dug furiously down to the Warwick River, which was dammed near its mouth and at several points up-stream to create an intermittent moat in front of the high ground leading south-ward to the James. This was the first peninsular line, fourteen miles in length: a great deal too long for the number of men available to defend it. Its principal drawback, however, was that the flanks were open to naval bombardment if the Union warships decided to brave the *Virginia* on the right or the additional wa-ter battery on the left, across the York at Gloucester Point. Ten miles in his rear, just east of Williamsburg, Magruder was constructing a second defensive line, though in fact it was not so much a line as it was a sort of rally-point in case the first gave way. Here he had two streams to protect his flanks from infantry as-sault, one flowing north, the other south. On the high ground in the center, just in front of the old colonial capital, he was improvising a bastioned earth-work which he or his officers, after the Thespian custom of sometimes naming a theater for a star, christened Fort Magruder. This second peninsular line had all the drawbacks of the first, plus certain intrinsic weaknesses all its own. Magruder was not a skilled engineer; he admitted it, and even complained about it. But he tried to make up in energy for what he lacked in skill. A dozen small redoubts were scattered about for the fort's protection; fields of fire were cleared by felling trees; additional rifle pits were dug, extending the line behind the tidal creeks. Magruder was doing the best he could.

In case that best was not enough — which seemed likely, considering the odds and limitations — Lee had a third line under construction, forty miles behind the second and within ten miles of Richmond. Its right was anchored on the James and its left on the Chickahominy, a boggy stream which also covered a portion of the front with a tributary known as White Oak Swamp. This was

★

the strongest of the three peninsular lines, being immune from naval attack, but Lee did not want to use it until he had to. Resistance below would give him time to bring up whatever troops he could spare from other points and to complete the reorganization now in progress while Congress debated conscription. That was why he was sending all the men he could lay hands on, including half of Johnston's army, down to Yorktown.

For a time he feared that he had guessed wrong. The Federals were strangely inactive at Fort Monroe. Then on April 4 he received word from Jeb Stuart, on outpost duty north of the Rappahannock, that another relay of transports was on its way down the Potomac. Simultaneously, Magruder reported heavy blue columns moving in his direction. These two pieces of evidence were strong, but Lee was still not sure that this was McClellan's main effort. Then five days later, on the heels of the depressing news that Albert Sidney Johnston had fallen at Shiloh, a minister who had escaped from Alexandria gave a detailed account of Unionist activities at that port of embarkation, adding that he personally had seen McClellan himself board one of the steamers for the journey down the coast. For Lee, this was conclusive. He went to

Two 32-pounder guns of a Confederate battery overlook the York River at Yorktown, Virginia.

Davis with the evidence, and that same day — April 9 — the President ordered Johnston to report at once to Richmond, bringing his two strongest divisions along for duty on the Peninsula.

He arrived on the 12th. Two of his divisions, under Major Generals G. W. Smith and Longstreet, were in his wake; the third, under Major General Richard Ewell, stayed where it was, with instructions to coöperate with Jackson if the necessity arose. Informed that his command now included the Peninsula and Norfolk, Johnston left Richmond that same day for an inspection of the Yorktown and Williamsburg lines. Two mornings later, April 14, he was back again, waiting in the presidential office when Davis arrived for work. The bleakness of his outlook matched the brevity of his absence. Both of Magruder's defensive lines were utterly untenable, he told Davis. Not only were they improperly sited and too long; vulnerable as they were to artillery in front and amphibious landings in the rear, they would most likely prove a trap for any army that tried to hold them. In short, he favored an immediate withdrawal to the third line of defense. Davis, somewhat taken aback at this suggestion that the war be brought forthwith to the gates of Richmond, asked the general to return at 11 a.m. and present his views to Lee and Secretary George W. Randolph. This being the case, Johnston asked that Smith and Longstreet also be invited, thus to preserve the balance. Davis agreed.

When the six men assembled at the specified hour it was evident that the general had chosen his supporters wisely. Longstreet had won considerable renown as a poker player, but had given it up three months ago, on the eve of his forty-first birthday, when his three children died of scarlet fever, all within a week. Grief had given him a stolid and ponderous dignity, augmented by a slight deafness which he could sit behind, when he chose, as behind a wall of sound-proof glass. He chose to sit so now. A large, square-built, hairy man, a native of the Deep South — born in South Carolina, raised in Georgia, and appointed to West Point from Alabama — he left the talking to Smith, who was a year younger but had been trained for disputation as Street Commissioner of New York City. Like Mansfield Lovell, his New York deputy, Smith had joined the Confederacy late, after waiting to see what his native Kentucky would do. Two months after Manassas he made his choice, which Davis applauded by making him a major general and giving him a division under Johnston, who admired him; the two were "Joe" and "G.W." to each other. A big-framed man with a large nose and firm-set lips, a West Pointer and a Mexico veteran, a former assistant professor of engineering at the Academy, Smith had been a civilian for the past eight years and was quite accustomed to attending such high-level councils as this. With Davis's and Johnston's permission, he said, he would like to submit a memorandum he had prepared. Johnston looked it over, then passed it to Davis, who read it aloud.

★

It was as if the ghost of Beauregard had been transported eastward 700 air-line miles from Mississippi. What Smith proposed, in essence, was a withdrawal from Norfolk and the lower Peninsula, a concentration of all available troops, and then a sudden strike, either against McClellan as he came up, or against the northern heartland beyond the Potomac. Smith was convinced that the fast-marching southern army could occupy Philadelphia or New York before McClellan could take Richmond. Johnston, questioned by Randolph, said he agreed — up to a point. He was not anxious to march on New York but he did want to cripple McClellan, and this was the way to do it; Norfolk and Yorktown were untenable anyhow. Randolph, a former navy man, protested that the loss of Gosport Navy Yard would mean the loss of the *Virginia*, which could neither put to sea nor ascend the James, unseaworthy and deep-drafted as she was, as well as the loss of all hope of ever building a real Confederate fleet. Johnston replied that it could not be helped. To attempt to hold positions that could readily be flanked would be to invite the destruction not only of the future navy but also of the present army.

All day the discussion continued, Randolph and Lee against Johnston and Smith, with Longstreet saying little and Davis acting as moderator. At suppertime they recessed for an hour, then reassembled at the Executive Mansion, where the argument continued into the night, apparently without affecting the convictions of any of the six. Then at 1 a.m. Davis adjourned the meeting with the decision to hold both Norfolk and Yorktown by uniting Johnston's and Magruder's armies on the lower Peninsula, under instructions to resist all Federal attempts to advance. Johnston thus was being sent to defend a position which he had declared untenable. He would have been removed, Davis later wrote, except that "he did not ask to be . . . and I had no wish to separate him from troops with whom he was so intimately acquainted." Johnston had his reasons, though he did not give them then. "The belief that events on the Peninsula would soon compel the Confederate government to adopt my method of opposing the Federal army," he wrote later, "reconciled me somewhat to the necessity of obeying the President's order."

As the general returned to Yorktown, convinced that things would work out his way in the end, Longstreet's men were marching through Richmond to join him. "The Walking Division," they called themselves, and one of them grumbled: "I suppose that if it was intended to reinforce Savannah, Mobile, or New Orleans with our division, we would be compelled to foot it all the way." But now that they were nearing the end of the march their spirits rose. It was the anniversary of Virginia's secession and the whole city had turned out to greet them with cheers and armloads of early spring flowers. Jonquils, hyacinths, narcissuses, and violets were tossed and caught, looped into wreaths or stuck into rifle muzzles. The drab mud-stained column seemed to burst into bloom as it swung down Main Street, a riot of colors dominated by the bright nodding yellow of the jonquils. Bands played "Dixie" and "The Bonnie Blue Flag," and the men returned the cheers of the crowd along the way. At one window they saw a lady and a pale young man waving handkerchiefs, and one of the bearded veterans shouted: "Come right along, sonny. The lady'll spare ye. Here's a little musket for ye!" The answer came back: "All right, boys. Have you got a leg for me, too?" As he spoke he placed on the window sill the stump of the leg he had lost at Manassas. The battalion made an effective apology. Wheeling spontaneously into line, it halted, presented arms, and rattled the windows of the block with cheering.

Johnston found a quite different spirit around Yorktown, fifty miles below. Magruder and his men were worn out by the strain of the long bluff. Their food was poor and their uniforms in rags. What was more, the enemy had begun to probe the Warwick River line with field artillery. There were night alarms and occasional stampedes, one including a work party of several hundred slaves, who broke for the rear and in their flight swept away part of the infantry support. Whatever his vaunted gallantry in the open field, the southern volunteer did not relish this kind of warfare, huddling under bombardments and waiting to be overrun. One detachment gave way completely under the tension, a member of the relief party reporting that he had found "some of these poor lads . . . sobbing in their broken sleep, like a crying child just before it sinks to rest. It was really pathetic. The men actually had to be supported to the ambulances sent down to bring them away."

They had the sympathy of their new commander, who was convinced that they should not have stayed there in the first place. To the War Department the last ten days of April brought word of the fall of New Orleans and the opening of Halleck's campaign against Corinth, as well as a trickle of I-told-you-so dispatches from the lower Peninsula. Johnston declared that Magruder's lines were even more defective than he had supposed when he made his first inspection. "No one but McClellan could have hesitated to attack," he reported on the 22d, and urged that some bridges across the Chickahominy, twenty-odd miles in his rear, should be repaired at once. Two days later he was suggesting that supplies be sent to meet the army on its way to the gates of the city "in the event of our being compelled to fall back from this point." On the 27th he instructed Huger to prepare to evacuate Norfolk. Two days later he wrote to Lee in the plainest language he had yet employed: "The fight for Yorktown, as I said in Richmond, must be one of artillery, in which we cannot win. The result is certain; the time only doubtful. . . . We must abandon the Peninsula at once."

There they had it; he had been right all along. May Day was a time of gloom in the southern capital. Ball's Bluff seemed far away and long ago.

★

★ ★ ★ **O**ne source of consolation existed, but it was unknown in Richmond, being hidden in the fog of war, far down the James and beyond the enemy lines. Johnston's worries were balanced — more than balanced, at least in number — by the woes of his opponent, which differed as much in quality as they did in multiplicity. The southern commander's fretfulness was based almost exclusively on strictly tactical considerations: the weakness of the Yorktown defenses and the shortage of troops to man them. But McClellan's was the product of a variety of pressures, roughly divisible under three main headings: 1) downright bad luck, 2) Lincoln, and — as always — 3) his own ripe imagination.

The first of a rapid succession of blows, like the preliminary tap of a farrier taking aim, landed the moment he stepped off the steamer at Old Point Comfort. Flag Officer Goldsborough, up from the North Carolina sounds to provide naval support for the movement up the narrow tongue of land, met him with word that the fleet would not be able to assist in reducing the enemy batteries on the York or the James. The navy already had its hands full, he said, patrolling Hampton Roads to neutralize the *Merrimac-Virginia*. One of the primary conditions of success, as stated by the corps commanders on the eve of departure, thus was removed before the campaign had even begun. Fortunately, McClellan had a full day in which to absorb the shock of this. But after that brief respite the blows began to land with trip-hammer rapidity.

On the second day, April 4, as he started his army forward — much gratified by the "wonderfully cool performance" of the trio of foragers who brought him the still-warm 12-pound shot — he made two dreadful discoveries. The first was that his handsome Coastal Survey maps were woefully inaccurate. The roads all ran the wrong way, he complained, and the Warwick River, shown on the maps as an insignificant creek flowing parallel to the James, was in fact a considerable barrier, cutting squarely across his line of march. To add to its effectiveness as an obstacle, the Confederates had dammed it in five places, creating five unwadable lakes and training their heavy artillery on the boggy intervals. McClellan was amazed at the river's location and condition; "[It] grows worse the more you look at it," he wailed.

As he stood gazing forlornly at this waste of wetness in his path, another unexpected development overtook him, also involving water. It began to rain. And from this there grew an even worse disclosure. Those fine sandy roads, recommended as being "passable at all seasons on the year," turned out to be no such thing. What they were was gumbo — and they were apparently bottomless. Guns and wagons bogged past the axles, then sat there, immovably

Federal soldiers stack logs to improve one of the Peninsula's muddy wagon tracks in preparation for their advance on Richmond.

stuck. One officer later testified that he saw a mule go completely out of sight in one of the chunk-holes, "all but the tips of its ears," but added, in the tall-tale tradition, that the mule was a rather small one.

No navy, no fit maps, no transportation: McClellan might well have thought the fates had dealt him all the weal they intended. Writing to his wife of his unenviable position — "the rebels on one side, and the abolitionists and other scoundrels on the other" — he said, "Don't worry about the wretches; they have done nearly their worst, and can't do much more." He was wrong, and before the day was over he would discover just how wrong he was. The people he referred to could do a great deal more. If McClellan did not realize this, Lincoln's two young secretaries knew it quite well already. "Gen McC is in danger," one was telling the other. "Not in front, but in rear."

Returning to army headquarters at the close of that same busy day — his first in bristling proximity to the enemy since the campaign in West Virginia, almost nine months ago — McClellan found the atmosphere of the lantern-hung interior as glum as the twilit landscape of rain-soaked fields and dripping woods through which he had just ridden. Sorrow and anger, despair and incredulity were strangely combined on the faces of his staff. Soon the Young Napoleon was sharing these mixed emotions; for the answer, or answers, lay in a batch of orders and directives just off the wire from Washington. The first was dated yesterday, April 3: Fort Monroe and its garrison of 12,000, placed under McClellan two weeks ago as a staging area and a pool from which to draw replacements, were removed forthwith from his control. Before he could recover from the shock of learning that he had lost not only that number of troops, but also command of his present base of operations, he was handed a second order, more drastic than the first. McDowell's corps of 38,000, still awaiting sailing orders at Alexandria — McClellan intended to bring it down in mass as soon as he decided where to land it, whether on the south bank of the York, for operations against Yorktown, or on the north bank, against Gloucester Point — was detached and withheld as part of the force assigned to provide close-in protection for the capital. This action was given emphasis by a supplementary order creating what was called the Department of the Rappahannock, under McDowell, as well as another new one, called the Department of the Shenandoah, under Banks, whose corps was also declared no longer a part of the Army of the Potomac. McClellan was floored. Even without the loss of Banks, which made no actual change in dispositions, the combined detachments of Blenker, McDowell, and the Fort Monroe garrison — an approximate total of 60,000 fighting men — reduced by well over one third the 156,000 he had said at the outset would be necessary for the success of his Peninsula campaign.

Nor was this all. As he took to his troubled bed that night he had something else to think about: something that seemed to him and his staff conclusive proof that the Administration, disapproving of the campaign in the first place, was determined to assure its failure before the opening shot was fired. A final order, dated yesterday and signed by the Adjutant General for distribution to the governors of all the loyal states, put an end to the recruiting of volunteers throughout the Union. All recruiting offices were closed, the equipment put up for sale to the highest bidders, and all recruiting personnel were reassigned to other duties. In some ways this was the hardest blow of all, or anyhow the most incredible. At a time when the Confederate authorities, sixty miles away in Richmond, were doing all they could to push through the first conscription law in American history — a law which could be expected to swell the ranks of the army facing him — it seemed to McClellan that his Washington superiors, twice that distance in his rear, had not only taken a full one third of his soldiers from him, but then had proceeded to make certain that they could never be replaced. The fact was, on the eve of bloody fighting, Lincoln and Stanton had seen to it that he would not even be able to replace his casualties. So it seemed to McClellan. At any rate, as he went to bed that night he could say, "They have done nearly their worst," and be a good deal closer to the truth.

Next morning, if somewhat daunted by all the knocks he had had to absorb in one short night, he was back at the front, probing the enemy defenses with his three remaining corps. Heintzelman and Keyes, on the right and left, had two divisions each, with a third on the way down Chesapeake Bay for both. Sumner, in the center, had only one; his second was en route, and his third had been Blenker. All three of these brigadiers were hard-shell regulars — Sumner had put in seven of his forty-three years of army service before McClellan was born, and both of the others were thirty-year men or better — but after coming under heavy fire from long-range guns and bogging down in the flooded approaches, all agreed with the Chief Engineer's report that the rebel line was "certainly one of the most extensive known to modern times." If the navy had been there to wreck the batteries on the flanks, or if the weight of McDowell's corps, the largest of the original four, could be added to the pressure the army could exert, things might be different. As it was, however, all felt obliged to agree with Keyes, who later reported bluntly: "No part of [the Yorktown-Warwick River] line, so far discovered, can be taken by assault without an enormous waste of life."

If the Confederate defenses could not be broken by flanking operations, if assault was too doubtful and expensive, only one method remained: a siege. McClellan would do it that way if he had to; he had studied siege tactics at Sebastopol. But he much preferred his original plan, which he now saw was impractical without his original army. As he rode back to headquarters this second night he decided to make a final appeal to Lincoln. Under the heading "Near Yorktown, 7.30 p.m." he outlined for the President the situation as he saw it, neglecting none of the drawbacks, and begged him to "reconsider" the order detaching McDowell. "In my deliberate judgment," he wrote, "the success of our cause will be imperiled by so greatly reducing my force when it is actually under the fire of the enemy and active operations have commenced. . . . I am now of the opinion that I shall have to fight all the available forces of the rebels not far from here. Do not force me to do so with diminished numbers."

Lincoln's reply, the following day, was a brief warning that delay on the Peninsula would benefit the Confederate defenders more than it would the Federal attackers: "You now have over 100,000 troops with you. . . . I think you better break the enemy's line from Yorktown to Warwick River at once." McClellan's first reaction, he told his wife, was "to reply that he had better come and do it himself." Instead, he wired on the 7th that, after the three recent detachments, his "entire force for duty" amounted to about 85,000 men, more than a third of whom were still en route from Alexandria. Lincoln took a day to study this, then replied on the 9th at considerable length. He was puzzled, he said, by "a curious mystery." The general's own report showed a total strength of 108,000; "How can the discrepancy of 23,000 be accounted for?"

Beyond this, however, the President's main purpose was to point out to McClellan that more factors were involved in this war than those which might occur to a man with an exclusively military turn of mind. In other words, this was a Civil war. The general was aware of certain pressures in his rear, but

Lincoln suggested in a final paragraph that he would gain more from studying those pressures, and maybe finding ways to relieve them, than he would from merely complaining of their presence. It was a highly personal communication, and in it he gave McClellan some highly personal advice:

"Once more let me tell you that it is indispensable to *you* that you strike a blow. *I* am powerless to help this. You will do me the justice to remember I always insisted that going down the bay in search of a field, instead of fighting at or near Manassas, was only shifting and not surmounting a difficulty; that we would find the same enemy and the same or equal intrenchments in either place. The country will not fail to note — is now noting — that the present hesitation to move upon an intrenched enemy is but the story of Manassas repeated. I beg to assure you that I have never written you or spoken to you in greater kindness of feeling than now, nor with a fuller purpose to sustain you, so far as, in my most anxious judgment, I consistently can. But you must act."

★　★　★　That "most anxious judgment" had been under considerable strain ever since McClellan's leading elements started down the coast in transports. Ben Wade and Zachariah Chandler were bombarding Lincoln with protests that the general's treasonable intent was plain at last for any eye to see: The whole campaign had been designed to sidetrack the main Union army by bogging it down in the slews southeast of Richmond, thus clearing the path for a direct rebel sweep on Washington, with little to stand in its way. Stanton not only encouraged the presentation and acceptance

McClellan (center) poses with his generals in Northern Virginia
before his campaign to capture Richmond. To his distress, several
of them would be detached before his army began its advance.

★

of this view, but also enlarged it by assigning additional motives to account for his former intimate's treachery: McClellan was politically ambitious, "more interested in reconstructing the Democratic party than the Army of the Potomac."

Lincoln wondered. He did not believe McClellan was a traitor, but in suggesting that the capital was in danger the Jacobins had touched him where he was tender. "This is a question which the country will not allow me to evade," he said. He could not afford the slightest risk in that direction; too much hung in the balance — including war with England and France as a result of the recognition both would almost certainly give the Confederacy once its army had occupied Washington. Then, as he pondered, an alarm was sounded which seemed to give substance to his fears.

On the day McClellan landed at Old Point Comfort, Brigadier General James Wadsworth, the elderly commander of the Washington defenses and one of the founders of the Republican Party, came to Stanton complaining that his force was inadequate for its task, both in numbers and in training. The Secretary sent his military assistant, the hapless Hitchcock, and Adjutant General Lorenzo Thomas to investigate, and when they confirmed Wadsworth's report that the capital was in danger, Stanton took him triumphantly to Lincoln. McClellan's note of the day before, claiming that he had left 77,456 men behind to give Washington the stipulated "entire feeling of security," was checked for accuracy. Certain discrepancies showed at once, and the harder the three men looked the more they saw. In the first place, by an arithmetical error, the troops at Warrenton had been counted twice. Proposed reinforcements from Maryland, Pennsylvania, and New York had not arrived, though they were listed. Blenker's division, on the way to Frémont, had also been included, on grounds that Banks could interrupt its march if it was needed. All these had to be subtracted. And so for that matter did the two divisions already with Banks in the Valley; Patterson's army, out there in July, had done nothing to protect the capital after the debacle at Bull Run. In fact, by actual count as Lincoln saw it, once McClellan's whole army had gone down the coast, there would be fewer than 29,000 men in all to stand in the way of a direct Confederate drive on Washington: 11,000 less than the general's own corps commanders had said were necessary.

The way to keep this from happening was to stop one corps from going to join McClellan, and that was what Lincoln did, creating in the process the Departments of the Rappahannock and the Shenandoah to give McDowell and Banks their independence. The former would make his headquarters at Falmouth, opposite Fredericksburg, and in time — conditions permitting — march overland to join his former chief in front of Richmond. That way, he would always be in a position to strike the front or flank of any rebel force that tried a direct lunge at Washington, and yet he would still be in on the kill when the time came. Lincoln did not want to hurt McClellan any more than he had to. In fact, on the day after telling him, "You must act," he released McDowell's lead division, under Franklin — a great favorite of McClellan's, who asked in a final desperate plea that this, at least, not be withheld — to proceed by the water route as originally planned. Exuberantly grateful, McClellan wired on April 13: "We shall soon be at them, and I am sure of the result."

Lincoln had heard him say such things before; they were part of what made the Young Napoleon at once so likeable and exasperating. The President knew by now not to put much stock in such expressions, which after all only meant that McClellan was feeling good again. Lincoln himself was not. The past week had been a strain, in some ways harder than the strain which had followed defeat on the plains of Manassas. His sadness had deepened, along with the lines in his face, though he still kept his wry sense of humor. A country editor called at the White House, claiming to have been the first to suggest Lincoln's nomination for President. Lincoln was busy, but when he tried to escape by saying he had to go over to the War Department on business, the editor offered to accompany him. "Come along," Lincoln said. When they got there he told his visitor, "I shall have to see Mr Stanton alone, and you must excuse me." He turned to enter, but then, perhaps considering this too abrupt, turned back and took the editor by the hand. "Goodbye," he said. "I hope you will feel perfectly easy about having nominated me. Don't be troubled about it. I forgive you."

★ ★ ★   **A**s April wore on and the rains continued, so did the **siege preparations;** McClellan was hard at work. He had not wanted this kind of campaign, but now that he had it he was enjoying it immensely. Back in the West Virginia days he had said, "I will not throw these raw men of mine into the teeth of artillery and intrenchments if it is possible to avoid it." He still felt that way about it. "I am to watch over you as a parent over his children," he had told his army the month before, and that was what he was doing. If it was to be a siege, let it be one in the grand manner, with fascines and gabions, zigzag approaches, and much digging and shifting of earth, preparatory to blasting the rebel fortifications clean out of existence. "Do not misunderstand the apparent inaction here," he wired Lincoln on the 23d, concerned lest a civilian fail to appreciate all this labor. "Not a day, not an hour has been lost. Works have been constructed that may almost be called gigantic."

Gigantic was particularly the word for the fifteen ten-gun batteries of 13-inch siege mortars being installed within two miles of Yorktown; on completion, they would be capable of throwing 400 tons of metal daily into the rebel defenses. Six were installed and ready before the end of the month, but McClellan held his fire, preferring to open with all of them at once. Meanwhile he neglected nothing which he thought would add to the final effect. On the 28th he wired Stanton: "Would be glad to have the 30-pounder Parrotts in the works around Washington. Am short of that excellent gun." When Lincoln saw the request, his thin-stretched patience snapped. "Your call for Parrott guns . . . alarms me," he answered on May Day, "chiefly because it argues indefinite procrastination. Is anything to be done?" McClellan replied that the Parrotts would hasten, not delay, the breaking of the enemy lines; "All is being done that human labor can accomplish." The build-up continued. Then suddenly, May 4, it paid off. The noonday Sabbath quiet of the War Department telegraph office was broken by the brief, jubilant clatter of a message from the Peninsula: "Yorktown is in our possession. Geo. B. McClellan."

That there was more to it than that, in fact a great deal more, became apparent from the messages which followed. McClellan had not "taken" Yorktown; he had received it by default. Joe Johnston had been observing all those large-scale preparations, then had pulled back on the eve of what was to have been the day of his destruction. It was Centreville-Manassas all over again, except this time the guns he left behind were real ones: 56 heavy siege pieces, many with their ammunition still neatly stacked and only three of them damaged. However, he had saved all of his field artillery and given his army a head start toward whatever defensive line he intended to occupy next. McClellan did not mean for him to do so unmolested. He sent the cavalry in pursuit at once, despite a thunderstorm that approached cloudburst proportions, and followed it with the whole army, under Sumner, while he himself remained at Yorktown to launch an amphibious end run up the York, attempting to cut off Johnston's retreat by landing Franklin's division in his rear. The result was a bloody rear-

Union artillery and Brigadier General Winfield Scott Hancock's brigade repel the attack of Jubal Early's Confederates at Williamsburg in this sketch by Alfred Waud. The artist noted "enemies dead and wounded covering the field."

★

guard action next day in front of Williamsburg, anticipated and reviewed in two telegrams he sent, the first at 9 a.m. and the last at 9.40 p.m. The former was to Stanton, an announcement of intention: "I shall push the enemy to the wall." The latter was to Franklin, who was coming up by water while McClellan himself hurried overland to where Sumner's guns were growling: "We have now a tangent hit. I arrived in time."

Johnston, whose men were plodding along the single miry road behind their slow-grinding wagon train, had not planned a halt until he crossed the Chickahominy, but the Union infantry was closing fast, unimpeded by wagons, and the cavalry was taking potshots at his rear guard before sundown. So he instructed Longstreet's division to delay the pursuit by holding Fort Magruder long enough to give the rest of the army time to draw off. When Sumner's men came slogging up they were met by a spatter of musketry that stopped them for the night. The fight next day — dignified by time into the Battle of Williamsburg — was confusion from start to finish, with lunges and counterlunges and a great deal of slipping and sliding in the mud. Cannonfire had a metallic ring in the saturated air, and generals on both sides lost their sense of direction in the rain. Sumner kept pushing and probing; Longstreet had to call for help, and Major General D. H. Hill countermarched his whole division and joined the melee. In the end, the Confederates managed to hang on until nightfall, when they fell back and the Federals took possession of Fort Magruder. Both claimed a victory: the latter because they had gained the field, the former because they had delayed the pursuit. The only apparent losers were the casualties: 1703 for the South, 2239 for the North.

Whatever else it amounted to, and that seemed very little, the day-long battle had given the troops of both sides two clear gains at least. The first was that, as soldiers, they were tangibly worth their salt. Despite the confusion and the milling about, which gave the action a superficial resemblance to Bull Run, the men had fought as members of military units, not as panicky individuals. This in itself was a substantial gain, one they knew was beyond value. Training had paid off. But the second was even more appealing. This was a new confidence in their respective commanding generals, in spite of the fact that neither had been present for the fighting.

Johnston was toiling westward through the mud with his main body. Coming upon a deeply mired 12-pound brass Napoleon which a battery lieutenant was about to abandon in obedience to orders that nothing was to be allowed to impede the march, Johnston said: "Let me see what I can do." He dismounted, waded into the bog — high-polished boots, gold braid, and all — and took hold of a muddy spoke. "Now, boys: all together!" he cried, and the gun bounded clear of the chunk-hole. After that, one cannoneer said, "our battery used to swear by Old Joe."

McClellan's performance was no less endearing. Arriving just at the close of the battle, mud-stained from hard riding, his staff strung out behind him trying desperately to keep up, he went from regiment to regiment, congratulating his men for their victory and acknowledging their cheers. Often he paused for a question-and-answer exchange, strophe and antistrophe:

"How do you feel, boys?"

"We feel bully, General!" they cried.

"Do you think anything can stop you from going to Richmond?"

"No! No!" they shouted, all together.

Little Mac would give them his jaunty salute, made even flashier today by the glazed waterproof cover he was wearing on his cap, and be off down the line at a gallop, to halt again in front of another regiment:

"How do you feel, boys?"

"We feel bully, General!"

"Do you think anything can stop you from going to Richmond?"

"No! No!"

Rain-soaked and hungry, but glad to be out of the trenches, the Confederates continued their march toward the Chickahominy. Smith, in the lead, was instructed to halt at Barhamsville, eighteen miles beyond Williamsburg, and guard against a flank attack from the direction of York River while the other three divisions were catching up. He got there on the afternoon of the 6th, just as Franklin's men were coming ashore at Eltham Landing, six miles away, to execute the movement Johnston feared. Informed of this, Johnston ordered Magruder, Longstreet, and Hill to hurry forward. While they were doing so, Smith moved toward Eltham to attack. Deciding that it would be better not to try to stop the Yankees within range of their gunboats, he waited until next morning when they were a couple of miles from the landing, then hit them with Hampton's Legion and a brigade of Texans and Georgians under a 30-year-old West Pointer named John Bell Hood, a prewar junior lieutenant in Sidney Johnston's 2d Cavalry. Franklin's men, deep in unfamiliar country and not knowing how many graybacks might be coming at them, gave ground rapidly until they regained the covering fire of the gunboats.

They had been hit harder than Johnston intended, anxious as he was to avoid the delay another general engagement would have entailed. Later he admonished the blond-bearded six-foot-two-inch Kentucky brigadier: "General Hood, have you given an illustration of the Texas idea of feeling an enemy gently and falling back? What would your Texans have done, sir, if I had ordered them to charge and drive back the enemy?" Hood's blue eyes were somber. He said gravely, "I suppose, General, they would have driven them into the river, and tried to swim out and capture the gunboats."

At any rate Smith was satisfied; Franklin was disposed of, and the wagon train was well along the road. He led his and Magruder's divisions on through New Kent Courthouse and made camp the following night beside the road, nineteen miles from Barhamsville and within easy reach of Bottom's Bridge across the Chickahominy. Five miles downstream, at Long Bridge, the divisions of Hill and Longstreet tried to sleep in a torrent of rain which finally sent them sloshing off in search of higher ground. Whatever their discomfort, Johnston's reaction was primarily a feeling of relief that his 54,000 soldiers had escaped a trap laid by twice their number. Not that he was through retreating. Already he had notified Lee in Richmond: "The want of provision and of any mode of obtaining it here, still more the dearth of forage, makes it impossible to wait to attack [the enemy] while landing. The sight of the ironclad boats makes me apprehensive for Richmond, too, so I move on. . . ."

The Federals were after him, moving slowly, however, along the cut-up roads. Sumner at Williamsburg and Franklin at Eltham Landing had failed to bag the retreating enemy, but McClellan was not discouraged. His men had shown all the dash a commander could ask for, and the rebels were dribbling casualties and equipment as they fled. "My troops are in motion and in magnificent spirits," he informed the War Department. "They have all the air and feelings of veterans. It will do your heart good to see them." The frontal attack, up the middle of the Peninsula, had left the foe no time to get set for another prolonged resistance, and the long end run, despite the savage repulse next day, had "fully served its purpose in clearing our front to the banks of the Chickahominy." In accordance with plans made months ago, when Urbanna was the intended place of debarkation, he set up his base at West Point, the terminus of the 35-mile-long Richmond & York River Railroad. Here the Mattapony and the Pamunkey converged to form the York, which afforded a deep-draft supply line all the way back to Chesapeake Bay. Regiment after regiment, division after division of reinforcements could be landed here, fresh for combat, and McClellan was quick to suggest that this be done. May 8 he wired Stanton: "The time has arrived to bring all the troops in Eastern Virginia into perfect coöperation. I expect to fight another and very severe battle before reaching Richmond and with all the troops the Confederates can bring together. . . . All the troops on the Rappahannock, and if possible those on the Shenandoah, should take part in the approaching battle. We ought immediately to concentrate everything."

★ ★ ★   **T**he wire did not have to go all the way to Washington; the Secretary was at Fort Monroe. He had arrived two days ago with Lincoln and Chase, primarily for relaxation and a look-see, but as it turned out was lending a hand in the direction of one of the strangest small-scale campaigns in American military history.

Amazed to find that McClellan had made no provision for the capture of Norfolk, outflanked by the drive up the opposite bank of the James, the President decided to undertake the operation himself, employing the fortress garrison under Major General John E. Wool. Wool was 78, two years older than Winfield Scott, and though he was more active physically than his fellow veteran of the War of 1812 — he could still mount a horse, for instance — he had other infirmities all his own. After twenty-five years as Inspector General, his hands trembled; he repeated things he had said a short while back, and he had to ask his aide if he had put his hat on straight. However, there was no deficiency of the courage he had shown under Anthony Wayne. He said he would gladly undertake the movement his Commander in Chief proposed.

The first trouble came with the navy: Goldsborough thought it would be dangerous to ferry the men across the Roads with the *Merrimac* still on the loose. But Lincoln not only overruled him, he and Chase got in separate tugs and reconnoitered the opposite shore for a suitable landing place. When they returned, however, they found that Wool had already chosen one from the chart and was embarking with the troops who were to seize it. Chase went along, but Lincoln and Stanton stayed behind to maintain a command post at the fort and question various colonels and generals who, the President thought, were to follow in support.

"Where is your command?" he asked one, and got the answer: "I am awaiting orders." To another he said, "Why are you here? Why not on the other side?" and was told: "I am ordered to the fort." Experiencing for the first time some of the vexations likely to plague a field commander, Lincoln lost his temper. He took off his tall hat and slammed it on the floor. "Send me someone who can write," he said, exasperated. When the someone came forward — a colonel on Wool's staff — the President dictated an order for the advance to be pushed and supported.

As things turned out, no push or support was needed. The Confederates had evacuated Norfolk the day before, leaving only a handful of men behind to complete the wrecking of Gosport Navy Yard. Chase and Wool were met just short of the city limits by a municipal delegation, including the mayor, who carried a large bunch of rusty keys and a sheaf of documents which he insisted on reading, down to the final line, before making the final formal gesture of handing over the keys. Unknown to Wool and the Secretary, while the mayor droned on, the rebel demolition crew was completing its work and setting out for Richmond. Then Chase and the general moved in with their troops and took charge, sending word back to Lincoln that his first field campaign had been a complete success, despite vexations.

★ ★ ★ One demolition job remained, and it was done that night. No nation ever owed more to a single ship than the Confederacy owed the *Merrimac-Virginia;* yet, with Norfolk gone, she had not only lost her home, she had lost her occupation. Josiah Tattnall, who had dipped his colors in salute to his old friend Du Pont at Port Royal and had been in command of the ironclad since late March, saw two choices: either to steer her out into the Roads for a suicidal finish, taking as many of the enemy with her as possible when she sank, or else to try and lighten her enough to ascend the James. In point of fact, however, there was really no choice. No matter how fitting the former seemed as a death for a gallant vessel, it obviously would not benefit the country; whereas the latter course would preserve her for future service, a second career. She now drew twenty-three feet as a result of recent additions to her armor, but the pilots assured the commodore that if she could be lightened to eighteen feet before daylight they would take her up to Harrison's Landing or City Point, where she could be put in fighting trim again. Tattnall assembled the crew and told them what had to be done. They gave three cheers and got to work, heaving everything movable over the side except her powder and shot. She had been lightened three feet by midnight — when the pilots announced that a strong west wind had reduced the tide so much that she could not be taken up at all.

The first choice was gone with the second, for the work had exposed two feet of her hull below the shield, and to let in water ballast to settle her again would be to flood her fires and magazines. Now that she could neither run nor fight, a third choice, unconsidered at the outset, was all that remained: to destroy her. Tattnall gave the necessary orders. The *Virginia* was run ashore near Craney Island and set afire. By the light of her burning, the crew set out on their march to Suffolk, where they took the cars for Richmond. There they were ordered to Drewry's Bluff, whose batteries now were all that stood between the Confederate capital and the Federal fleet, including their old adversary the *Monitor.*

Those batteries were of primary concern to Lee, who also had lost a good part of his occupation when Johnston came down and took command on the Peninsula. All through late April and early May, while Johnston was warning that he was about to bring the war to the outskirts of Richmond, Lee had been supervising work on the close-in defenses, of which the installations at Drewry's were a part, and now that Johnston was falling back with all the speed the mud allowed, Lee continued to do what he could to protect his ancestral capital from assault. Called on at a cabinet meeting to say where the next stand could be made if the city had to be abandoned, he made an unaccustomed show of his emotions. It would have to be along the Staunton River, he said calmly, a hundred miles southwest. Then suddenly his eyes brimmed with tears. "But Richmond must not be given up; it shall not be given up!" he exclaimed.

Davis felt much the same way about it. Twice he had ridden down to Drewry's with Lee to inspect the work in progress there, the hulks being sunk alongside pilings driven across the channel and the heavy naval cannon being emplaced on the high bluff. But in spite of hearing that Butler's men, with Farragut on his way up the Mississippi, were sacking and looting Briarfield, he kept an even closer rein on his emotions than did the Virginian who had been nicknamed "The Marble Monument" while they were at the Academy together. Many interpreted this calmness to mean a lack of concern by the Chief Executive, and when he was baptized and confirmed at St Paul's on the 9th, the *Examiner* took him to task for finding time for such ministrations on the day of Norfolk's evacuation. Faced with imminent assault by land and water, the people wanted assurance from Davis that Richmond would be defended, block by block and house by house. A committee called at his office on the morning of May 15, inquiring whether the government shared their determination, but their spokesman was interrupted by a messenger who came to inform the President that the masts of Federal warships had been sighted on the James from the hills of the city. "This manifestly concludes the matter," Davis said, dismissing the committee.

Soon the guns began to roar, clangorous on the hilltops and reverberant in the hollows. They kept it up for three full hours and twenty minutes, rattling Richmond windows from a distance of eight miles. It was deafening; people trembled at the sound. Then suddenly it stopped, and that was worse. With the abrupt descent of silence, they took their hands down from their ears

★

Federal gunboats, including the ironclads Galena and Monitor, endure Confederate artillery fire from Drewry's Bluff on the James River below Richmond. After more than three hours of action the battered vessels were forced to withdraw.

and looked at one another, not knowing which to expect: a messenger announcing that the assault had been repulsed, or the gunboats celebrating a victory by lobbing 11-inch shells into the city. Presently they had the answer.

The attack had been led by two ironclads, the *Monitor* and the *Galena*, supported by two wooden vessels. The latter kept their distance, but the armored ships began the bombardment at a range of 800 yards. The *Monitor* soon retired, unable to elevate her guns enough to reach the batteries on the bluff. The *Galena* stayed and took twenty-eight hits, including eighteen perforations which cost her 13 killed and 11 wounded, before she dropped back down the river with the others, winding lamely out of sight around the bend. The Confederate gunners leaped on the unfinished parapets, cheering and tossing their caps: especially the sailors off the *Virginia,* who at last had scored the triumph that had been beyond their reach at water level.

Richmond had been delivered, at least for a day. But Johnston was still retreating. That same morning he abandoned the middle and lower stretches of the Chickahominy, taking up an intermediary position which he abandoned in turn, two days later, because he found it tactically weak and inadequately supplied with drinking water. What he would do next he would not say, not even to the President. A South Carolinian recalled that before the war Wade Hampton had brought Johnston down there on a bird hunt, but Johnston had not fired a shot all day. "The bird flew too high or too low; the dogs were too far or too near. Things never did suit exactly." It seemed to be that way with him now, but one thing at least was clear. The next withdrawal would have to be beyond the capital. His present left was at Fairfield Race Course, just outside the northeast city limits, and his right was on the near bank of the James, across from Drewry's Bluff. Richmond was beleaguered. At nightfall people saw from her hills the semicircular twinkle of the campfires of the Army of Northern Virginia. Beyond them, a greater refulgence along the eastern and northeastern sky reflected the glow of campfires kindled by McClellan's hundred thousand.

★ ★ ★ *I*n preparation for what he believed might be the last great battle of the war, the Federal commander had reorganized his army while it was still on the march toward the Chickahominy crossings. Shuffling and reconsolidating while in motion, he created two new corps, one under Fitz-John Porter, the other under Franklin — both of them original pro-McClellan brigadiers — which gave him five corps in all, each with two three-brigade divisions. The order of battle, as reported in mid-May:

SUMNER	HEINTZELMAN	KEYES	PORTER	FRANKLIN
Richardson	Hooker	Couch	Morell	Slocum
Sedgwick	Kearny	Casey	Sykes	Smith

gave him a tightly knit yet highly flexible fighting force of 102,236 front-line soldiers and 300 guns. Another 5000 extra-duty men, including cooks and teamsters, laborers and suchlike, were with the advance, while 21,000 more had been left at various points along the road from Fort Monroe, sick or absent without leave or on garrison duty, to give him an over-all total of 128,864.

McClellan did not consider this a man too many. In fact he was convinced it was not enough. Pinkerton was at work again, questioning prisoners and contrabands and totting up figures he received from his operatives beyond the enemy lines. A month ago, in front of Yorktown, he had said that the Confederates were issuing 119,000 daily rations. Presently this grew to 180,000, reported along with a warning that the figure was probably low, since 200 separate regiments of southern infantry had already been identified on the Peninsula, plus assorted battalions of artillery, cavalry, and combat engineers. One corps commander wrote in his journal that 240,000 rebels were concentrated in front of the northern army. McClellan never believed the figure was quite that high, but he clearly believed it might be. Complaining to the War Department on May 10 that he himself could put barely 70,000 on the firing line, he continued to plead for more: "If I am not reinforced, it is probable that I will be obliged to fight nearly double my numbers, strongly intrenched."

Whatever their strength, the Confederates kept falling back and McClellan continued to follow. By May 15 he had advanced his base another fifteen miles along the railroad, from West Point to the head of navigation on the Pamunkey, which gave him both water and rail facilities for bringing supplies forward. Here was a large southern mansion called the White House, where the nation's first President had courted the Widow Custis, and there was a note attached to the front door. "Northern soldiers who profess to reverence Washington," it read, "forbear to desecrate the home of his first married life, the property of his wife, now owned by her descendants. A Grand-daughter of Mrs Washington." The author of the note was Mrs R. E. Lee. She had already lost one home in the path of war — Arlington, near Alexandria — and McClellan respected her wishes in regard to this one. He pitched his headquarters tents in the yard and set up a permanent supply dump at the landing, but he stationed guards around the house itself to keep out prowlers and souvenir-hunters, and provided an escort with a flag of truce to see the lady through the lines to join her husband.

Glad of this chance to show that the practice of chivalry was not re-stricted to soldiers dressed in gray, he then enjoyed a brief sojourn among the relics. Even though the house itself was a reconstruction, the sensation of being on the site where Washington had slept and eaten and taken his ease gave the youthful commander a feeling of being borne up and on by the stream of histo-ry; he hoped, he said, "that I might serve my country as well as he did." Riding toward the front on May 16, he came to old St Peter's Church, where Washing-ton was married. Here too he stopped, dismounted, and went in. That night he wrote his wife: "As I happened to be there alone for a few minutes, I could not help kneeling at the chancel and praying."

What followed next day was enough to convince an agnostic of the ef-ficacy of prayer. Officially and out of the blue, he heard from Stanton that Mc-Dowell was being reinforced by a division already on its way from Banks in the Shenandoah Valley. As soon as it got there, McClellan was told, McDowell would move south to join him in front of Richmond with an additional 40,000 men.

★ ★ ★   **T**his was the one calamity beyond all others Lee had been seeking for means to avoid. McClellan was a hover-ing threat — his front-line troops could hear the clocks of Richmond strike the hours — but at least Johnston stood in his path; whereas at present there was nothing between McDowell and Richmond that he could not brush aside with an almost careless gesture, and if Johnston sidled to block him too, the capital's defenses would be stretched beyond the snapping point. The fall of the city would follow as surely as nightfall followed sunset of the day Mc-Dowell got there.

For possible deliverance, Lee looked north. Numerically the odds were even longer in Northern Virginia than they were on the Peninsula — three-to-two against Johnston, three-to-one against the troops he had left be-hind — but Johnston was wedged tight in coffin corner, while northward there was still room for maneuver. If anything, there was too much room. A brigade of 2500 under Brigadier General Charles Field — another of Sidney Johnston's ubiquitous former U.S. Cavalry lieutenants — had been left on the Rappahannock to watch McDowell. Jackson's command, grown by now to about 6000, opposed Banks in the Valley. Ewell's 8500 were posted at Gordonsville, equidistant from both, instructed to be ready to march in support of whichever needed him worse. Beyond Jackson, Edward Johnson with 2800 was observing Frémont's Allegheny preparations. McDowell, with Franklin detached, had 30,000; Banks had 21,000; Frémont had 17,000 and more on the way. Numerically, then — with 68,000 Federals distributed along a perimeter guarded by just under 20,000 Confederates — the outlook was as gloomy there as elsewhere, even gloomier. But Lee saw possibilities through the gloom. If the two largest southern commands, under Jackson and Ewell, could be combined, they might be able to hit one of the three opposing forces hard enough to alarm the Union high command into delaying the advance of all the rest: including McDowell. That is, Lee would stop McDowell not by striking him — he was too strong — but by striking Banks or Frémont, who would call on him for help.

Daring as the conception was, a great deal more than daring would be needed before it could be translated into action. Field, for instance, would have to be reinforced. To leave him where he was, without support from Ewell, would be to invite McDowell to smother him. But when Lee appealed to Johnston to spare the men from the Yorktown intrenchments, Johnston would not hear of it. "To detach troops from this position would be ruin to those left," he said. Once more Lee had to improvise, robbing Peter to pay Paul, and this he did. Burnside's aggressiveness having subsided, he took three brigades from North and South Carolina, 10,000 men in all, and sent them up to Fredericksburg under Brigadier General J. R. Anderson, who combined them with Field's brigade and assumed command by seniority. Ewell could now slide westward toward the Blue Ridge and conjunction with Jackson.

They were a strange pair: so strange, indeed, that perhaps the most daring thing about Lee's plan was that he was willing to trust it to these two to carry out. Dick Ewell was an eccentric, a queer-looking forty-five-year-old bachelor who spoke with a sort of twittering lisp and subsisted on a diet of cracked wheat to palliate the tortures of dyspepsia. With his sharp nose and bald-domed head, which he frequently let droop far toward one shoulder, he reminded many people of a bird — an eagle, some said; others said a woodcock. He was a West Pointer, but a generation of frontier duty, he declared, had taught him all about handling fifty dragoons and driven all other knowledge from his mind. So far, his only appreciable service in the war had been at the Battle of Manassas, where he crossed and recrossed Bull Run, far on the right, and never came to grips with the enemy at all. He had a habit of interjecting odd remarks into everyday conversations: as for instance, "Now why do you suppose President Davis made me a major general anyway?"

Stonewall seemed about as bad. The fame he had won along with his nickname at Manassas had been tarnished by last winter's fruitless Romney expedition, which resulted in much friction with the War Department, as well as by the bloody repulse he had blundered into recently at Kernstown. His abrupt cashiering of Garnett after that fight had caused his officers to think of him distastefully, and quite accurately, as a man who would be quick to throw the book at a subordinate who stepped or wandered out of line. Like Ewell, who was three months his junior in rank and seven years his senior in age, he had adopted a peculiar diet to ease the pains of dyspepsia: raspberries and plain bread and milk, supplemented by lemons — many lemons — though he

Dick Ewell was an eccentric, a queer-looking forty-five-year-old bachelor. . . . With his sharp nose and bald-domed head, which he frequently let droop far toward one shoulder, he reminded many people of a bird — an eagle, some said; others said a woodcock.

would take no seasoning in his food: pepper made his left leg ache, he said. Nor was his appearance reassuring. His uniform was a single-breasted threadbare coat he had worn in the Mexican War, a rusty V.M.I. cadet cap, which he wore with the broken visor pulled well down over his weary-looking eyes, and an outsized pair of flop-top cavalry boots. A religious fanatic, he sometimes interrupted his soldiers at their poker and chuck-a-luck games by strolling through camp to hand out Sunday School pamphlets. They did not object to this so much, however, as they did to the possible truth of rumors that he imagined himself a southern Joshua and in combat got so carried away by the notion that he lost his mental balance. They feared it might be so with him, for they had seen his pale blue eyes take on a wild unearthly glitter in the gunsmoke; Old Blue Light, they called him. And there was substance for their fears. Just now he was writing his wife that he hoped to make his Valley command "an army of the living God as well as of its country."

Such as they were, they were all Lee had — and strictly speaking he did not even have them. Both were still a part of Johnston's army, subject to

★

Johnston's orders, and Johnston was extremely touchy about out-of-channels interference. Whatever was to be done in Northern Virginia would have to be done with his coöperation, or anyhow his acquiescence, which he seemed likely to withhold in the case of a proposal that violated, as this one did, his cherished principles of "concentration." On the other hand, Lee had Davis to sustain him. Unlike Lincoln, who did not count a soldier as part of the Washington defenses unless he could ride out and touch him in the course of an afternoon's round-trip carriage drive from the White House, Davis could see that a man a hundred miles away might do more to relieve the pressure, or stave off a threat, than if he stood on the capital ramparts. With the President's approval, Lee went ahead, trusting that he and Johnston would not issue conflicting orders — or, in Lee's case, suggestions — to the generals out in the Valley.

April 21 he wrote to Jackson, outlining the situation at Richmond and emphasizing the need for holding McDowell on the Rappahannock line. The key force, as he saw it, was Ewell's, which could be used in one of three ways: either by leaving it where it was, or by reinforcing Field — Anderson was still on the way — or by reinforcing Jackson. Lee preferred this last, and he was writing to find out whether Stonewall thought it practicable: "If you can use General Ewell's division in an attack on General Banks, and to drive him back, it will prove a great relief to the pressure on Fredericksburg." A letter went to Ewell that same day, stressing the necessity for "a speedy blow." Four days later this emphasis on the necessity for speed was added in another note to Jackson: "The blow, wherever struck, must, to be successful, be sudden and heavy. The troops used must be efficient and light."

Jackson replied that he did indeed think an attack was practicable, either against Banks, who had advanced to Harrisonburg, or against Frémont's lead division, which was threatening Edward Johnson near the village of McDowell, west of Staunton. In fact, now that Ewell was at hand, Jackson had formulated three alternate plans of attack: 1) to reinforce Johnson for a sudden lunge at Frémont, leaving Ewell to watch Banks; 2) to combine with Ewell for a frontal assault on Banks; or 3) to march far down the Valley and strike Banks' rear by swinging around the north end of Massanutten Mountain. For the present, he wrote, he preferred the first; "for, if successful, I would afterward only have Banks to contend with, and in doing this would be reinforced by General Edward Johnson."

That was the last Lee heard from Stonewall for a while, though on May Day Ewell informed him, in a postscript to a report: "He moves toward Staunton and I take his position." Plan One was in the course of execution. Ten days later the silence was broken by a wire from Jackson himself. Routed through Staunton, it was dated the 9th: "God blessed our arms with victory at McDowell yesterday."

In normal times the dispatch would have been received with an exultation to match the sender's, but this was the day the Federals took Norfolk, forcing the *Virginia*'s destruction, and Pensacola toppled, down on the Gulf. From Mississippi came news that Farragut had followed his occupation of New Orleans by forcing the upriver surrender of Baton Rouge and Natchez, while Halleck's ponderous southward advance inched closer and closer to Corinth. Worse still, from Richmond's point of view, Johnston's army was crossing the Chickahominy, near the end of its muddy retreat up the Peninsula. The government archives were being loaded onto canal boats for shipment to Lynchburg, in anticipation of the fall of the capital; the Treasury's gold reserve was packed aboard a special train with a full head of steam kept in its boiler, ready to whisk it out of the city ahead of the Yankees. President Davis had sent his wife and children to North Carolina, and there was talk that he and the cabinet were soon to follow. The soldiers seemed disheartened by their long retreat, and their general had submitted his resignation in a fit of pique because men under his command on the south side of the James had been ordered about by Lee. "My authority does not extend beyond the troops immediately around me," Johnston wrote. "I request therefore to be relieved of a merely nominal geographical command."

Lee managed to calm Johnston down — "suage him" was the term he generally employed in such cases — but the flare-up seemed likely to occur again whenever the general thought he detected signs of circumvention; which he well might do if he looked out toward the Valley. It was a testy business at best. By now, too, details of Jackson's "victory at McDowell" had shown it to be less spectacular than the brief dispatch had indicated. As at Kernstown, more Confederates than Federals had fallen. In fact, except that the outnumbered enemy had retreated, it hardly seemed a victory at all. Meanwhile, alarming news had come from Ewell: Banks was moving northward down the Valley toward the Manassas Gap Railroad, which could speed his army eastward to reinforce McDowell or McClellan. Apparently Jackson's strategy had soured. His attack on Frémont's van seemed to have had an effect quite opposite from the one he had intended.

Lee did not despair. On May 16, the day after the repulse of the Union gunboats on the James — perhaps as McClellan knelt in prayer at the chancel of St Peter's — he wrote to Stonewall, urging an immediate attack: "Whatever may be Banks' intention, it is very desirable to prevent him from going either to Fredericksburg or the Peninsula. . . . A successful blow struck at him would delay, if it does not prevent, his moving to either place." A closing sentence opened vistas; Banks was not the only high-ranking Federal the Valley blow was aimed at. "Whatever movement you make against Banks do it speedily, and if successful drive him back toward the Potomac, and create the impression, as far as practicable, that you design threatening that line."

★ ★ ★

★

Shelby Foote

The macadamized Valley turnpike was vital to both Union and Confederate military operations in the Shenandoah Valley.

Valley Campaign; Seven Pines

1862 ★ ★ ★ ★ ★ McDowell, the sharp but limited engagement fought twenty-five miles beyond Staunton on May 8, was in the nature of a prologue to the drama about to be performed in the Shenandoah Valley. Jackson at any rate thought of it as such, and though, like a good actor, he gave it his best effort, all through it he was looking forward to the larger action whose cast and properties — Ewell and Banks, with their two armies, and the mountains and rivers with their gaps and bridges — were already in position, awaiting the entrance of the star who would give them their cues and put them to use. In the wings there were supernumeraries, some of whom did not yet know that they were to be called on stage: McDowell, for example, who by coincidence shared his surname with the furious little battle that served as prologue and signaled the raising of the curtain.

As such it held the seeds of much that followed, and this was especially true of the manner in which Stonewall put his army in motion to reinforce Edward Johnson for the attack on Frémont's van. Staunton lay to the southwest, with Johnson west of there; but Jackson marched southeast, toward Richmond, so that his men, along with whatever Federal scouts and spies might be observing, thought they were on the way to help Joe Johnston stop McClellan. Leaving his

★

cavalry with Ewell, who moved in through Swift Run Gap to take over the job of watching Banks while he was gone, the Valley commander took his 5000 infantry through Brown's Gap, then — apparently in rehearsal for the boggy work awaiting them on the Peninsula — exposed them to a three-day nightmare of floundering through eighteen miles of ankle-deep mud before they struck the Virginia Central Railroad, ten miles short of Charlottesville, and boarded a long string of boxcars, doubleheaded for speed with two locomotives. When the train jerked into motion the men cheered; for it headed not east, toward Richmond, but west toward Staunton. Sunday, May 4, they got there — to the delight of the townspeople, who had thought they were being left at the mercy of Frémont, whose 3500-man advance under Brigadier General Robert Milroy was already pressing Johnson back. In compensation for the violated Sabbath, Jackson gave his men two days' rest, acquired a new uniform — it was homespun and ill-fitting, but at least it was regulation gray — then marched westward to combine with Johnson for a surprise attack that would outnumber the enemy better than two-to-one.

Numerically it did not work out that way; nor was it a surprise. Despite Stonewall's roundabout approach and careful picketing of the roads, Federal scouts and spies had informed Milroy of the odds he faced. He fell back to the village of McDowell — a sort of miniature Harpers Ferry, surrounded by heights — and called for help from his fellow brigadier, Robert Schenck, thirty-four miles away at Franklin. Schenck got started before midday of May 7, made a driving all-night march with 1500 men, and arrived next morning, just as Jackson was assembling his 8000 for a downhill charge against Milroy, who was in position on the outskirts of McDowell, firing gamely with the trails of his guns set in trenches to elevate the tubes. Reinforced to 5000, he decided to attack before the Confederates got their artillery on the heights. It was done with spirit, catching Jackson off balance and rocking him on his heels. But Milroy fell back on the town, lacking the strength for anything more than one hard punch, and retreated toward Franklin under cover of darkness, having inflicted 498 casualties at a cost of 256.

Jackson took up the pursuit next morning and continued it for three days, including another violated Sabbath, but gained nothing from it except some abandoned wagons. Milroy was not only too quick for him; to make matters worse, he set the woods afire along the road, causing the rebels to dance on embers as they groped their way through eye-stinging clouds of smoke. With regretful admiration, Stonewall called a halt near Franklin and issued a congratulatory order, urging his men "to unite with me, this morning, in thanksgiving to Almighty God, for having thus crowned your arms with success." Having done what he came west to do — knock Frémont back from Staunton — he now was ready, as he later reported, to "return to the open country of the Shenandoah Valley, hoping, through the bless-

Jackson's Valley campaign took the form of a series of rapid maneuvers against three Federal armies. Despite his repulse at Kernstown, Jackson crossed the Alleghenies to block Milroy at McDowell before marching north to smash Banks at Winchester. Withdrawing up the Valley to avoid Shields and Frémont, he defeated them at Cross Keys and Port Republic.

ing of Providence, to defeat Banks before he should receive reinforcements."

It was open only by comparison, but it had opened itself to him. Long and painful hours spent committing its geography to memory with the assistance of mileage charts, listing the distance between any two points in the region, had enabled him to quote from the map as readily as he could quote from Scripture, sight unseen. From Staunton to Winchester, eighty miles, the Valley turnpike led northeast, cradled by the Blue Ridge and the Alleghenies. Whoever controlled the macadamized pike could move the fastest, particularly in rainy weather; but there were possibilities for maneuver. East of the pike, from Harrisonburg to Strasburg, lay a smoke-colored ridge forty miles long, called Massanutten Mountain, and an alternate road led through the narrow valley just beyond it, connected to the turnpike by roads leading westward from Conrad's Store and Front Royal, around the upper and lower ends of the mountain. Embraced by the twin forks of the Shenandoah, which combined at Front Royal and flowed northward into the Potomac, the ridge could be crossed at only one point, about midway, by a road connecting New Market and Luray. Here was where Jackson fixed his eye, and the harder he looked the more he saw in the way of opportunities. The road net thus inclosing Massanutten resembled an elongated italicized capital *H*:

The crossbar was the key. Whoever held it could move up or down either shank of the *H*, not only with his own flank protected, but also with an excellent chance of striking the flank of an enemy in motion on the opposite side. Then too, the narrow eastern valley afforded an ideal covered approach for gaining the rear of an army coming southward up the pike, as Banks had done. Afterwards, if necessary, the attacker could make a quick escape by retracing his steps and swinging eastward through the passes of the Blue Ridge while the enemy was trying to get at him by marching around either end of the forty-mile-long mountain.

Ripe as were the opportunities awaiting him back in the Valley, they would never be available to an army that straggled as badly as his had done on the march to Kernstown. Since then, the marching had improved; but not enough. Mindful of Lee's suggestion that the troops must be "efficient and light," Jackson issued on May 13, while his men were clearing their lungs of the smoke they had breathed in pursuit of Milroy, an order requiring strict discipline on the march. The troops were to fall in at attention, step off in cadence, hold it for two or three hundred yards before shifting to route step, and maintain pre-scribed intervals thereafter. No one was to leave the column for any reason whatever, except by express permission from an officer. Fifty minutes of each hour they were to march. The other ten were for rest, which preferably was to be taken prone. "A man rests all over when he lies down," Jackson said. He had little patience with frailty; a broken-down man and a straggler were two of a kind to him. As one of his officers remarked, "He classed all who were weak and weary, who fainted by the wayside, as men wanting in patriotism. If a man's face was as white as cotton and his pulse so low you could scarcely feel it, he looked upon him merely as an inefficient soldier and rode off impatiently." The men grumbled, seeing in the order further evidence of their general's crackbrained meticulosity; but, having no choice, they obeyed. In time they even saw sense in it, especially after compliance had transformed them into such rapid marchers that they became known as "foot cavalry."

Having prescribed the exact manner in which it was to be conduct-ed, Stonewall was ready that same day to begin his march back to Staunton and beyond. Whatever its shortcomings as a tactical victory, the Battle of McDowell had earned him certain definite advantages. Despite his losses, he would be re-turning to the Valley with about 2500 more soldiers than he had had when he left, two weeks ago. Johnson himself would not be coming — he had suffered a bad leg wound in the fight — but his men would, in spite of the fact that it meant leaving Frémont's advance down the Alleghenies unopposed. As far as Jackson was concerned, there was no longer much danger from that direction. He could turn his back on Frémont and walk off, as if dismissing him absolutely from his mind. In bullfight terms — or, for that matter, in veterinary jargon — he had "fixed" him.

★ ★ ★ *F*or Ewell, back at Conrad's Store, the past two weeks had been "the most unhappy I ever remember. . . . I never suffered as much with dyspepsia in my life." He had cause. Recently he had learned that one of Banks' two divisions was preparing to march east to join McDowell. According to Johnston's orders, this would require him to follow, but Jackson had left strict instructions for him to stay where he was until the rest of the Valley command returned. Ewell hardly knew what to do; "I have been keeping one eye on Banks, one on Jackson, all the time jogged up from Richmond, until I am sick and worn down." Stonewall — "that enthusiastic fanatic," Ewell called him — was keeping his intentions to himself, limiting his communications mostly to announcements of things past: as for instance a dispatch informing his lieutenant that, with the aid of di-vine Providence, he had captured much of Milroy's wagon train. Ewell could find little comfort in this, nor could he fathom the connection. "What has

Providence to do with Milroy's wagon train?" he asked, distracted and outdone.

On May 17 the crisis became acute with the arrival of definite information that one of Banks' divisions, under Major General James H. Shields, had already crossed the Blue Ridge, on its way to Fredericksburg. Though Johnston's orders left him no choice except to follow, Ewell saw that to do so would be to give up a rare chance to annihilate Banks, who was pulling his remaining division back down the pike toward Strasburg. Deciding to delay his departure at least long enough for a talk with Jackson, next morning Ewell rode west, beyond Harrisonburg, and met the Valley commander approaching that place at the head of his marching men. Stonewall's eyes flashed at the news of Banks' depletion, but then were clouded with regret that Johnston's orders denied him the chance to take advantage of it. Infected by his enthusiasm, Ewell offered to stay and lend a hand if Jackson would cover him with a letter of instructions. Quickly this was done, and Ewell returned to Conrad's Store, much happier than when he left that morning. Jackson had given him orders to prepare to march, as well as a dazzling glimpse into the secret corners of his mind.

Before the war, Nathaniel Banks had risen from bobbin boy in a cloth mill to governor of Massachusetts.

Banks now had 9000 men occupying the three points of a triangle which rested against the northern face of Massanutten Mountain: 1500 at Winchester, his main base of supplies, 1000 at Front Royal, where the vital Manassas Gap Railroad crossed the Shenandoah River, and 6500 at Strasburg, intrenched to block an attack down the Valley pike. As protection against guerilla raids, these dispositions were judicious, but they were something less than that against anything more substantial. Banks was quite aware of this, and as a result had been feeling apprehensive ever since he learned of Ewell's arrival at Conrad's Store. In point of fact, however, he had brought this predicament on himself. A self-made man at forty-six, he had risen rapidly in politics and business. Three times governor of Massachusetts, speaker of the Federal House of Representatives, and president of the Illinois Central Railroad, he was determined to do as well in his new career, which might bring him the largest rewards of all.

On April 28 he had wired the War Department that he was "entirely secure" at Harrisonburg. "The enemy is in no condition for offensive movements," he declared. Two days later, while Jackson was setting out on his roundabout march to Staunton, Banks reported him "bound for Richmond. This is the fact, I have no doubt. . . . There is nothing to be done in this Valley." There was the rub. He wanted to be where guns were booming and reputations could be gained, not off in an inactive theater, watching the war go by. That night he wired again, suggesting that his corps be sent to join McDowell or McClellan. Satisfied that this would be "the most safe and effective disposition possible," he added: "I pray your favorable consideration. Such order will electrify our force."

Stanton took him at his word — but not to the extent he had intended. After conferring with Lincoln, the Secretary instructed Banks to send (not bring) one (not both) of his divisions beyond the Blue Ridge to McDowell, who would move south to join McClellan's assault on Richmond as soon as the Valley troops arrived to reinforce him. Here, then, was the natural explanation for the seemingly miraculous response to McClellan's prayers at the chancel of St Peter's. As for Banks, his plan for gaining a share of the glory available on the Peninsula had resulted in nothing, so far, but the loss of half his force — and the better half at that, for it was Shields who had whipped Jackson at Kernstown, back in March. Meanwhile, Ewell had come onto the scene, replacing the vanished Stonewall, who was presently making havoc west of Staunton. Banks, growing cautious, drew back to Strasburg and dug in, preparing to fight whatever came at him down the pike.

★ ★ ★   **T**he electrification he had sought was closer than he knew, and it would not come from Washington. After sending Ewell back to Conrad's Store with instructions to advance two of his three brigades to Luray, Jackson continued his march through Harrisonburg, preceded by a screen of cavalry, and made camp just south of New Market on May 20. Later that day, Ewell's third brigade joined him after a trek around the south end of the mountain. Jackson sat on a rail fence, sucking thoughtfully at a lemon as he watched the troops arrive. Bayonets glinting steely in sunlight, 3000 neat gray uniforms glided past in strict alignment above the cadenced flash of white gaiters. They were Louisianians: Creoles and Irishmen, plus a battalion of New Orleans wharf rats under Roberdeau Wheat, who had put his case on record at Manassas. When they reached their assigned bivouac areas, the commands to halt were given in French — gobble-talk, the Valley soldiers called it, and hooted at the sound. Presently they had more to hoot about. The bands switched to polkas; the men broke ranks, clasped each other about the waist, and began to dance. Stonewall sat and watched in silence, the lemon gleaming yellow in his beard. "Thoughtless fellows for serious work," he said.

Another command crisis was threatening to cost him their services even now. Some hours before, a courier from Ewell had crossed the mountain with a dispatch just received from Johnston, vetoing the proposed attack and ordering him to follow Shields across the Blue Ridge while Jackson stayed behind to observe Banks. This meant that the plan to "drive him back toward the Potomac" would have to be abandoned: Ewell had no choice except to obey, unless the peremptory order was countermanded by higher authority: meaning Davis himself. Jackson moved swiftly, wiring an appeal to Lee in Richmond — "Please answer by telegraph at once," it ended — and instructing Ewell to stay where he was, pending the outcome of the plea for intercession. Now there was the strain of waiting. None of it showed, however, as Stonewall sat on the rail fence pulling thoughtfully at the lemon. When the commander of the Louisianians, Brigadier General Richard Taylor, requested instructions for tomorrow's march, Jackson merely informed him that it would begin at earliest dawn and the newly arrived brigade would head the column. When Taylor asked — not unreasonably, it seemed to him — in which direction they would move, Jackson replied that he would be with him by then to point the way.

He was there before daylight glimmered, and if there was extreme pleasure in his face this morning he had reason: Lee had conferred with Davis and wired back, countermanding Johnston's orders. The march would be north, Jackson told Taylor, and sat his horse beside the pike to watch the gaitered dandies set off down it. His mount was a close-coupled thick-necked ox-eyed creature, taken from the enemy a year ago this month; Little Sorrel was its name, but the men called it "Fancy" in derision. They made a strange pair, the undersized, rather muscle-bound horse and the tall, angular rider with his ill-fitting clothes and his taciturnity. A certain aura was gathering around him, a magnetism definite but impersonal. "No one could love the man for himself," one of his officers wrote home. "He seems to be cut off from his fellow men and to commune with his own spirit only, or with spirits of which we know not." Another put it more briefly, calling him "a one-idea-ed man." Two things he believed in absolutely, "the vigorous use of the bayonet and the blessings of Providence," and he would not be distracted in his efforts to employ them. Lately he had inquired sharply about a missing courier and was told that the boy had just been killed while delivering a message under fire. "Very commendable. Very commendable," Jackson muttered, and went back to the matter at hand.

A mile beyond New Market, just as Taylor's men settled down for the twenty-five-mile march he thought would end with an assault on Banks' main body in its Strasburg intrenchments, the Louisiana brigadier got orders to swing right and take the road across Massanutten — back into the narrow valley he had left the day before. He scarcely knew what to make of this, but presently, hiking through the lofty gap that gave simultaneous breath-taking views of the Blue Ridge and the Alleghenies, he decided that Stonewall was "an unconscious poet" who "desired to give strangers an opportunity to admire the beauties of his Valley." Though his father and his brother-in-law, Zachary Taylor and Jefferson Davis, had been professional soldiers, Taylor himself had attended Yale and Harvard, not West Point. He could not yet see that his arrival had thickened the column which, by now, Banks' scouts would have reported advancing northward on the pike: an illusion that was being continued by the cavalry, which had been left on the west side of the mountain, under orders to keep up the threatening movement, letting no one through or past with information that the infantry had turned off.

It was a hard, leg-throbbing march, steeply uphill, then steeply down, but at its end the two wings of the Army of the Valley were united at Luray. When the cavalry crossed the ridge tomorrow morning Jackson would have 17,000 soldiers concentrated for a strike at Banks' dispersed 9000. Rewarded at last for sticking by a man he swore was crazy, Ewell had absorbed his commander's spirit to such an extent that he spoke with his very accent. "We can get along without anything but food and ammunition," he warned his subordinates; "The road to glory cannot be followed with much baggage." Not only Ewell but a good part of the men in the ranks could appreciate now what Stonewall had wrought, usually to their bewilderment and over their muttered objections. Twenty miles ahead lay Front Royal. Once its 1000-man garrison had been scattered or wiped out, Jackson would be on Banks' flank and astride the Manassas Gap Railroad, blocking his path of retreat across the Blue Ridge. If he stayed to fight, outnumbered worse than two-to-one, with his back to his Strasburg intrenchments, he would be overwhelmed. Or if he fled northward down the pike toward the Potomac, he might be caught in motion and destroyed. Jackson had the answer to his prayers. Meanwhile — as always — his principal concern was secrecy, and for this he had the covered approach of the Luray Valley, leading directly to Front Royal.

Next day, May 22, while the cavalry was fading back from Strasburg to rejoin the main body, the infantry marched to within ten miles of Front Royal — near enough to get there early the following afternoon, with plenty of daylight left for fighting, yet far enough back to keep from alarming the unsuspecting garrison — then halted for a good night's sleep before the day of battle. Up and on the way by dawn, with Ewell in the lead, Jackson sent his troopers ahead to circle east and west of the town, tearing up sections of railroad track and clipping telegraph wires to prevent the arrival of reinforcements from Strasburg or Manassas and the spreading of alarm in either direction. The odds being what they were, seventeen-to-one, the fight could have only one outcome. But Stonewall wanted more than a lopsided victory that would yield him nothing more than control of an isolated outpost. He wanted to kill or capture every bluecoat in the place.

★

That was about what it came to, in the end, though for a time the thing was touch and go. Learning that the garrison was the Federal 1st Maryland, Ewell halted his column long enough to pass the Confederate 1st Maryland to the front. They came at a trot, anxious to have at the "homemade Yankees," as they called them. About 2 o'clock they struck the advance picket, drove it back through the streets of Front Royal, and came upon the main body, drawn up north of town, preparing to resist what its colonel thought was a guerilla raid. He soon found out better, but he continued fighting, determined to hold his ground, whatever the odds. Both forks of the Shenandoah were at his back, crossable only by three narrow bridges, two over the South Fork and one over the North; so that when he saw a body of grayback cavalry riding hard to cut him off, he knew it was no use. Falling back, he won the race for the North Fork bridge, crossed it, and held off the troopers with his two rifled guns while his rear guard set the wooden span afire.

Jackson looked down from the heights south of town and saw the Federals escaping, a compact blue column hurrying north beyond the spiral of smoke from the burning bridge whose flames kept the Confederates from pursuit. "Oh, what an opportunity for artillery! Oh that my guns were here!" he

FRONT ROYAL, VIRGINIA, LOOKING SOUTH.—Sketched by C. L. B.—[See Page 411.]

Front Royal, Virginia, lies beneath Massanutten Mountain at the confluence of the North and South Forks of the Shenandoah River.

★

cried, and turning to his staff he shouted, "Order up every rifled gun and every brigade in the army!" It was easier said than done; the guns were far back, and only three of the forty-eight were rifled. But Stonewall did not wait for their arrival. He rode down the hill and beyond the town, where a glad sight awaited him. The skirmishers had beaten out the flames, preserving enough of the damaged span to permit a crossing by horsemen. The general sent about 250 cavalry in pursuit of the Federals, who had disappeared over a ridge. They soon caught up, forcing a stand, and charged. The bluecoats broke, tried another stand, were charged again, and scattered. By now the infantry had caught up. Gleefully the rebel Marylanders beat the bushes, rounding up their late compatriots and neighbors. Out of 1063, the Federals lost 904 killed or captured. Jackson had fewer than 50 casualties, all told. Mostly they were cavalry, shot from their saddles in the two headlong charges that made his victory complete.

★ ★ ★   **W**hen first reports of the disaster reached Strasburg that same Friday, Banks informed Washington that the attack had been made by a rebel force of 5000, which "had been gathering in the mountains, it is said, since Wednesday. Reinforcements should be sent us if possible." Troops would be sent, he was told in reply; "Do not give up the ship before succor can arrive." He had no intention of giving up the ship, but by the following morning his estimate of the enemy strength had risen to "not less than 6000 to 10,000. It is probably Ewell's force, passing through the Shenandoah Valley. Jackson is still in our front." He added: "We shall stand firm."

Presently the ugly truth came home. Jackson was not "in our front," nor was Ewell merely "passing through." They were not only united, they were united on Banks' flank: moving, he heard, toward Middletown, which was six miles in his rear, one third of the way to Winchester, his main supply base. Still, Banks was determined not to budge. "I must develop the force of the enemy," he kept saying. When one of his brigade commanders, Colonel G. H. Gordon, who had attended West Point with Jackson, came to reason with him, urging that the proper action would be to fall back in an attempt to save his men and supplies, the former governor said he would not hear of it; he intended to stand firm.

"It is not a retreat," Gordon explained, "but a true military movement to escape from being cut off — to prevent stores and sick from falling into the hands of the enemy."

"By God, sir!" Banks cried hotly, "I will not retreat. We have more to fear from the opinions of our friends than the bayonets of our enemies!"

Gordon now saw what the trouble was: Banks was afraid of being accused of being afraid. The colonel rose. "This, sir, is not a military reason for occupying a false position," he said. He returned to his camp, saw to the packing of his stores and baggage, got the wagons headed for Winchester, and alerted his men for the order he knew was inevitable. At last it came. The army would fall back, Banks informed him.

★ ★ ★ *J*ackson spent a good part of the night staring thoughtfully into a campfire, exploring a problem in geometry. At Strasburg and Front Royal, opposite ends of the base of the triangle resting against the northern face of Massanutten, he and Banks were equidistant from the apex at Winchester. By marching fast he could get there first and capture or destroy the Federal supply dump. But Stonewall wanted more than Banks' supplies; he wanted his army too. There was the nub of the problem. If he set out north in a race for Winchester, Banks might move eastward, across his wake, and get away eastward beyond the Blue Ridge. Or if he marched west, against Strasburg, Banks might flee northward, down the pike, and save both his army and his stores. Morning came before the problem had been solved, but at least it had been explored. The latter being the graver risk, Jackson decided to take the former. With luck — or, as he preferred to express it, "with the assistance of an ever kind Providence" — he might still accomplish both his goals.

Luck or Providence seemed at first to be against him. The weather had turned blustery overnight, and the wind was whipping rain in the men's faces. Slow to fall in, they were even slower in getting started. Before long, the rain turned to hail, plopping into the mud and pelting the marchers. "Press on, men; press on," Jackson urged them, riding alongside. His impatience increased when he received a cavalry report that Banks was blowing up his Strasburg ammunition dump, preparing to evacuate. In hopes of catching the Federals in motion on the pike, he sent a section of artillery, supported by Wheat's Tigers, on a road that branched west to Middletown, seven miles away, while the rest of the army continued slogging north, straining to outstrip the head of the Federal column somewhere short of Winchester, where their paths converged.

Almost nothing went right for the Southerners today, and to lengthen the odds — in spite of his original reluctance, which had given him an even later start than his opponent — Banks was showing a real talent for retreat. His rested men hiked fast on the macadamized pike, while Stonewall's plodded wearily through mud. Twice the Union column was cut, at Middletown and five miles beyond, with resultant slaughter and confusion, but both were basically rear-guard actions, marred by the fact that the hungry Confederates could not be kept from plundering abandoned wagons instead of forging ahead after more, and the cavalry practically disbanded as the troopers set out for their nearby homes with captured horses. Jackson was furious, but neither he nor Taylor, who brought his brigade across country to join the pursuit along the turnpike, could deal with more than a handful at a time, and even these returned to their looting

★

as soon as the generals' backs were turned. They would fight when they had to — as for instance in repulsing a 2000-man cavalry charge, which they did in style, emptying hundreds of saddles — but otherwise they were concerned with nothing they could not stuff in their mouths or pockets.

For all their slackness, the pursuers were gleaning a rich harvest of prisoners and equipment. Too badly outnumbered to turn and fight until he gained a strong defensive position, Banks was sacrificing companies in rear-guard ambuscades and dribbling wagons in his wake like tubs to Jackson's whale. With them he was buying time and distance so successfully that by sunset it was obvious that his main body was winning the race for Winchester, where just such a strong position awaited him. Even Stonewall was obliged to admit it. But he had no intention of allowing his quarry any more time than he could

---

"Colonel, I yield to no man in sympathy for the gallant men under my command, but I am obliged to sweat them tonight that I may save their blood tomorrow."

— Thomas J. Jackson

---

possibly avoid. He pushed his weary brigades through the gathering twilight. "Press on. Press on, men," he kept saying. Impatiently he rode with the handful of cavalry in advance, when suddenly the darkness ahead was stitched with muzzle flashes. The troopers drew rein. "Charge them! Charge them!" Jackson shouted. A second volley crashed ahead; bullets whistled past; the horsemen scattered, leaving the general alone in the middle of the road. "Shameful!" he cried after them in his shrill, womanish voice. "Did you see anybody struck, sir? Did you see anybody struck?" He sat there among the twittering bullets, still complaining. "Surely they need not have run, at least until they were hurt."

Sheepishly the troopers returned, and Jackson sent them forward, following with the infantry. Kernstown lay dead ahead, the scene of blundering in March. Tonight — it was Sunday again by now, as then — there was only a brief skirmish in the darkness. Winchester lay four miles beyond, and he did not intend to allow Banks time to add to the natural strength of the double line of hills south of town. When one officer remarked that his men were "falling by the roadside from fatigue and loss of sleep. Unless they are rested," he complained, "I shall be able to present but a thin line tomorrow," Jackson replied: "Colonel, I yield to no man in sympathy for the gallant men under my command, but I am obliged to sweat them tonight that I may save their blood tomorrow." He pressed on

★

through Kernstown, but eventually saw that the colonel was right. If he kept on at this rate he would arrive with almost no army at all. He called a halt and the men crumpled in their tracks, asleep as soon as their heads touched the ground.

Jackson did not share their rest. He was thinking of the double line of hills ahead, outlining a plan of battle. At 4 o'clock, unable to wait any longer, he had the sleepy men aroused and herded back onto the road. Before the stars had paled he was approaching the high ground south of Winchester. To his re-lief he saw that Banks had chosen to make his stand on the second ridge, leaving only a few troops on the first. Quickly Stonewall threw out skirmishers, drove the pickets off, and brought up guns to support the assault he would launch as soon as his army filed into position. Banks had his cannon zeroed in, blasting away at the rebel guns while the infantry formed their lines. Jackson saw that the work would be hot, despite his advantage of numbers. Riding back to bring up Taylor, whose Louisianians he planned to use as shock troops, he passed some Virginia regiments coming forward. They had been ordered not to cheer, lest they give away their position, but as Jackson rode by they took off their hats in salute to the man who had driven them, stumbling with fatigue, to where the guns were growling. He removed his battered cap, riding in silence past the un-covered Virginians, and came upon Taylor, whom he greeted with a question:

"General, can your brigade charge a battery?"

"It can try."

"Very good; it must do it then. Move it forward."

Taylor did so. Passing along the ridge the Louisianians came under fire from the Union guns. Shells screamed at them, tearing gaps in their ranks, and the men began to bob and weave. "What the hell are you dodging for?" Taylor yelled. "If there is any more of it, you will be halted under this fire for an hour!" As they snapped back to attention, he felt a hand on his shoulder. He looked around.

"I am afraid you are a wicked fellow," Jackson said, and rode away.

What followed was brief but decisive. Taylor's charge, on the left, was a page out of picture-book war: a long line of men in gray sweeping forward after their commander, who gestured on horseback, pointing the way through shellbursts with his sword. On the opposite flank, Ewell had come into position up the Front Royal road in time to share in the assault. In the center, the Stonewall Brigade surged forward, down the first slope and up the second, where 7000 Federals were breaking for the rear at the sight of 16,000 Confeder-ates bearing down on them — or, strictly speaking, up at them — from three different directions. The attackers swept over the second ridge and charged through Winchester, firing after the bluecoats as they ran. Jackson rode among his soldiers, his eyes aglow at the sight.

"Order forward the whole line! The battle's won!" he shouted. All around him, men were kneeling to fire after the scampering Yankees. He

*Citizens of Winchester cheer Stonewall
Jackson after his defeat of Nathaniel Banks'
Federals on May 25, 1862.*

snatched off his cap and waved it over his head in exultation. "Very good!" he cried. "Now let's holler!" The men took it up, and the Valley army's first concerted rebel yell rang out so loud it seemed to rock the houses. Stonewall cheered as wildly as the rest. When a staff officer tried to remonstrate with him for thus exposing himself, he paid him no mind except to shout full in his face: "Go back and tell the whole army to press forward to the Potomac!"

The Potomac was thirty-six miles ahead, but distance meant nothing to Jackson so long as an opportunity like the present was spread before his eyes. North of Winchester, all the way to the horizon, Banks' army was scattered in headlong flight, as ripe for the saber this fine May morning as grain for the scythe in July. At Front Royal his artillery had failed him; today it was his cavalry. As he watched the blue fugitives scurry out of musket range, the Valley commander clenched his fists and groaned: "Never was there such a chance for cavalry! Oh that my cavalry were in place!" Attempting to improvise a horseback pursuit, he brought up the nearest batteries, had the teams uncoupled, and mounted the cannoneers. But he soon saw it would not do; the horses were worn out, wobbly from fatigue, and so were the men. The best he could manage was to follow at a snail's pace through the waning Sunday afternoon, picking up what the fleeing enemy dropped.

Added to what had already been gleaned in three days of marching and fighting, the harvest was considerable, entirely aside from the Federal dead, the uncaptured wounded, and the tons of goods that had gone up in smoke. At a cost of 400 casualties — 68 killed, 329 wounded, and 3 missing — Jackson had taken 3030 prisoners, 9300 small arms, two rifled cannon, and such a wealth of quartermaster stores of all descriptions that his opponent was known thereafter as "Commissary" Banks.

★ ★ ★ *T*hose were only the immediate and material fruits of the opening phase of the campaign. A larger gain — as Lee had foreseen, or at any rate had aimed at — was in its effect on Lincoln, who once more swung round to find the Shenandoah shotgun loaded and leveled at his head. Banks put on a brave face as soon as he got what was left of his army beyond the Potomac. "It is seldom that a river crossing of such magnitude is achieved with greater success," he reported. Though he admitted that "there were never more grateful hearts in the same number of men than when at midday of the 26th we stood on the opposite shore," he denied that his command had "suffered an attack and rout, but had accomplished a premeditated march of nearly 60 miles in the face of the enemy, defeating his plans and giving him battle wherever he was found."

Lincoln was not deceived. Anxious though he was for reassurance, he saw clearly that Banks was in no condition to repulse the rebels if they continued their advance beyond the Potomac. In fact, he had already reacted exactly as Lee had hoped and intended. Shields had reached McDowell, and they had set out to join McClellan in front of Richmond; but on Saturday, as soon as news reached Washington of the disaster at Front Royal, they were halted six miles south of the Rappahannock and ordered to countermarch for operations against Jackson. McDowell replied with "a heavy heart" that he would attempt what the President commanded, though he did not believe the movement would succeed. "I am entirely beyond helping distance of General Banks," he told Lincoln; "no celerity or vigor will avail so far as he is concerned." Nor did he have a high opinion of Lincoln's scheme to use him to recover control of the Valley. "I shall gain nothing for you there, and shall lose much for you here. . . . I feel that it throws us all back, and from Richmond north we shall have our large masses paralyzed." The Commander in Chief thanked him for his promptness, but rejected his advice. "For you it is a question of legs," he urged as soon as McDowell's men were on the march for the Valley. "Put in all the speed you can."

Lincoln had something more in mind than the relief of pressure on Banks or even the salvation of Washington. He wanted to capture Jackson, bag and baggage. Poring over maps of Northern Virginia, he had evolved a plan whereby he would block the rebel general's retreat and crush him with overwhelming numbers. McDowell's command, advancing on the Valley from the east, was one jaw of the crusher; Frémont's was the other. Concentrated at Franklin, the Pathfinder was thirty miles from Harrisonburg, which was eighty miles in Stonewall's rear. Lincoln wired instructions for him "to move against Jackson at Harrisonburg, and operate against the enemy in such a way as to relieve Banks." He added: "This movement must be made immediately. You will acknowledge the receipt of this order and specify the hour it is received by you." Frémont replied within the hour that he would march at once. "Put the utmost speed into it. Do not lose a minute," Lincoln admonished. And having ordered the combination of two large forces in the presence of the enemy — the movement Napoleon characterized as the most difficult in the art of war — he sat back, like a long-distance chess player, to await results.

Not that he was not kept busy with other matters growing out of this one. The North was in turmoil. "Intelligence from various quarters leaves no doubt that the enemy in great force are advancing on Washington," Stanton wired the governors of thirteen states, asking them to send him whatever militia they could lay hands on. Three others were told, "Send all the troops forward that you can immediately. Banks is completely routed. The enemy in large force are advancing upon Harpers Ferry." Recruiting offices were reopened. The railroads were taken over to provide speedy transportation for reinforcements before the capital was beleaguered. Rumors spread fast on Monday, so quickly had Sunday's bolt come tumbling. The New York *Herald,* whose morning edition had carried an editorial captioned "Fall of Richmond," replaced it with a report that the whole rebel army was on the march for the Potomac. Harried by congressmen and distraught citizens, Lincoln hoped that his opponent in the Confederate seat of government could be given a hard time, too. To McClellan in front of Richmond went a wire: "Can you get near enough to throw shells into the city?"

The Young Napoleon was scarcely in a mood to throw anything at anybody: except possibly at Lincoln. When he first got the news that McDowell would not be joining him just yet, after all, his first reaction was, "Heaven save a country governed by such counsels!" On second thought, however, he could see at least one benefit proceeding from the panic in the capital: "A scare will do them good, and may bring them to their senses." But the President wired on

After the battle at Front Royal, Banks ordered his outflanked Federals to march rapidly north from Strasburg to Winchester. Jackson sent his forces in pursuit, striking at Banks' rear guard before fighting a decisive battle at Winchester that drove the Federals across the Potomac into Maryland.

Sunday that the enemy movement was "general and concerted," not merely a bluff or an act of desperation — "I think the time is near," he wrote, "when you must either attack Richmond or else give up the job and come to the defense of Washington." McClellan reacted fast. The last thing he wanted in this world was to return to "that sink," within reach of "those hounds." Replying that "the time is very near when I shall attack," he added that he disagreed with Lincoln's appraisal of Confederate strategy: "The object of the movement is probably to prevent reinforcements being sent to me. All the information from balloons, deserters, prisoners, and contrabands agrees in the statement that the mass of the rebel troops are still in the immediate vicinity of Richmond, ready to defend it."

Lincoln knew how to translate "very near" and also how to assess McClellan's estimates as to the strength of an enemy intrenched to his front; he had encountered both before. Just now, though, his attention was distracted. On Tuesday, May 27, he received from Frémont a message that alarmed him: not because of what it said, but because of the heading, which showed that the Pathfinder had moved north instead of east. "I see that you are at Moorefield," Lincoln wired. "You were expressly ordered to march to Harrisonburg. What does this mean?" Frémont replied that it meant the road leading east from

Franklin was "impossible," that he had swung north to pick up food for his men, who otherwise would have starved, and that he was obeying instructions to "relieve Banks" in the best way he saw fit: by marching on Strasburg. "In executing any order received," he declared, "I take it for granted that I am to exercise discretion concerning its literal execution, according to circumstances. If I am to understand that literal obedience to orders is required, please say so."

The reply threw Lincoln into much the same state as when he flung his hat on the floor at Fort Monroe, three weeks ago. Frémont now had seventy miles to march instead of thirty. However, McDowell was closing in fast from the east, and Jackson was still reported near Harpers Ferry. There was plenty of time to cut him off, if the troops marched on schedule. On May 30 Lincoln sent two wires, one to Frémont: "You must be up in the time you promised," the other to McDowell: "The game is before you." Three days later he had Stanton give them both a final warning: "Do not let the enemy escape you."

★ ★ ★ For once, Jackson — "the game," as Lincoln styled him — was exactly where the Federal high command had him spotted: at Charles Town, with his infantry thrown forward to demonstrate against Harpers Ferry, seven miles away. Though he had known for two days now of the forces moving east and west toward a convergence that would put 35,000 soldiers in his rear, nothing in his manner showed that the information bothered him at all. After setting Monday aside for rest and prayer, in compensation for another violated Sabbath, he had come on by easy marches, driving the enemy not merely "toward the Potomac," as Lee had suggested, but to and beyond it. While the reassembled cavalry was pressing northward down the Valley pike, through Martinsburg and on to the Williamsport crossing, the infantry took the fork that branched northeast to Harpers Ferry. It was all rather anticlimactic, though, even lackadaisical, compared to what had gone before, and on the 28th — the day he was warned of the movement that threatened to cut off his retreat — he ordered his troops to resume the prescribed four hours of daily drill. Howls went up from the ranks at this, but the howls availed the outraged soldiers no more than did the complaints of the staff that the present delay would result in utter ruin. If Jackson was oblivious to the danger in his rear, they certainly were not. Once more they called him crackbrained, and one young officer muttered darkly: "*quem Deus vult perdere, prius dementat.*"

There was no middle ground for confidence where Stonewall was concerned; you either trusted him blindly, or you judged him absolutely mad. That was the obverse of his method, never better illustrated than now. It was true that he had already wrung every possible psychological advantage from his present exposed position, which he knew was growing more perilous by the hour, but there were other considerations. He had 2300 unparoled prisoners on his hands, each of whom could be exchanged for a southern soldier now in a northern prison camp, and near Winchester his chief of transportation was assembling a double line of wagons eight miles long, loaded with a wealth of captured goods, including 9000 badly needed rifles, mostly new, and invaluable medical equipment shut off from the Confederacy by blockade. All this took time, but Jackson was determined to give the grinding column of spoils and captives a head start up the Valley turnpike before he attempted to bring his army out of the two-jawed trap about to snap shut in its rear.

On May 30, when the long train started rolling south, there were even more urgent reasons for the army to follow in its wake at once. Intelligence reports placed the advance of McDowell's column within a day's march of Front Royal and Frémont's about the same distance from Strasburg, both of which places were more than forty miles in Jackson's rear. Banks had been reinforced at Williamsport and presumably was about ready to take the field again, tamping the Confederates into the grinder that would be created when Frémont and McDowell met in the shadow of the northern face of Massanutten Mountain. Nothing in Stonewall's manner expressed concern, however, when he emerged from his tent this Friday morning. After receiving a delegation of Charles Town ladies who called to pay their respects, he rode toward Harpers Ferry and watched some desultory skirmishing. When a shower of rain came up, he stretched out under a tree for shelter and presently fell asleep.

He woke to find A. R. Boteler, a Valley congressman who had volunteered for duty on his staff, making a sketch of him. Jackson studied it, then remarked: "Colonel, I have some harder work than this for you to do, and if you'll sit down here now I'll tell you what it is. . . . I want you to go to Richmond for me; I must have reinforcements. You can explain to them down there what the situation is here." Boteler replied that he would be glad to go, but that he was not sure he understood the situation: whereupon Jackson outlined it for him. "McDowell and Frémont are probably aiming to effect a junction at Strasburg, so as to cut us off from the upper Valley, and are both nearer to it now than we are. Consequently, no time is to be lost. You can say to them in Richmond that I'll send on the prisoners, secure most if not all of the captured property, and with God's blessing will be able to baffle the enemy's plans here with my present force, but that it will have to be increased as soon thereafter as possible." If Boteler thought the general wanted to use those reinforcements merely to help stand off the various columns now converging on him, he was much mistaken — as he discovered from what Stonewall said in closing: "You may tell them, too, that if my command can be gotten up to 40,000 men a movement may be made . . . which will soon raise the siege of Richmond and transfer this campaign from the banks of the Potomac to those of the Susquehanna."

★

★ ★ ★ **R**iding south with all the speed he could manage — by rail to Winchester, by horseback to Staunton, by rail again to Richmond — the congressman-colonel arrived to find that the eastern theater's first major engagement since Manassas, eighty miles away and ten full months ago, had been fought at the city's gates while he was traveling. With his back to the wall and the choice narrowed to resistance or evacuation, Johnston at last had found conditions suitable for attack.

In point of fact, despite his fondness for keeping the tactical situation fluid — in hopes that his opponent would commit some error or be guilty of some oversight and thereby expose a portion of the blue host to destruction — Johnston really had no choice. With McDowell poised for a southward advance, a junction that would give the Federals nearly a three-to-one advantage over the 53,688 Confederates drawn up east of Richmond, not even evacuation would assure the salvation of Johnston's army, which now as always was his main concern: McClellan would still be after him, and with overwhelming numbers. The only thing to do, he saw, was to strike one Mac before the other got there. Besides, the error he had been hoping for seemed already to have been committed. McClellan's five corps were unequally divided, three north and two south of the Chickahominy. Normally a sluggish stream, not even too broad for leaping in the dry months, the river was greatly swollen as a result of the continual spring rains, and thus might serve to isolate the Union wings, preventing their mutual support and giving the Confederates a chance to slash at one or the other with equal or perhaps superior numbers. Johnston would have preferred to attack the weaker south-bank wing, keeping Richmond covered as he did so; but this would not only leave McDowell's line of advance unblocked, it would probably also hasten the junction by provoking a rapid march from Fredericksburg when McClellan yelled for help. By elimination, then, Johnston determined to strike down the north bank, risking uncovering Richmond for the sake of wrecking McClellan's right wing and blocking McDowell's advance at the same time.

He had his plan, a product of necessity; but as usual he took his time, and kept his counsel as he took it. Least of all did he confer with the President, afterwards explaining: "I could not consult him without adopting the course he might advise, so that to ask his advice would have been, in my opinion, to ask him to command for me." The result, with the Federals a rapid two-hour march away, was a terrible strain on Davis. Unable to get the general's assurance that an all-out defense of the city would be attempted, he never knew from day to day which flag might be flying over the Capitol tomorrow. May 22, riding out the Mechanicsville turnpike with Lee, he found few troops, no fortifications, indeed no preparations of any kind, as he wrote Johnston, for blocking a sudden Union drive "toward if not to Richmond." Two days later Johnston came to town for a conference, but he told his superior nothing except that he intended to be governed by circumstances. To make matters worse, while he was there the Federals seized Mechanicsville, five miles north, just as Davis had predicted. Not only was this an excellent location for a hook-up when McDowell made his three- or four-day march from Fredericksburg, but now there was nothing at all to stand in the way of such an advance, Johnston having instructed Anderson to fall back from the line of the Rappahannock.

Two days later, May 26, while he was reviewing the situation with Lee, the President's anxiety over Johnston's undivulged intentions was so obviously painful that Lee proposed, "Let me go and see him, and defer this discussion until I return." When he was gone a dispatch arrived from Jackson, who broke his silence with an outright shout of joy. "During the past three days," it began, "God has blessed our arms with brilliant success." Banks had been routed and Stonewall was in pursuit, "capturing the fugitives." Whether this would have the intended effect of frightening the Union high command into holding back McDowell remained to be seen, but the news was a tonic for Davis, arriving as it did at the very crisis of his concern. Presently Lee returned, to be heartened by this early yield from the seeds of strategy he had sown in the Valley and to deliver tidings that bore directly on the subject of the President's anxiety. Johnston at last had announced his decision to attack. Intended to crumple McClellan's right wing, which brushed the purlieus of the city, the strike would be made on the 29th.

That was Thursday; today was Monday. Davis braced himself for the three-day wait.

★ ★ ★ *M*cClellan was quite aware of the danger of straddling what he called "the confounded Chickahominy," but his instructions left him no choice. In the dispatch of the 17th, rewarding his prayers with the announcement that McDowell would be moving south as soon as Shields arrived, Stanton had told McClellan: "He is ordered — keeping himself always in position to save the capital from all possible attack — so to operate as to place his left wing in communication with your right wing, and you are instructed to coöperate, so as to establish this communication as soon as possible, by extending your right wing to the north of Richmond."

That was that, and there was nothing he could do to change it, though he tried. Next day, as if he knew how little an appeal to Stanton would avail him, he wired Secretary Seward: "Indications that the enemy intend fighting at Richmond. Policy seems to be to concentrate everything there. They hold central position, and will seek to meet us while divided. I think we are committing a great military error in having so many independent columns. The great battle

★

should be fought by our troops in mass; then divide if necessary." Three days later, when this had brought no change in his instructions, he wrote to his friend Burnside: "The Government have deliberately placed me in this position. If I win, the greater the glory. If I lose, they will be damned forever, both by God and men."

Consoled by this prediction as to the verdict that would be recorded in history as in heaven, and reassured the following day by a message from Fredericksburg — "Shields will join me today," McDowell wrote, and announced that he would be ready to march on the 24th with 38,000 men and 11,000 animals — McClellan took heart and labored to make the dangerous waiting peri-

"The Government have deliberately placed me in this position. If I win, the greater the glory. If I lose, they will be damned forever, both by God and men."

— George B. McClellan

od as brief as possible. On the scheduled date he sent his cavalry to drive the rebels out of Mechanicsville, thus extending his grasp north of Richmond in accordance with Stanton's instructions. Before the day was over, however, he received a telegram from the President which informed him that he was clutching at emptiness: "In consequence of General Banks' position, I have been compelled to suspend McDowell's movements." Next day, with Banks "broken up into a total rout," Lincoln explained his action by combining a justification with an appeal: "Apprehensions of something like this, and no unwillingness to sustain you, have always been my reason for withholding McDowell from you. Please understand this, and do the best you can with the force you have."

That was what McClellan did. Though he found the order "perfectly sickening," he took comfort at least in the fact that McDowell's southward movement had been "suspended," not revoked, and he worked hard to strengthen his army's position astride the river and to pave the way for the eventual junction on the right as soon as the Fredericksburg command got back from what McDowell himself considered a wild-goose chase. Eleven new bridges, "all long and difficult, with extensive log-way approaches," were erected across the swollen Chickahominy between Mechanicsville and Bottom's Bridge, twelve miles apart. It was an arduous and unending task, for the spans not only had to be constructed, they often had to be replaced; the river, still rising though it was already higher than it had been in twenty years, swept them away about as fast as they were built. While thus providing as best he could for mutual support by the two wings in event

★

that either was attacked, he saw to the improvement of the tactical position of each. Keyes, supported by Heintzelman on the south bank, pushed forward along the Williamsburg road on the 25th and, a mile and a half beyond Seven Pines, constructed a redoubt within five miles of the heart of the enemy capital. Though McClellan could not comply with Lincoln's request next day that he "throw some shells into the city," he could see Richmond's tallest steeples from both extremities of his line, north and south of the river, and hear the public clocks as they struck the quiet hours after midnight.

On the north bank, Porter was farthest out; behind him were Franklin, in close support, and Sumner, who occupied what was called the center of the position, eight miles downstream from Mechanicsville. The latter's corps was theoretically on call as a reserve for either wing, though the rising flood was steadily increasing its pressure on the two bridges he had built for crossing the river in event of an attack on Keyes or Heintzelman. To protect his rear on the north bank, and to shorten McDowell's march from Fredericksburg, McClellan on the 27th had Porter take a reinforced division twelve miles north to Hanover Court House, where a Confederate brigade had halted on its fifty-

Cavalry and artillery, part of Major General Fitz-John Porter's advance guard, skirmish with Confederate infantry at Winston's Farm, south of Hanover Court House.

★

mile retreat from Gordonsville. Porter encountered the rebels about noon, and after a short but sharp engagement drove them headlong, capturing a gun and two regimental supply trains. At a cost of 397 casualties, he inflicted more than 1000, including 730 prisoners, and added greatly to the morale of his corps.

It was handsomely done; McClellan was delighted. The sizeable haul of men and equipment indicated a decline of the enemy's fighting spirit. Lying quiescent all this time in the Richmond intrenchments, despite his reported advantage in numbers, Joe Johnston seemed to lack the nerve for a strike at the divided Federal army. At this rate, the contest would soon degenerate into a siege — a type of warfare at which his young friend George was an expert. "We are getting on splendidly," McClellan wrote his wife before he went to bed that night. "I am quietly clearing out everything that could threaten my rear and communications, providing against the contingency of disaster, and so arranging as to make my whole force available in the approaching battle. The only fear is that Joe's heart may fail him."

★ ★ ★ *T*hat seemed to be about what had happened Thursday morning when, after hurrying through some office work, Davis rode out to observe the scheduled attack, but found the troops lounging at ease in the woods and heard no sound of gunfire anywhere along the line. Johnston had told him nothing of canceling or postponing the battle; Davis was left to wonder and fret until late in the day, when investigation uncovered what had occurred.

At a council of war held the previous night for issuing final instructions, something in the nature of a miracle had been announced. Only the day before, Johnston had been given definite information that McDowell was on the march; already six miles south of Fredericksburg, his advance was within thirty miles of Hanover Court House, where Porter had been waiting since his midday repulse of the Confederate brigade. But now, at the council held on Wednesday evening, a dispatch from Jeb Stuart announced that McDowell, with nothing at all between him and a junction with McClellan, had halted his men and was countermarching them back toward the Rappahannock. It seemed entirely too good to be true; yet there it was. Johnston breathed a sigh of relief and canceled tomorrow's attack. That was why Davis heard no gunfire when he rode out next morning, expecting to find the battle in full swing.

Johnston did not abandon his intention to wreck one wing of McClellan's divided army, but he was doubly thankful for the delay. For one thing, it gave him additional time, and no matter how he squandered that commodity while backing up, time was something he prized highly whenever he considered moving forward. For another, with McDowell no longer a hovering threat, he could shift the attack to the south bank of the Chickahominy, where the Federals were less numerous and reportedly more open to assault. With this in mind he drew up a plan of battle utilizing three roads that led eastward out of the capital so patly that they might have been surveyed for just this purpose. In the center was the Williamsburg road, paralleling the York River Railroad to the Chickahominy crossing, twelve miles out. On the left was the Nine Mile road, which turned southeast to intersect the railroad at Fair Oaks Station and the Williamsburg road at Seven Pines, halfway to Bottom's Bridge. On the right, branching south from the Williamsburg road about two miles out, was the Charles City road, which reached a junction six miles southeast leading north to Seven Pines and Fair Oaks. Thus all three roads converged upon the objective, where the advance elements of the Federal left wing were intrenched. The attack could be launched with all the confidence of a bowler rolling three balls at once, each one down a groove that had been cut to yield a strike.

A third advantage of the delay was that it brought in reinforcements. R. H. Anderson's command, at the end of its long withdrawal from the line of the Rappahannock, was combined with the brigade that had been thrown out of Hanover Court House, thus creating a new division for A. P. Hill, a thirty-seven-year-old Virginia West Pointer just promoted to major general. Another division was on the way from Petersburg under Huger, who had stopped there after evacuating Norfolk. These additions would bring Johnston's total strength to nearly 75,000 men, giving him the largest army yet assembled under the Stars and Bars. What was more, the six divisions were ideally located to fit the plan of battle. A. P. Hill and Magruder, north of Richmond, could maintain their present positions, guarding the upper Chickahominy crossings. Smith and Longstreet were camped in the vicinity of Fairfield Race Course, where the Nine Mile road began; Longstreet would move all the way down it to strike the Union right near Fair Oaks, while Smith halted in reserve, facing left as he did so, to guard the lower river crossings. D. H. Hill was east of the city, well out the Williamsburg road; he would advance and deliver a frontal attack on signal from Huger, who had the longest march, coming up from the south on the Charles City road. The object was to maul Keyes, then maul Heintzelman in turn as he came up, leaving McClellan a single wing to fly on.

It was a simple matter, as such things went, to direct the attacking divisions to their separate, unobstructed routes. On the evening of May 30, as Johnston did so, a pelting rainstorm broke, mounting quickly to unprecedented violence and continuing far into the night. This would no doubt slow tomorrow's marches on the heavy roads and add to the difficulty of deploying in the sodden fields, but it would also swell the Chickahominy still farther and increase the likelihood that the Federal right wing would be floodbound on the northern bank, cut off from rendering any help to the assailed left wing across the river. Johnston was glad to see the rain come down, and glad to see it continue; this was "Confederate

★

weather" at its best. Some of the instructions to his six division commanders were sent in writing. Others were given orally, in person. In either case, he stipulated that the attack, designed to throw twenty-three of the twenty-seven southern brigades against a single northern corps, was to be launched "early in the morning — as early as practicable," he added, hearing the drumming of the rain.

★ ★ ★ The most remarkable thing about the ensuing action was that a plan as sound as Johnston's appeared at the outset — so simple and forthright, indeed, as to be practically fool-proof, even for green troops under green commanders — could produce such an utter brouhaha, such a Donnybrook of a battle. Seven Pines, or Fair Oaks as some called it, was unquestionably the worst-conducted large-scale conflict in a war that afforded many rivals for that distinction. What it came to, finally, was a military nightmare: not so much because of the suffering and bloodshed, though there was plenty of both before it was over, but rather because of the confusion, compounded by delay.

Longstreet began it. Since his assigned route, out the Nine Mile road, would put him under Smith, who outranked him, he persuaded Johnston to give him command of the forces on the right. As next-ranking man he was entitled to it, he said, and Johnston genially agreed, on condition that control would revert to him when the troops converged on Seven Pines. Longstreet, thus encouraged, decided to transfer his division to the Williamsburg road, which would give him unhampered freedom from Smith and add to the weight of D. H. Hill's assault on the Union center. He did not inform Johnston of this decision, however, and that was where the trouble first began. Marching south on the outskirts of Richmond, across the mouth of the Nine Mile road, he held up Smith's lead elements while his six brigades of infantry trudged past with all their guns and wagons.

This in itself amounted to a considerable delay, but Longstreet was by no means through. When Huger prepared to enter the Williamsburg road, which led to his assigned route down the Charles City road, he found Longstreet's 14,000-man division to his front, passing single file over an improvised bridge across a swollen creek. Nor would the officers in charge of the column yield the right of way; first come first served, they said. When Huger protested, Longstreet informed him that he ranked him. They stood there in the morning sunlight, the South Carolina aristocrat and the broad, hairy Georgian, and that was the making of one career and the wrecking of another. Huger accepted the claim as true, though it was not, and bided his time while Longstreet took the lead.

The morning sun climbed up the sky, and now it was Johnston's turn to listen, as Davis had done two days ago, for the boom of guns that remained silent. As he waited with Smith, whose five brigades were in position two miles short of Fair Oaks Station, his anxiety was increased by the fact that

★

Federal gunners lounge near their
24-pounder howitzer in the earthworks east
of the "twin houses" at Seven Pines.

he had lost one of his divisions as completely as if it had marched unobserved into quicksand. Nobody at headquarters knew where Longstreet was, nor any of his men, and when a staff officer galloped down the Nine Mile road to find him, he stumbled into the enemy lines and was captured. When at last Longstreet and his troops were found — they were halted beside the Williamsburg road, two miles out of Richmond, while Huger's division filed past to enter the Charles City road — Johnston could only presume that Longstreet had misinterpreted last night's verbal orders. The delay could be ruinous. Everything depended on the action being completed before nightfall; if it went past that, McClellan would bring up reinforcements under cover of darkness and counterattack with superior numbers in the morning. As the sun went past the overhead, Johnston remarked that he wished his army was back in its suburban camps and the thing had never begun.

He could no more stop it, however, than he could get it started. All

★

he could do was wait; and the waiting continued. Lee rode out from Richmond, determined not to spend another day like the office-bound day of Manassas. Johnston greeted him courteously, but spared him the details of the mix-up. Presently there came from the southeast an intermittent far-sounding rumble of cannon. It grew until just after 3 o'clock, with ten of the fifteen hours of daylight gone, the rumble was vaguely intensified by a sound that Lee believed was musketry. No, no, Johnston told him; it was only an artillery duel. Lee did not insist, although it seemed to him that the subdued accompaniment was rising in volume. Then at 4 o'clock a note came from Longstreet, informing the army commander that he was heavily engaged in front of Seven Pines and wanted support on his left.

That was the signal Johnston had been awaiting. Ordering Smith's lead division to continue down the Nine Mile road until it struck the Federal right, he spurred ahead to study the situation at first hand. As he rode off, the President rode up; so that some observers later said that the general had left in haste to avoid an irksome meeting.

Davis asked Lee what the musketry meant.

Had he heard it, too? Lee asked.

Unmistakably, Davis said. What was it?

★ ★ ★ *M*ostly it was **D. H. Hill.** He had been in position for six hours, awaiting the signal from Huger as instructed, when at 2 o'clock he ran out of patience and surged forward on his own. (It was just as well; otherwise the wait would have been interminable. Cutting cross-country to take his assigned position on Hill's right, Huger had become involved in the upper reaches of White Oak Swamp. He would remain so all through what was left of this unhappy Saturday, as removed from the battle — except that the guns were roaring within earshot — as if he had been with Jackson out in the Shenandoah Valley.) Hill's attack was no less furious for being unsupported on the flanks. A forty-year-old North Carolinian, a West Point professional turned schoolmaster as a result of ill health, he was a caustic hater of all things northern and an avid critic of whatever displeased him anywhere at all. Dyspeptic as Stonewall Jackson, his brother-in-law, he suffered also from a spinal ailment, which gave him an unmilitary bearing whether mounted or afoot. His friends called him Harvey; that was his middle name. A hungry-looking man with haunted eyes and a close-cropped scraggly beard, he took a fierce delight in combat — especially when it was hand to hand, as now. His assault swept over the advance Federal redoubt, taking eight guns and a brigade camp with all its equipment and supplies. Scarcely pausing to reform his line, he went after the rest of Keyes' corps, which was drawn up to receive him just west of Seven Pines.

★

North Carolinian Daniel Harvey Hill was a West Point graduate turned school-master. In 1861 he offered his services to the Confederacy, as did his brother-in-law, Thomas J. "Stonewall" Jackson.

Here too the fight was furious, the Federals having the advantage of an abatis previously constructed along the edge of a line of woods, while the Confederates, emerging from a flooded swamp, had to charge unsupported across an open space to reach them. Longstreet's complaint, made presently when he appealed to Johnston for help on the left, that green troops were "as sensitive about the flanks as a virgin," did not apply to Hill's men today. Especially it did not apply to the lead brigade, four regiments from Alabama and one from Mississippi, under Brigadier General Robert E. Rodes. Inexperienced as they were, their only concern was the tactics manual definition of the mission of the infantry in attack: "to close with the enemy and destroy him." Advancing through the swamp, thigh-deep in mud and stagnant water, they propped their wounded against the trunks of trees to keep them from drowning, and came on, yelling as they came. They reached the abatis, pierced it, and drove the bluecoats back again.

It was gallantly done, but at a dreadful cost: Rodes' 2000-man command, for instance, lost 1094 killed, wounded, or drowned. And there were no replacements near at hand. Out of thirteen brigades available to Longstreet here on the right — his six, Hill's four, and Huger's three — less than half went into action. Three of his six he had sent to follow Huger into the ooze of White Oak Swamp, and a fourth he had posted on the left to guard against a surprise attack, in spite of the fact that there was nothing in that direction except the other half of the Confederate army. However, the Federals were forming a new line farther back, perhaps with a counterattack in mind, and he was not so sure. Huger was

★

lost on the right; so might Smith be lost on the left. At any rate, that was when he sent the note to Johnston, appealing for the protection of his virginal left flank.

Smith's division, reinforced by four brigades from Magruder and A. P. Hill, followed the army commander down the Nine Mile road toward Fair Oaks, where the leading elements were formed under his direction for a charge that was intended to strike the exposed right flank of Keyes, whose center was at Seven Pines, less than a mile away. Late as the hour was, Johnston's juggernaut attack plan seemed at last to be rolling toward a repetition of his triumph at Manassas. But not for long. Aimed at Keyes, it struck instead a substantial body of men in muddy blue, who stood and delivered massed volleys that broke up the attack before it could gather speed.

They were strangers to this ground; the mudstains on their uniforms were from the Chickahominy bottoms. It was Sumner's corps, arrived from across the river. Commander of the 1st U.S. Cavalry while Albert Sidney Johnston commanded the 2d — Joe Johnston was his lieutenant-colonel, McClellan one of his captains — Sumner was an old army man with an old army notion that orders were received to be obeyed, not questioned, no matter what obstacles stood in the way of execution. "Bull" Sumner, he was called — in full, "the Bull of the Woods" — because of the loudness of his voice; he had a peacetime custom of removing his false teeth to give commands that carried from end to end of the regiment, above the thunder of hoofs. Alerted soon after midday (Johnston's aide, who had ridden into the Union lines in search of Longstreet, had told his captors nothing; but his presence was suspicious, and the build-up in the woods and swamps out front had been growing more obvious every hour) Sumner assembled his corps on the north bank, near the two bridges he had built for this emergency. Foaming water had buckled them; torn from their pilings, awash knee-deep in the center, they seemed about to go with the flood. When the order to support Keyes arrived and the tall white-haired old man started his soldiers across, an engineer officer protested that the condition of the bridges made a crossing not only unsafe, but impossible. "Impossible?" Sumner roared. "Sir, I tell you I *can* cross! I am ordered!"

Marching toward the sound of firing, he got his men over the swaying bridges and across the muddy bottoms, on to Fair Oaks and the meeting engagement which produced on both sides, in about equal parts, feelings of elation and frustration. If Sumner had kept going he would have struck the flank of Longstreet; if Smith had kept going he would have struck the flank of Keyes. As it was, they struck each other, and the result was a stalemate. Smith could make no headway against Sumner, who was content to hold his ground. Hill, to the south, had shot his bolt, and Keyes was thankful that the issue was not pressed beyond the third line he had drawn while waiting for Heintzelman, who had sent one division forward to help him but did not bring the other up till dusk.

★

By then the battle was practically over. Seven Pines, the Southerners called it, since that was where they scored their gains; to the Northerners it was Fair Oaks, for much the same reason. The attackers had the advantage in spoils — 10 guns, 6000 rifles, 347 prisoners, and a good deal of miscellaneous equipment from the captured camp — but the price was excessive. 6134 Confederates were dead or wounded: well over a thousand more than the 5031 Federals who had fallen.

These were the end figures, not known or attained until later, but they included one casualty whose fall apparently tipped the balance considerably further in favor of the Yankees. Near Fair Oaks, Johnston watched as the uproar swelled to a climax; then, as it diminished, he rode closer to the battle line, and perceiving that nothing more could be accomplished — the flame-stabbed dusk was merging into twilight — sent couriers to instruct the various commanders to have their men cease firing, sleep on their arms in line of battle, and prepare to renew the contest in the morning. Just then he was hit in the right shoulder by a bullet. As he reeled in the saddle, a shell fragment struck him in the chest and un-

At Fair Oaks, General Joseph E. Johnston, commander of the Confederate Army of Northern Virginia, was severely wounded by a shell fragment. Johnston, the son of a Revolutionary War cavalry officer, refused to leave the field without his father's sword.

★

horsed him. Two aides carried the unconscious general to a less exposed position and were lifting him onto a stretcher when the President and Lee came riding up. As they dismounted and approached, Johnston opened his eyes and smiled. Davis knelt and took his hand, beginning to express his regret that the general had been hit. This affecting scene was interrupted, however, by Johnston's shock at discovering that he had lost his sword and pistols: the "unblemished" sword of which he had written in protest at being oversloughed by the man who now held his hand and murmured condolences. "I would not lose it for $10,000," he said earnestly. "Will not someone please go back and get it and the pistols for me?" They waited then while a courier went back under fire, found the arms where they had fallen, and returned them to Johnston, who rewarded him by giving him one of the pistols. This done, the stretcher-bearers took up their burden and set off.

Davis and Lee went looking for Smith, who as the next-ranking field commander would now take charge of the uncompleted battle. Presently they found him. But the man they found bore little resemblance to the stern-lipped, confident "G.W." who the month before had urged an all-or-nothing assault on Philadelphia and New York. He had learned of Johnston's misfortune and he counted it as his own. It made him tremble. He looked sick. In fact he *was* sick: not from fear, or anyhow not from any ordinary fear (he was brave as the next man in battle, if not braver) but from the strain of responsibility suddenly loaded on his shoulders. The effect was paralyzing — quite literally — for within two days he would leave the army, suffering from an affliction of the central nervous system. Just now, when Davis asked what his plans were, he replied that he had none. First he would have to discover Longstreet's situation on the right, of which he knew nothing. He might have to withdraw; on the other hand, he might be able to hold his ground. . . . Davis suggested that he take the latter course. The Federals might fall back in the night; if the Confederates stayed they would gain the moral effect of a victory. Smith said he would if he could.

The best that could be hoped for under present circumstances was that the army would be able to disengage itself tomorrow, without further excessive losses, for a future effort under a new commander. As Davis and Lee rode together up the Nine Mile road, clogged like all the others tonight with wounded and disheartened men who had stumbled and hobbled out of the day-long nightmare of bungled marches and mismanaged fire-fights, one thing at least was clear. The new commander would not be Smith, who had had retreat in the front of his mind before he even knew the situation. The two men rode in silence under a sickle moon: Davis was making his choice. If he hesitated, there was little wonder. His companion was the obvious candidate; but he could easily be by-passed. Davis, knowing better than anyone how well Lee had served in his present advisory capacity, could as logically keep him there as he kept Samuel Cooper at the Adjutant General's post. "Evacuating Lee," the press had called the fifty-five-year-old graybeard, and with cause. Disappointing lofty expectations, he had shown a woeful incapacity to deal with high-strung subordinates in the field — and Johnston's army had perhaps the greatest number of high-strung troop commanders, per square yard, of any army ever assembled. Besides, in the more than thirteen months of war, Lee had never taken part in a general engagement. Today in fact, riding about the field as an observer, he had been under close-up rifle fire for the first time since Chapultepec, nearly fifteen years ago.

Nevertheless, by the time the lights of beleaguered Richmond came in sight Davis had made his decision. In a few words lost to history, but large with fate for the two riders and their country, he informed Lee that he would be given command of the army known thereafter as the Army of Northern Virginia.

★ ★ ★   *I*n a telegram to McClellan, written while the guns were roaring around Seven Pines and Sumner was assembling his corps for its march across the Chickahominy, Lincoln described the geometrical dilemma he had created for the Confederates in the Shenandoah Valley: "A circle whose circumference shall pass through Harpers Ferry, Front Royal, and Strasburg, and whose center shall be a little northeast of Winchester, almost certainly has within it this morning the forces of Jackson, Ewell, and Edward Johnson. Quite certainly they were within it two days ago. Some part of their forces attacked Harpers Ferry at dark last evening and are still in sight this morning. Shields, with McDowell's advance, retook Front Royal at 11 a.m. yesterday . . . and saved the bridge. Frémont, from the direction of Moorefield, promises to be at or near Strasburg at 5 p.m. today. Banks, at Williamsport with his old force, and his new force at Harpers Ferry, is directed to coöperate." He added, by way of showing that the picture was brightening all over: "Corinth is certainly in the hands of General Halleck."

The circle was not quite complete, however. There was still the Front Royal-Strasburg gap, and Jackson — who knew as well as Lincoln that for him, as for the blue columns attempting a convergence, the question was one of "legs" — was making for it with all the speed he could coax from his gray marchers. Leaving the Stonewall Brigade to continue the demonstration against Harpers Ferry, he had boarded the train yesterday at Charles Town for a fast ride to Winchester, where the rest of the army was being assembled for the race up the Valley turnpike. Time was running out now and he knew it. Still, nothing in his manner showed distress. Folding his arms on the back of the seat ahead, he rested his face on them and went to sleep. He was wakened by a mounted courier, who flagged the train to a stop and handed him a message through the window. Jackson read it without comment, then tore it up and dropped the pieces on the floor. "Go on, sir, if you please," he told the conductor. He put his head on his arms again, and soon was rocked to sleep by the vibration of the train.

At Winchester, when the other passengers learned the contents of the dispatch that had been delivered en route, they wondered that Stonewall had not blenched. Shields had turned the tables on him. Marching fast from the east through Manassas Gap, the leader of McDowell's advance had surprised the Front Royal garrison, a regiment of Georgians whose colonel fled at the first alarm, leaving his men and $300,000-worth of captured goods to be scooped up by the Yankees. Jackson interviewed the runaway colonel that night — "How many men did you have killed?" "None"; "How many wounded?" "None, sir"; "Do you call that much of a fight?" — and put him in arrest. Fortunately, the senior captain had taken command, burned the supplies, and brought the troops out. But the damage was done, and the implications were ominous. Shields stood squarely across the entrance to the narrow eastern valley with its many avenues of escape through the passes of the Blue Ridge. Stonewall's only remaining line of retreat was up the Valley pike, through Strasburg. At Front Royal, Shields was only eleven miles from there: Jackson, at Winchester with his wagon train and prisoners and the main body of his army, was seventeen. Worst of all, the Stonewall Brigade, still menacing Harpers Ferry, had forty-four miles to go before it reached that mid-point in the narrowing gap where Shields and Frémont would converge. Jackson sent a staff officer to bring up the brigade with all possible speed. "I will stay in Winchester until you get here if I can," he told him, "but if I cannot, and the enemy gets here first, you must bring it around through the mountains."

The army was moving by dawn, May 31: first the wagon train, a double column eight miles long, loaded with captured goods that were literally priceless; then the prisoners, a brigade-sized throng of men in blue, who, having missed the pell-mell northward retreat from here to the Potomac the week before, would march faster under Jackson than they had ever done before: and finally the main body, the "foot cavalry," already looking a little larger than life because of the fame they were beginning to share with their strange captain. By early afternoon they had cleared the town, all but a couple of cavalry regiments left to wait for the Stonewall Brigade. Winchester's seven days of liberation were about over. Ahead lay Strasburg, which they might or might not clear before Lincoln's steel circumference was closed. They did not worry about that, however. They left such worries to Jackson, who knew best how to handle them. The worst it could mean was fighting, and they had fought before. Nor did they worry about the rain, a slow drizzle that gave promise of harder showers to come. In fact, they welcomed it. They had the macadamized pike to march on, while their opponents slogged through mud. "Press on; press on, men," Stonewall urged them.

★

They pressed on, halting for ten minutes out of every hour, as prescribed, and joking among themselves that Jackson would never allow the train to be captured; he had his reserve supply of lemons in one of the wagons. Presently, sure enough, good news was passed back down the line. The head of the column had entered Strasburg — and found the gap unclosed. To the east and west, the cavalry was skirmishing within earshot, but the infantry saw no sign of bluecoats as they swung into sight of the little town and made camp for the night. Eighteen miles they had marched today, despite the long wait for the wagons and the prisoners to clear the road ahead, and now they had reached the rim of the map-drawn circle. They were into the clear.

Good news came from the rear as well. By midnight the Stonewall Brigade was four miles south of Winchester, the men dropping dog-tired in their tracks after a record-breaking march of thirty-five miles. Next morning they were off again on wobbly legs, cursing their old commander for having left them far in the rear to fight the whole compounded Yankee army. Always he gave them the dirty end of the stick, lest he be accused of favoritism — and now they were to be sacrificed for the sake of this glory-hunter's mad gyrations. So they complained. Approaching Strasburg, however, they heard a spatter of musketry from the west,

Stonewall Jackson's supply train passes Strasburg on its way southwest along the Valley turnpike. The Confederates outmarched their opponents and slipped between the converging Federal columns of Frémont and Shields.

mixed in with the boom of guns. It was Jackson, fighting to hold the gap ajar for the men of his old brigade. Their hearts were lifted. Once more they sang his praises. "Old Jack knows what he's about! He'll take care of us, you bet!"

It was a strange day, this June 1 Sunday: particularly for Ewell. Except for a feint by one brigade, repulsed the afternoon before, Shields seemed to be resting content with the retaking of Front Royal; but Frémont was hovering dangerously close in the opposite direction, as if he were tensing his muscles for a leap at the west flank of the long column. Ewell was given the task of holding him back while the Stonewall Brigade caught up with the main body, plodding southward up the pike behind the train and the leg-weary captives. He was warned not to bring on a general engagement; all Jackson wanted was a demonstration that would encourage the Pathfinder to hesitate long enough for the Stonewall Brigade to pass through Strasburg. The warning seemed superfluous, however. Contact was established early, but nothing would provoke Frémont into close-up fighting. He stopped as soon as his skirmishers came under fire.

If Frémont was not provoked, Ewell was. "I can't make out what those people are about," he said. "They won't advance, but stay out there in the woods, making a great fuss with their guns." Taylor suggested that he place his brigade on the Federal flank and then see what developed. "Do so," Old Baldy told him; "that may stir them up, and I am sick of this fiddling about." Taylor gained the position he wanted, then walked down Frémont's line of battle until he came under fire from Ewell's other brigades; there he stopped and they came up alongside him. Frémont gave ground, refusing to be provoked into what he evidently thought was rashness. After all that marching, seventy miles in seven days, lashed by rain and pelted by hail as he picked his way over mountain roads, the Pathfinder seemed to want no part of what he had been marching toward. It was strange.

At last, about midafternoon, the Stonewall Brigade passed Strasburg. Ewell broke off the fight, if it could be called that, and followed the main body up the turnpike. Frémont again became aggressive, slashing so savagely at the rear of the moving column that Taylor's men and the cavalry had all they could do to hold them off. Up front, Jackson was having his troubles, too. Twelve miles beyond Strasburg, a portion of the train fell into confusion and presently was overtaken by the lead brigade. The result was turmoil, a seemingly inextricable mix-up of wagons and men and horses. Stonewall came riding up and rebuked the infantry commander:

"Colonel, why do you not get your brigade together, keep it together, and move on?"

"It's impossible, General. I can't do it."

"Don't say it's impossible! Turn your command over to the next officer. If he can't do it, I'll find someone who can, if I have to take him from the ranks."

He got the tangle straightened out and pressed on southward under a scud of angry-looking clouds and jagged streaks of lightning. Soon after sunset the tempest broke. Rain came down in torrents. (Near Strasburg, Frémont called a halt for the night, wiring Lincoln: "Terrible storm of thunder and hail now passing over. Hailstones as large as hens' eggs.") Jackson kept moving, having just received word that he was now involved in another race. McDowell had joined Shields at Front Royal, and had sent him south up the Luray valley to parallel Jackson's advance on the opposite side of Massanutten Mountain. If Shields marched fast he would intercept the rebels as they came around the south end of the ridge; or he might cross it, marching from Luray to New Market, and thus strike the flank of the gray column moving along the turnpike. Either way, Jackson would have to stop and deploy, and Frémont could then catch up and attack his rear, supported perhaps by Banks, who had reëntered Winchester, urged by Lincoln to lend a hand in accomplishing Jackson's destruction.

Once more it was "a question of legs," and Stonewall was duly thankful for the downpour. Even though it bruised his men with phenomenal hailstones, it would deepen the mud in the eastern valley and swell the South Fork of the Shenandoah, which lay between Shields and the mountain. To make certain he

After all that marching, seventy miles in seven days, lashed by rain and pelted by hail as he picked his way over mountain roads, the Pathfinder seemed to want no part of what he had been marching toward.

did not cross it, Jackson sent a detail to burn the bridges west of Luray. That way, he would have only Frémont to deal with, at least until he passed Harrisonburg. When he finally stopped for the night, the Sabbath was over; he could write a letter to his wife. "[The Federals] endeavored to get in my rear by moving on both flanks of my gallant army," he told her, "but our God has been my guide and saved me from their grasp." And he added, with a tenderness that would have shocked the men he had been driving southward through rain and hail, under sudden forks of lightning: "You must not expect long letters from me in such busy times as these, but always believe your husband never forgets his little darling."

All next day the rain poured down; "our God," as Stonewall called Him, continued to smile on the efforts of the men in gray. Jackson, never one to neglect an advantage, continued to press the march of his reunited army along the all-weather pike. There was an off chance that Shields, within earshot of Frémont's guns as he slogged through the mud in the opposite valley, might somehow have managed to rebuild the Luray bridges and thereby have gained access to the road across the mountain. A staff officer, sent to check on the work of destruction, returned and reported it well done, but Jackson did not rest easy until he entered New Market with the advance and found the mountain road empty.

Meanwhile, far back down the pike, the rear guard was having its hands full. Shields had sent his troopers around through Strasburg to coöperate with Frémont, and they were doing their work with dash and spirit. Several times that day they charged the Confederate rear guard, throwing it into confusion. Late in the afternoon they made their most effective attempt, breaking through the scattered ranks and riding hard up the pike until they struck a Virginia regiment, which had halted to receive them with massed volleys. The result was as if they had ridden into a trip wire. Saddles were emptied and horses went down screaming; all except one of the attackers were killed or captured. That night, reporting the incident to Jackson, the Virginia colonel expressed his regret at having had to deal so harshly with such gallantry. The general heard him out, then asked: "Colonel, why did you say you saw those Federal soldiers fall with regret?" Surprised at Stonewall's inability to appreciate chivalrous instincts, the colonel said that it was because he admired their valor; he hated to have to slaughter such brave men. "No," Jackson said dryly. "Shoot them all. I do not wish them to be brave."

He had in mind the expectation that he would soon be facing them in battle: not a series of piecemeal rear-guard actions, fought to gain time for retreating, but a full-scale conflict into which he would throw every soldier in his army. Having employed defensive tactics to escape the first and second traps at Strasburg and New Market, he now was thinking of ways to assume the offensive in dealing with the third, which he would encounter somewhere beyond Harrisonburg when he rounded the south end of Massanutten. At that point he might be able to turn on one or another of the Federal columns and give it a mauling before the other could come to its relief. He would await developments; meanwhile that was what he had in mind.

Before it could be attempted, however, he would have to give his men a chance to rest. Next day — June 3 — they got it. The North Fork of the Shenandoah intersected the Valley turnpike just above the railroad terminus at Mount Jackson, and as Frémont's advance approached that place, the last gray cavalrymen crossed the bridge and set it afire, leaving their pursuers stranded on the northern bank. Stonewall took advantage of this to give his men a full day's badly needed rest and the wagon train and prisoners a substantial head start toward the Virginia Central, where they could be loaded for shipment by rail to warehouses and prisons down near Richmond. If there seemed to be a considerable risk in this delay, he felt he could afford it. Beyond the mountain, Shields was toiling through the mud; he would be at least a day behind and badly worn by the time he reached Conrad's Store, where he would reënter the tactical picture. On this side, there was the danger that Frémont might bridge the swollen river — he had brought a pontoon train across the Alleghenies for just such an emergency — but Jackson doubted if this could be successful, considering all the water that was trickling down the slopes of all the mountains. It was not. Frémont got his pontoon bridge across, all right, but before he could make much use of it, the North Fork rose twelve feet in four hours. He had to cut it loose from the southern bank to keep it from being swept away and lost in the raging water.

While his men were taking their ease beyond New Market, and leg-weary stragglers were catching up to share in the first hot meals the army had had since leaving Winchester four days ago, Jackson took out his Valley map and resumed his study of geography. As always, the harder he looked the more he saw. Resting against the southern face of Massanutten there was a road-net triangle much like the one at the opposite end, which he had used to discomfort Banks; and as Stonewall pored over the map he began to see possibilities for using this upper triangle in an even more ambitious venture against Shields and Frémont. Its base ran from Harrisonburg to Conrad's Store; its apex was at Port

★

Republic, which lay at the tip of a tongue of land where North and South Rivers joined to form the South Fork of the Shenandoah. A bridge spanned North River, connecting the town with Harrisonburg, nine miles away, but all the other crossings were badly swollen fords. Once the South Fork bridge at Conrad's Store was destroyed, this upper bridge at Port Republic would be Shields' only way of joining Frémont. If Jackson's army got there first, he would be between the two, and therefore able to deal with them one at a time. Defensively, too, the position was a sound one. If Frémont attempted an advance on Staunton, Jackson would be on his flank; or if Shields somehow managed to cross the South Fork and marched toward a junction at Harrisonburg, he could then be served in the same fashion. Or if everything went wrong and disaster loomed, Jackson could make a quick getaway by moving southeast through Brown's Gap, as he had done the month before on his roundabout march to fight the Battle of McDowell. All this was much, but mainly he prized the offensive advantages of the position, which would put his army between Frémont and Shields, with a chance to strike at one or the other; or both.

Resuming the march that afternoon, he dispatched two mounted details to perform two separate but allied tasks: one to burn the bridge at Conrad's Store, the other to establish a signal station on the southernmost peak of Massanutten Mountain. The first would frustrate Shields when he attempted to turn west. The second would observe his reaction. Meanwhile, fed and rested, each man carrying two days' cooked rations and a fresh supply of ammunition on his person, the main body made good time up the turnpike. The rain had slacked to a drizzle, which meant that Frémont would soon be able to recommission his pontoon bridge, but for the present the Valley soldiers enjoyed an unmolested march. After stopping for the night just short of Harrisonburg, they entered that place next morning, June 5, and turned southeast toward Port Republic and the execution of Stonewall's design.

As soon as they left the turnpike they encountered what Shields had had to cope with all along: Napoleon's "fifth element," mud. Presently it became obvious that they were not much better at coping with the stuff than they had been on the nightmare march near here five weeks ago. By nightfall the head of the column was approaching North River, but the tail was no more than a mile from Harrisonburg, while the rest of the army was strung out along the six or seven intervening miles of boggy road. Jackson's wrath was mollified, however, by the return of the detail he had sent to Conrad's Store. They had won the race and done their job. From the signal station, high on Massanutten, came a message that Shields had halted two miles north of the burned bridge, which placed him fourteen muddy miles from Port Republic. Frémont was a good deal farther back. He had crossed North Fork above Mount Jackson, but the cavalry was hacking away at the head of his column, impeding his progress up the pike. Reassured, though still regretful, Stonewall called a halt. The rain had slacked to a mizzle by now; perhaps tomorrow the road would be firmer.

It was. Saturday, after an early start, Ewell's division stopped just beyond the hamlet of Cross Keys, six miles from Harrisonburg, to stand in Frémont's path when he came up. Jackson's plodded another three miles and went into position on the heights above the confluence of the rivers at Port Republic, overlooking the low-lying opposite bank of the South Fork, where the road wound southwest from Conrad's Store; this would be Shields' line of advance, and the guns on the heights would enfilade his column at close range. Neither of the Union forces was yet in sight, however, so the Valley soldiers had time for reading their mail, which had just been forwarded along with the latest newspapers. Elated by their victories, the editors had broken out their blackest type. The Charleston *Mercury* called Stonewall "a true general" and predicted that he would soon be "leading his unconquerable battalions through Maryland into Pennsylvania." By way of contrast, gloomy reports from the northern press were reprinted in adjoining columns, and the Richmond *Whig* combined a mock protest with a backhand swipe at the Administration: "This man Jackson must be suppressed, or else he will change the humane and Christian policy of the war, and demoralize the Government." The men, of course, enjoyed this flood of praise. Jackson, too, had an ache for fame — "an ambition boundless as

Cromwell's," Taylor called it, "and as merciless" — but he considered this a spiritual infirmity, unbecoming in a Christian and a deacon of the Presbyterian Church. Also, he was pained that the glory was not ascribed to its true source: God Almighty. Members of his staff observed that from this time on he gave up reading the papers — perhaps for the same reason he had given up drinking whiskey: "Why, sir, because I like the taste of [it], and when I discov-

Irish by birth, James Shields was elected to the U.S. Senate from both Illinois and Minnesota and served as a brigadier general in the Mexican War.

ered that to be the case I made up my mind to do without [it] altogether."

Included in the packet of mail was a congratulatory letter in the handwriting of the President. Congressman Boteler had delivered Jackson's request for more troops; Davis regretted that none were available. "Were it practicable to send you reinforcements it should be done, and your past success shows how surely you would, with an adequate force, destroy the wicked designs of the invader of our homes and assailer of our political rights." For the present, however, the Chief Executive added, "it is on your skill and daring that reliance is to be placed. The army under your command encourages us to hope for all which men can achieve."

Welcome though the praise was, the letter itself was disappointing. Without substantial reinforcements Jackson knew he could not hope to drive Shields and Frémont from the Valley as he had driven Banks. In fact, unless they came against him in his present strong position — which seemed unlikely, considering their caution; neither was yet in sight — he could scarcely even hope to give them a prod. So he began thinking of alternatives, including the possibility of taking his little army down to the Peninsula for a knockout combination against his old academy classmate, McClellan. Replying that same day (not to Davis, but to Johnston, who he thought was still in charge despite his wound) Stonewall wrote: "Should my command be required at Richmond I can be at Mechum's River Depot, on the Central Railroad, the second day's march, and part of the command can reach there the first day, as the distance is 25 miles. At present," he added, unhappy in the middle of what seemed to be a stalemate, "I do not see that I can do much more than rest my command and devote its time to drilling."

★ ★ ★ *I*n this he was much mistaken. He could, and indeed would have to, do a great deal more — as he found out next morning in a most emphatic manner. Shields was a politician, having represented both Illinois and Minnesota in the U.S. Senate, but he was also a veteran of the Black Hawk War and a Mexico brigadier. A fifty-six-year-old native of Tyrone County, Ireland, he had proved his fighting ability by whipping Jackson at Kernstown back in March, and now that his opponent's fame had risen he was anxious to prove it again in the same way. From Conrad's Store, where he had paused to let his division catch its breath near the end of its wearing march up the narrow valley, he sent two brigades forward along the right bank of the South Fork to explore the situation at Port Republic. Stonewall was there already and might launch a sudden attack across the river, so Shields sent a message requesting coöperation from Frémont, whose guns he had been hearing intermittently for a week: "If he attempts to force a passage, as my force is not large there yet, I hope you will thunder down on his rear. . . . I think Jackson is caught this time."

★

He very nearly was: quite literally. The Valley chieftain had spent the night at Port Republic, saddened by the death of his cavalry commander, Brigadier General Turner Ashby, who had fallen that afternoon in a skirmish just this side of Harrisonburg. Ashby had had his faults, the main one being an inability to keep his troopers on the job when there was loot or applejack within reach, but he had established a reputation for personal bravery that was never outdone by any man in either army. In death the legend was complete; "Charge, men! For God's sake, charge!" he cried as he took the bullet that killed him; now only the glory remained. "As a partisan officer I never knew his superior," Jackson declared. Next morning, June 8, when the chief of staff — a theologian who, conditions permitting, did double duty by preaching Sunday sermons in the camps — inquired if there would be any military operations today, Stonewall told him there would not; "You know I always try to keep the Sabbath if the enemy will let me."

The men put no stock in this at all. Convinced by now that Jackson thought he enjoyed an advantage when fighting on the Lord's day, they believed that he did so every time he got the chance. Statistics seemed to bear them out, and presently this statistical trend was strengthened. As the minister-major went back into the house to compose his sermon and the rest of the staff prepared to ride out for an inspection of the camp on the northward ridge, a rattle of musketry shattered the Sunday-morning stillness and a cavalryman came galloping with alarming news. The Federals had forded South River, scattering the pickets, and were entering the town! "Go back and fight them," Jackson snapped. He mounted and rode hard for the North River bridge, clattering across the long wooden structure just in time. A colonel and a lieutenant who brought up the rear were cut off and captured.

Gaining the heights, which overlooked the town, Jackson ordered his batteries to open fire on the bluecoats in the streets below, and sent two brigades of infantry to clear them out at the point of the bayonet. It was smartly done; the Federals fell back in haste, abandoning a fieldpiece and the prisoners they had taken. Stonewall, peering down from the ridge as his men advanced across the bridge and through the smoke that hung about the houses, dropped the reins on his horse's neck and lifted both hands above his head, palms outward. When the men looked up and saw him stark against the sky, invoking the blessing of the God of battle, they cheered with all their might. The roar of it reached him there on the heights, and the cannoneers swelled the chorus.

As the cheering subsided, the men on the ridge became aware of a new sound: the rumble and boom of cannon, swelling from the direction of Cross Keys. It was Frémont, responding to Shields' request that he "thunder down." Going forward, however, he struck not Jackson's rear but Ewell's front. The first contact, after a preliminary bombardment, was on the Confederate right, where Ewell had posted a Virginia brigade along a low ridge overlooking some fields of early grain. Frémont came on with unaccustomed vigor, a regiment of New Yorkers in the lead, their boots crunching the young stalks of buckwheat. As they started up the slope there was a sudden crash of gunfire from the

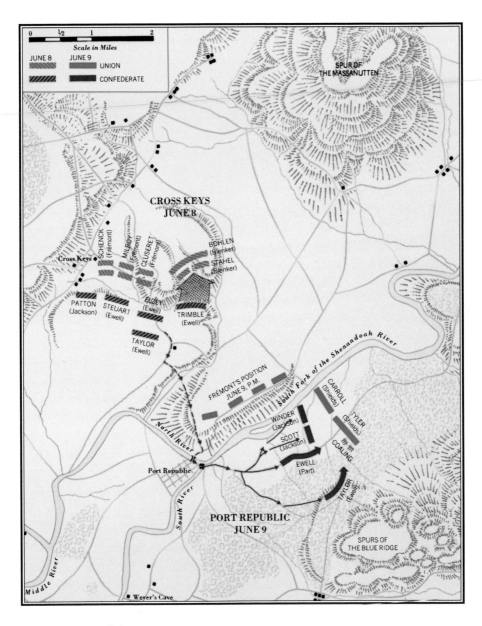

Facing converging Federal forces, Jackson blocked Frémont at Cross Keys on June 8th and crossed the Shenandoah River on June 9th to defeat Shields' Federals near Port Republic.

⭐

crest and the air was full of bullets. A second volley thinned the ranks of the survivors as they tried to re-form their shattered line. They fell back, what was left of them. Frémont, reverting to the form he had shown at Strasburg, settled down to long-range fighting with his artillery, which was skillfully handled. Out in the buckwheat the wounded New Yorkers lay under this fire, crying for water. Their cries decreased as the day wore on and Frémont continued his cannonade.

In essence that was all there was to the Battle of Cross Keys. Ewell, fretting because he could not get the Pathfinder to make another attack, at last pushed forward for more than a mile until he occupied the ground from which the Federals had advanced that morning. There he stopped, having been warned not to put too much space between the two wings of the army. Frémont, with 10,500 infantry effectives, faded back before Ewell's 5000. It was finished. The North had lost 684 men, nearly half of them lying dead of their wounds in the grainfields; the South had lost 288, only 41 of them killed. Jackson's trust in Old Bald Head was confirmed. Except for a quick ride out, to see how things were going, he had let Ewell fight his own battle while he himself remained on the heights above Port Republic. Asked if he did not think there was some danger that Shields would advance to help Frémont, whose guns were within earshot, Stonewall gestured toward his batteries and said grimly: "No, sir; no; he cannot do it! I should tear him to pieces." As he stood there, listening to the sound of Ewell's battle, intoxicated as if by music, he remarked to his ministerial chief of staff: "Major, wouldn't it be a blessed thing if God would give us a glorious victory today?" One who overheard him said that as he spoke he wore the expression "of a child hoping to receive some favor."

But, childlike, having received it, he was by no means satisfied. He wanted more. That night he issued orders for Ewell to leave a reinforced brigade in front of Frémont and march the rest of his division through Port Republic to join the other wing for a combined assault on the Union troops beyond the river. Once Shields was properly broken up, they could both return and fall on Frémont, completing the destruction Ewell had begun today.

The march began at earliest dawn of what was to be a lovely sun-drenched day. Jackson's division came down off the heights, crossed the North River bridge, filed through the town, and forded South River. The Stonewall Brigade was in the lead, under thirty-three-year-old Brigadier General Charles S. Winder, a tall, wavy-haired Maryland West Pointer who, by strict discipline and a resolute bearing under fire, had gained the respect of his men, despite their resentment at losing Garnett. For an hour the advance up the right bank of the South Fork continued. Then at 7 o'clock word came back that Federal pickets had been encountered. Jackson studied the situation briefly, then told Winder to go ahead and drive them. He did not know the enemy strength, but he believed more would be gained by a sudden assault than by a detailed reconnaissance of

★

the position. Besides, Ewell would soon be coming up, and Stonewall wanted to get the thing over with quickly, so as to return and deal with Frémont before the Pathfinder, discovering the weakness of the force to his front, pushed it back into Port Republic and burned the bridge.

Winder went forward, driving hard, but entered a maelstrom of bullets and shells that stopped the charge in its tracks. Once more, as at Kernstown against these same men, Jackson's old brigade had to pay in blood for his rashness. What was worse, by way of indignity — though he did not know it — there were only two small brigades before him, fewer than 3000 soldiers. But they made up in fury and grit for what they lacked in numbers. Their commander, Brigadier General E. B. Tyler, had placed six of his sixteen guns in a lofty charcoal clearing on his left. While the blue infantry held in front, these guns delivered a rapid and accurate fire, enfilading the stalled ranks of the attackers. Winder sent two regiments to flank and charge the battery, but they were met by volleys of grape and flung back with heavy losses. All this time the Stonewall Brigade was being decimated, its ranks plowed by shells from the guns in the coaling.

Jackson was dismayed, seeing his hopes dissolve in the boil and swirl of gunsmoke. Frémont by now must have attacked in response to the uproar, and Ewell was nowhere in sight. It seemed likely that McDowell might be coming up with the rest of his 20,000 troops: in which case there was nothing to do but concentrate everything against him for a decisive battle right here, or else retreat and put a sorry ending to the month-long Valley campaign. Stonewall chose the former course, sending couriers to hasten Ewell's march and inform the holding force at Cross Keys to fall back through Port Republic, burning the North River bridge behind them so that Frémont, at least, would be kept out of the action. Meanwhile, Winder must hang on. His men were wavering, almost out of ammunition, but he held them there, perhaps remembering what had happened to his predecessor after falling back from a similar predicament.

Presently the unaccustomed frown of fortune changed suddenly to a smile. Taylor appeared, riding at the head of his Louisianians; he had marched toward the sound of firing. Jackson greeted him with suppressed emotion, saying calmly: "Delightful excitement." Taylor looked at the hard-pressed front, then off to the right, where smoke was boiling up from the hilltop clearing. If those guns were not silenced soon, he said, the army "might have an indigestion of such fun." Stonewall agreed, and gave him the job.

While Taylor was setting out to perform it, the Valley commander joined Winder, whose men were dropping fast along the front. From his horseback perch Jackson saw enemy skirmishers beginning to creep forward. Quickly he ordered a charge, hoping to shock them into caution until Taylor reached their flank. The Stonewall Brigade gave him what he asked for. Winder's troops advanced, the skirmishers recoiling before them, and took up a new position behind a snake-rail fence. Here they were even worse exposed to the shells that tore along their line. Wavering, they began to leak men to the rear. A gap appeared. Rapidly it widened. Soon the brigade was in full retreat — past Winder, past Jackson, past whatever tried to stand in their way or slow them down. It was a rout worse than Kernstown.

But fortune's smile was steady. The men of Ewell's brigade, arriving on the left soon after Taylor's men filed off to the right, replaced Winder's and blocked a Federal advance. As they did so, a terrific clatter erupted at the far end of the line. It was Taylor; he had come up through a tangle of laurel and rhododendron. Three charges he made against double-shotted guns, and the third charge took them, though the cannoneers fought hard to the last, swinging rammer-staffs against bayoneted rifles. Then, as the Union commander attempted a left wheel, intending to bring his whole force against Taylor, Ewell's third brigade arrived in time to go forward with the second. Outnumbered three-to-one, fighting now with both flanks in the air and their strongest battery turned against them, the Federals fell back, firing erratically as they went. For the Confederates it was as if all the pieces of a gigantic jigsaw puzzle had fallen suddenly into place of their own accord. Eyes aglow, Stonewall touched Ewell's arm and pointed: "He who does not see the hand of God in this is *blind,* sir. Blind!"

It was now 11 o'clock; a good eight hours of daylight remained for pursuit. Pursue was easier said than done, however. Tyler's men withdrew in good order, covering the retreat with their ten remaining guns. Jackson had to content himself with gleaning 800 muskets from the field while the cavalry pressed the retreating column, picking up prisoners as they went. Soon the

ambulances were at work. When all the wounded Confederates had been gathered, the aid men gave their attention to the Federals. However, this show of mercy was interrupted by Frémont. Free at last to maneuver, he put his guns in position on the heights across the river and, now that the battle was over, began to shell the field. Jackson, much incensed, ordered the ambulances back. Federal casualties for the day were 1018, most of them inflicted during the retreat, including 558 prisoners; Stonewall's were in excess of 800, the heaviest he had suffered.

The battle was over, and with it the campaign. Jackson put his army in motion for Brown's Gap before sundown, following the prisoners and the train, which had been sent ahead that morning. By daylight he was astride the gap, high up the Blue Ridge, well protected against attack from either direction and within a day's march of the railroad leading down to Richmond, which the past month's fighting in the Valley had done so much to save. He intended to observe Shields and Frémont from here, but that

Federal batteries, part of Frémont's Federal army, exchange fire with Confederate artillery across Mill Creek during the battle fought near the village of Cross Keys, Virginia. Edwin Forbes sketched the opening of the battle from the center of the Union line.

turned out to be impossible: Lincoln ordered them withdrawn that same day. Frémont was glad to go — he had "expended [his troops'] last effort in reaching Port Republic," he reported — but not Shields, who said flatly: "I never obeyed an order with such reluctance." Jackson came down off the mountain, sent his cavalry ahead to pick up 200 sick and 200 rifles Frémont abandoned at Harrisonburg, and recrossed South River, making camp between that stream and Middle River. There was time now for rest, as well as for looking back on what had been accomplished.

"God has been our shield, and to His name be all the glory," he wrote his wife. Not that he had not coöperated. To one of his officers he confided that there were two rules to be applied in securing the fruits which the

---

"Always mystify, mislead, and surprise the enemy, if possible. And when you strike and overcome him, never let up in the pursuit so long as your men have strength to follow; for an army routed, if hotly pursued, becomes panic-stricken, and can then be destroyed by half their number."

— Thomas J. Jackson

Lord's favor made available: "Always mystify, mislead, and surprise the enemy, if possible. And when you strike and overcome him, never let up in the pursuit so long as your men have strength to follow; for an army routed, if hotly pursued, becomes panic-stricken, and can then be destroyed by half their number. The other rule is, never fight against heavy odds if by any possible maneuvering you can hurl your own force on only a part, and that the weakest part, of your enemy and crush it. Such tactics will win every time, and a small army may thus destroy a large one in detail, and repeated victory will make it invincible."

Application of these strategic principles, plus of course the blessing of Providence — particularly in the form of such meteorological phenomena as cloudbursts and hailstones large as hen-eggs — had enabled Stonewall, with 17,000 troops, to frustrate the plans of 60,000 Federals whose generals were assigned the exclusive task of accomplishing his destruction. Four pitched battles he had fought, six formal skirmishes, and any number of minor actions. All had been victories, and in all but one of the battles he had outnumbered the enemy in the field, anywhere from two- to seventeen-to-one. The exception was Cross

★

Keys, where his opponent showed so little fight that there was afterwards debate as to whether it should be called a battle or a skirmish. Mostly this had been done by rapid marching. Since March 22, the eve of Kernstown, his troops had covered 646 miles of road in forty-eight marching days. The rewards had been enormous: 3500 prisoners, 10,000 badly needed muskets, nine rifled guns, and quartermaster stores of incalculable value. All these were things he could hold and look at, so to speak. An even larger reward was the knowledge that he had played on the hopes and fears of Lincoln with such effect that 38,000 men — doubtless a first relay, soon to have been followed by others — were kept from joining McClellan in front of Richmond. Instead, the greater part of them were shunted out to the Valley, where, fulfilling their commander's prediction, they "gained nothing" and "lost much."

Beyond these tangibles and intangibles lay a further gain, difficult to assess, which in time might prove to be the most valuable of all. This was the campaign's effect on morale, North and South. Federals and Confederates were about equally fagged when the fighting was over, but there was more to the story than that. There was such a thing as a tradition of victory. There was also such a thing as a tradition of defeat. One provoked an inner elation, *esprit de corps,* the other an inner weariness. Banks, Frémont, and Shields had all three had their commands broken up in varying degrees, and the effect in some cases was long-lasting. The troops Stonewall had defeated at McDowell were known thereafter, by friend and foe, as "Milroy's weary boys," and he had planted in the breasts of Blenker's Germans the seeds of a later disaster. Conversely, "repeated victory" — as Jackson phrased it — had begun to give his own men the feeling of invincibility. Coming as it did, after a long period of discouragement and retreat, it gave a fierceness to their pride in themselves and in their general. He marched their legs off, drove them to and past exhaustion, and showed nothing but contempt for the man who staggered. When they reached the field of battle, spitting cotton and stumbling with fatigue, he flung them into the uproar without pausing to count his losses until he had used up every chance for gain. When it was over and they had won, he gave the credit to God. All they got in return for their sweat and blood was victory. It was enough. Their affection for him, based mainly on amusement at his milder eccentricities, ripened quickly into something that very closely resembled love. Wherever he rode now he was cheered. "Let's make him take his hat off," they would say when they saw him coming. Hungry as they often were, dependent on whatever game they could catch to supplement their rations, they always had the time and energy to cheer him. Hearing a hullabaloo on the far side of camp, they laughed and said to one another: "It's Old Jack, or a rabbit."

★　★　★

★

A Union work party strengthens
a log bridge over the Chickahominy
River, one of several bridges built
by McClellan's engineers during his
advance on Richmond.

Lee, McClellan: The Concentration

1862 ★ ★ ★ ★ ★ **C**onfederate authorities at the seat **of government** did what they could to keep the news of Johnston's wound and the subsequent change of commanders out of the papers. Enterprising news-boys sometimes wandered out beyond the fortifications, profitably hawking their journals in the Union camps, and the authorities feared that the enemy might find comfort and encouragement in the news. They were right. "I prefer Lee to Johnston," McClellan declared when he heard of the shift — meaning that he preferred him as an opponent. "The former is too cautious and weak under grave responsibility. Personally brave and energetic to a fault, he yet is wanting in moral firmness when pressed by heavy responsibility, and is likely to be timid and irresolute in action."

He wrote this under the influence of a new surge of confidence and elation. At the time of Fair Oaks, in addition to the depression he felt at hearing that McDowell was being withheld, he had been confined to bed with neuralgia and a recurrent attack of malaria, contracted long ago in Mexico; but he was feeling much better now. Pride in the reports of his army's conduct in that battle — so fierce that eight out of the nine general officers in Keyes' corps had been wounded or had had their horses shot from under them — restored his health

★

and sent his spirits soaring: as was shown in the congratulatory address he issued a few days later. "Soldiers of the Army of the Potomac!" it began. "I have fulfilled at least a part of my promise to you. You are now face to face with the rebels, who are held at bay in front of their capital. The final and decisive battle is at hand. Unless you belie your past history, the result cannot be for a moment doubtful. . . . Soldiers!" it ended. "I will be with you in this battle and share its dangers with you. Our confidence in each other is now founded on the past. Let us strike a blow which is to restore peace and union to this distracted land. Upon your valor, discipline and mutual confidence the result depends."

The men enjoyed the sound of this, the reference to their valor and the notion that the war was being fought for peace. Some of them had wondered; now they knew. It was being fought to get back home. That knowledge was a gain, and there were others. Having done well in one big battle, they felt they would do better in the next one. They could laugh now at things that had seemed by no means humorous at the time: for instance, the boy going up to the firing line with the fixed stare of a sleepwalker, pale as moonlight, moaning "Oh Lord, dear good Lord," over and over as he went. They had a familiarity with the mechanics of death in battle. Coming up the Peninsula they had passed a rebel graveyard with a sign tacked over the gate: "Come along, Yank. There's room outside to bury you." Since then, many of them had served on burial details, fulfilling the implication, and undertakers were doing a rush business with both the quick and the dead, embalming the latter and accepting advance payments from the former, in return for a guarantee of salvation from a nameless grave in this slough they called the Chicken Hominy. The going price was $20 for a private and up to $100 for an officer, depending on his rank.

Their main consolation was McClellan. He gave the whole thing meaning and lent a glitter to the drabness of their camps. They cheered him as he rode among them; they took their note of confidence from him. Presently, after fretful news from the Shenandoah Valley, they saw his confidence increase. He had just been informed that Lincoln had called off the goose-chase after Jackson and was bringing McDowell back to Fredericksburg, with orders to resume the advance on Richmond as soon as his men recovered from their exertions. Best of all, as a cause for immediate rejoicing, the 9500-man division of Brigadier General George A. McCall — left on the Rappahannock while the rest of the First Corps was crossing the Blue Ridge — had been ordered to join McClellan at once, moving by water to assure the greatest speed. Their transports began to arrive at White House June 11, five days after the march order was issued. As these reinforcements came ashore a dispatch arrived from Stanton: "Be assured, General, that there has never been a moment when my desire has been otherwise than to aid you with my whole heart, mind and strength since the hour we first met. . . . You have never had and never can have anyone more truly your friend or more anxious to support you."

Next day army headquarters moved to the south bank of the Chicka-hominy, where three of the five corps now were: Keyes on the left at White Oak Swamp, Heintzelman covering the Williamsburg road in the center, and Sumner on the right, astride the railroad. Porter and Franklin were still on the north bank, the former advanced to Mechanicsville, the latter in support. When Mc-Call arrived he would be assigned to Porter, whose strength would be 27,500 men, and Franklin would join the main body, taking position between Sumner and the river. The army then would present an unbroken front, anchored firmly on the left and extending a strong right arm to meet McDowell, who had wired on June 8: "McCall goes in advance by water. I will be with you in ten days with the remainder by land from Fredericksburg."

McClellan had plenty to do while he waited. The rains had returned with a vengeance, taking the bridges out again, flooding the bottoms, and sweeping away the corduroy approaches. "The whole face of the country is a perfect bog," he informed Washington. "The men are working night and day, up to their waists in water." Lincoln and Stanton kept wanting to know when he would be ready to attack, and he kept stalling them off with a series of loop-holed replies. A week after Fair Oaks he told them: "I shall be in perfect readi-ness to move forward and take Richmond the moment McCall reaches here and the ground will admit the passage of artillery." Six days later, with McCall on hand and four corps consolidated south of the Chickahominy, he declared: "I shall attack as soon as the weather and the ground will permit." June 18 the rain slacked and he wired: "After tomorrow we shall fight the rebel army as soon as Providence will permit."

It was a tantalizing progression of near-commitments and evasions: first McCall, then the weather, and finally Providence itself: Lincoln and Stanton scarcely knew what to think. McClellan knew, though. He had read rumors that the powers in Washington were engaged in a frenzy of backbiting over the recent fiasco in the Valley. "Alas! poor country that should have such leaders," he groaned, adding: "When I see such insane folly behind me I feel that the final sal-vation of the country demands the utmost prudence on my part, and that I must not run the slightest risk of disaster, for if anything happened to this army our cause would be lost." He saw his way to victory. According to the Pinkertons, the rebels had the advantage of numbers, but he had the advantage of superior train-ing and equipment. Therefore he would make the contest a siege. Employing "the utmost prudence" to avoid "the slightest risk," he had evolved a formula for victory, ponderous but sure. He kept it from Lincoln and Stanton, who would neither approve nor understand, but he told it gladly to his wife, who would do both: "I will push them in upon Richmond and behind their works. Then I will bring up my heavy guns, shell the city, and carry it by assault."

★ ★ ★ *W*hether Lee was "cautious . . . weak . . . wanting in moral firmness . . . timid and irresolute" remained to be seen, but part at least of McClellan's judgment of his opponent had already been confirmed. He was "energetic" — and southern soldiers agreed with the northern commander that it was "to a fault." Reverting to his former role as King of Spades, he had them digging as they had never dug before. Their reaction was the one he had encountered in the Carolinas: that intrenchments were cowardly affairs, and that shoveling dirt wasn't fit work for a white man. Lee's reply was that hard work was "the very means by which McClellan has [been] and is advancing. Why should we leave to him the whole advantage of labor? . . . There is nothing so military as labor, and nothing so important to an army as to save the lives of its soldiers." A third complaint, that digging would never drive the Yankees away from the gates of Richmond, he left for time to answer. Meanwhile there were those who, remembering his earnest statement back in May — "Richmond must not be given up; it shall not be given up!" — considered that he might be saving his soldiers' lives for a quite different purpose, entirely aside from the sheer humanity of the thing.

He saw the problem posed for him by his fellow engineer: "McClellan will make this a battle of posts. He will take position from position under cover of his heavy guns and we cannot get at him." What Lee needed in the face of this was time, and he got it. The first ten days of June were solid rain. "You have seen nothing like the roads on the Chicky bottom," he reported thankfully. McClellan's big guns were immobilized unless he brought them forward on the York River Railroad, and Lee moved quickly to block this route by mounting a long-range 32-pounder on a railway truck and running it eastward to outrange the swamp-bound Federal ordnance. This was the birth of the railroad gun, fathered by necessity and Lee.

The men could appreciate this kind of thing, its benefit being immediately apparent. They could appreciate, too, the new administrative efficiency which brought them better rations and an equitable distribution of the clothes and shoes it prised from quartermaster warehouses. There was a rapid improvement of their appearance and, in consequence, their tone. Lee himself was frequently among them, riding the lines to inspect the progress of their work on the intrenchments. Tall, handsome, robust, much younger-looking up close than from a distance, he had a cheerful dignity and could praise them without seeming to court their favor. They began to look forward to his visits, and even take pride in the shovel work they had performed so unwillingly up to now. The change for the better was there for everyone to see, including their old commander, convalescent in Richmond. "No, sir," Johnston said manfully when a friend remarked that his wound was a calamity for the South. "The shot that struck me down is the very best that has been fired for the southern cause yet. For I possess in no degree the confidence of

★

*"McClellan will make this a battle of posts.
He will take position from position under cover of
his heavy guns and we cannot get at him."*

— Robert E. Lee

*Of Robert E. Lee, newly appointed commander
of the Army of Northern Virginia, a fellow officer
remarked that "his name might be Audacity."*

our government, and now they have in my place one who does possess it, and who can accomplish what I never could have done: the concentration of our armies for the defense of the capital of the Confederacy."

This in fact was a main key to Lee's success in the course of his first weeks as head of the army in Virginia. He knew how to get along with Davis. Unlike Johnston, who had kept his intentions from the President as assiduously as if the two had been engaged as opponents in high-stakes poker, Lee sought his advice and kept him informed from day to day, even from hour to hour. One of the first letters he sent from the field was to Davis, describing certain administrative difficulties in one of the commands. "I thought you ought to know it," he wrote. "Our position requires that you should know everything and you must excuse my troubling you." Davis fairly basked in the unfamiliar warmth — and gave, as always, loyalty for loyalty received. Knowing him well, Lee knew that this support would never be revoked. Whatever lay before him, down the months and years, he knew that he would never have to look back over his shoulder as he went. Nor would he, like his opponent, have to step cautiously in anticipation of a fall from having the rug jerked from under him by wires leading back to his capital.

What lay before him now was McClellan, whose "battle of posts" would begin as soon as the weather turned Union and dried the roads. Such a battle could have only one outcome, the odds being what they were. As Lee saw it, he had but two choices: to retreat, abandoning Richmond, or to strike before his opponent got rolling. The former course had possibilities. He could fall back to the mountains, he said, "and if my soldiers will stand by me I will fight those people for years to come." However, it was the latter course he chose. At first he considered a repetition of Johnston's tactics, an attack on the Federal left, but he soon rejected the notion of making a frontal assault against an intrenched and superior enemy who, even if defeated, could retreat in safety down the Peninsula, much as Johnston had retreated up it. The flank beyond the Chicka-hominy was weaker and more exposed to attack, and once it was crushed or brushed aside, the way would be open for seizure of McClellan's base at White House. Cut off from his food and munitions, the Union commander would be obliged to come out of his intrenchments and fight the Confederates on ground of their choice, astride his lines of supply and communication.

When Lee submitted the plan for presidential approval, Davis raised a question. If McClellan behaved like an engineer, giving all his concern to his line of supply, the thing might work; but what if he assaulted the weakened line in front of Richmond while Lee was mounting the flank attack with troops stripped from the capital defenses? Would that not mean the fall of the city? Lee bridled at the reference to engineers, his own branch of the service as well as McClellan's, but said that he did not believe his opponent would attempt such a desperate venture. Besides, that was why he had put the men to digging: to enable a thin line to withstand an assault by superior numbers. It would not have to be for long. "If you will hold as long as you can at the intrenchments, and then fall back on the detached works around the city, I will be on the enemy's heels before he gets here." So he said, and Davis, after consideration, agreed that the long odds required long chances. He approved the plan of attack.

The first problem, once the plan had been approved, was the securing of reinforcements. No matter how ingenious the tactics, 61,000 Confederates could not hope to drive more than 100,000 Federals from a position they had been strengthening ever since their repulse of the full-scale assault two weeks before. As a problem it was thorny. South Carolina could spare no men at all, Charleston being menaced by an amphibious force assembling at Hilton Head; but Burnside seemed to be resting on his New Bern laurels, so that the rest of Holmes' division could be brought from North Carolina, adding 6500 bayonets to the ranks. Georgia could furnish a single brigade; Lee sent it to Jackson. "We must aid a gallant man if we perish," he said, having already weakened his army for this purpose. Besides, it was in the nature of a loan. Stonewall was to use the troops offensively if the opportunity arose, discouraging the Washington authorities from sending reinforcements to the Peninsula from the Valley or the line of the Rappahannock. Then, when everything was ready for the leap at McClellan, he was to leave his cavalry and his least effective infantry units in their present location, and take the cars for Richmond, adding 18,500 veterans to the column of assault.

This would bring Lee's total strength to 86,000: still about 20,000 short of McClellan's. Total strengths were not as important, however, as critical strengths at the point of vital contact — and that was where Lee proposed to secure the advantage. He would hold the Richmond intrenchments with the combined commands of Magruder, Huger, and Holmes, while those of Longstreet, the two Hills, and Jackson struck the isolated enemy corps on the north bank of the Chickahominy. In round figures, 30,000 men would be facing 75,000 to the east, while 55,000 assaulted 30,000 to the north; or, more roughly speaking, one third of Lee's army would resist three fourths of McClellan's, while the remaining two thirds attacked the remaining one fourth. The risk was great, as Davis said, but not so great as the possibilities for gain. As the Federal main body, its right wing crushed, fell back to recover or protect its seized or threatened base, the Confederates would catch it in motion and destroy it, flank and rear. Richmond would be delivered.

No matter how devoutly this consummation was to be wished, a great deal remained to be done before it could begin to be accomplished. Jackson's approach march from the railroad would be along the ridge between the Chickahominy River and Totopotomoy Creek, an affluent of the Pamunkey. Lee knew that McClellan had withdrawn Porter's troops from Hanover Court House soon after the junction with McDowell was suspended, but he did not know the present location of Porter's right or the condition of the roads in that direction. Both of these necessary pieces of information could be gathered, along with possibly much else, by a reconnaissance in force. That meant cavalry, and cavalry meant Jeb Stuart. Accordingly, on June 10, Lee sent for him and told him what he wanted.

Stuart was delighted. A brigadier at twenty-nine, square-built, of average height, with china-blue eyes, a bushy cinnamon beard, and flamboyant clothes — thigh-high boots, yellow sash, elbow-length gauntlets, red-lined cape, soft hat with the brim pinned up on one side by a gold star supporting a foot-long ostrich plume — he had had no chance for individual

A brigadier at twenty-nine, square-built, of average height, with china-blue eyes, a bushy cinnamon beard, and flamboyant clothes . . . he had had no chance for individual distinction since the charge that scattered the Fire Zouaves at Manassas.

distinction since the charge that scattered the Fire Zouaves at Manassas. He had a thirst for such exploits, both for his own sake and his troopers', whose training he was conducting in accordance with a credo: "If we oppose force to force we cannot win, for their resources are greater than ours. We must substitute *esprit* for numbers. Therefore I strive to inculcate in my men the spirit of the chase." That partly explained the gaudy fox-hunt clothes, and it also explained what he proposed as soon as Lee had finished speaking. Once he was in McClellan's rear, he said, it might be practicable to ride all the way around him.

Lee might have expected something of the sort, for Stuart had been an industrious collector of demerits as an adventurous cadet at the Point while his fellow Virginian was superintendent. At any rate, in the written instructions sent next day while Jeb was happily selecting and assembling 1200 troopers for the ride, the army commander warned him explicitly against rashness: "You will return as soon as the object of your expedition is accomplished, and you must bear constantly in mind, while endeavoring to execute the general purpose of

★

your mission, not to hazard unnecessarily your command or to attempt what your judgment may not approve; but be content to accomplish all the good you can, without feeling it necessary to obtain all that might be desired." These were sobering words, but Stuart was pleased to note that the general called the proposed affair an "expedition," not merely a scout or a raid.

At 2 a.m. on the 12th he passed the word to his unit commanders standing by: "Gentlemen, in ten minutes every man must be in the saddle." Within that time they set out, riding north out of Richmond as if bound for the Shenandoah Valley. Only Stuart, who rode at the head of the column, knew their true destination. His high spirits were heightened by the knowledge that his opposite number, commanding McClellan's cavalry, was Brigadier General Philip St George Cooke, his wife's father, an old-line soldier who, to his son-in-law's discomfort and chagrin, had stayed with the old flag. "He will regret it but once," Jeb said, "and that will be continuously."

The three-day wait, following Stuart's disappearance into the darkness, was a time of strain for Lee and the Army of Northern Virginia. For one thing, the weather turned Union; the roads were drying fast under the influence of a hot spell. For another, there was information that McClellan was receiving reinforcements; McCall's division had come up the York in transports, adding its strength to the preponderance of numbers already enjoyed by the blue army in front of Richmond. Taken together, these two factors indicated that the "battle of posts" was about to begin before Lee could put his own plan into execution. The strain was not considerably relieved by the arrival of a courier, late on the 14th, with the first news from Stuart since he left. Far in the Federal rear, after wrecking a wagon train and capturing more than 300 men and horses, he had decided that it would be safer to continue on his way instead of turning back to cut a path through the disrupted forces gathering in his rear. Accordingly, he had pushed on eastward, then veered south to complete his circuit of the enemy army. But when he reached the Chickahominy, thirty-odd miles below the capital, he found the bridges out and the water too swift and deep for fording. That had been his plight when the courier left him: a swollen river to his front and swarms of hornet-mad Federal horsemen converging on his rear. However, he was confident he would get out all right, he said, if Lee would only make a diversion on the Charles City road to distract the bluecoats while he continued his search for an escape route.

Lee was not given to swearing, or else he would have done so now. At any rate, the day was too far gone for the diversion Stuart requested, and next morning, before the order could be issued, Jeb himself came jingling up to headquarters. His fine clothes were bedraggled and the face above the cinnamon beard showed the effects of two nights in the saddle without sleep, but he was jubilant over his exploit, which he knew was about to be hailed and bewailed in southern and northern papers. Improvising a bridge, he had crossed the Chickahominy with his entire command, guns and all, then ridden up the north bank of the James to report to Lee in person. At a cost of one man, lost in a skirmish two days back, he had brought out 170 prisoners, along with 300 horses and mules, and added considerably to whatever regret his father-in-law had been feeling up to now. Beyond all this, he had also brought out the information Lee had sent him after. McClellan's base was still at White House, and there was no indication that he intended to change it. The roads behind the Federal lines, which the enemy would have to use in bringing his big guns forward, were in even worse shape than those in the Confederate front. And, finally, Porter's right did not extend to the ridge between the Chickahominy and Totopotomoy Creek. In fact, that whole flank was practically "in the air," open to Jackson's turning movement along the ridge.

The moment was at hand. After feeling out the enemy lines that afternoon to determine whether Stuart's ride around McClellan had alarmed the northern commander into weakening his front in order to reinforce his flank beyond the river — it had not — Lee wrote to Jackson next morning, June 16. Five days ago, congratulating Stonewall for the crowning double victory at Cross Keys and Port Republic, he had sent him a warning order, alerting him for the march toward Richmond. Now the instructions to move were made explicit, though in language that was courteous to the point of being deferential: "The present . . . seems to be favorable for a junction of your army with this. If you agree with me, the sooner you can make arrangements to do so the better. In moving your troops you can let it be understood that it was to pursue the enemy in your front. Dispose those to hold the Valley so as to deceive the enemy, keeping your cavalry well in their front, and at the proper time suddenly descending upon the Pamunkey. . . . I should like to have the advantage of your views and to be able to confer with you. Will meet you at some point on your approach to the Chickahominy."

With the date of the attack dependent on Jackson's rate of march, there was little for the southern commander to do now except wait, perfecting the details of the north-bank convergence, and hope that his opponent would remain astride the river with his right flank in the air. The strain of waiting was relieved by good news of a battle fought in South Carolina on the day Lee summoned Stonewall from the Valley. The Federals had mounted their offensive against Charleston, landing 6500 troops on James Island, but were met and repulsed at Secessionville by Shanks Evans with less than half as many men. Inflicting 683 casualties at a cost of 204, Evans increased the reputation he had won above the stone bridge at Manassas and on the wooded plateau above Ball's Bluff and was proclaimed the savior of Charleston. Though this minor action scarcely balanced the recent loss of Fort Pillow and Memphis, or the evacuation of Cumberland Gap two days later, it made a welcome addition to the little

Troopers of Stuart's cavalry rode around the Federal Army of the Potomac, accurately reporting on the extent of the enemy's position. The exploit boosted morale in Richmond.

string of victories won along the twin forks of the Shenandoah River. Lee was encouraged to hope that the tide was turning, at least in the East, and that the blue host in front of Richmond might soon be caught in the undertow and swept away or drowned. "Our enemy is quietly working within his lines, and collecting additional forces to drive us from our capital," he wrote in a private letter June 22, three weeks after taking command. "I hope we shall be able yet to disappoint him, and drive him back to his own country."

Next afternoon the possibility of such a deliverance was considerably enhanced by the arrival of a dusty horseman who came riding out the Nine Mile road to army headquarters. It was Jackson. Stiff from fourteen hours in the saddle, having covered fifty-two miles of road on relays of commandeered horses, he presently was closeted with Lee and the other three division commanders who would share with him the work of destruction across the river. Lee spread a crude map and explained the plan as he had worked it out.

Stonewall, coming down from the north with Stuart's troopers guarding his left, was to clear the head of Beaver Dam Creek, outflanking Porter and forcing him to evacuate his main line of resistance, dug in along the east bank of the stream. That way, there would be no fighting until the enemy had been flushed from his intrenchments, and by then the other three attack divisions would be on hand, having crossed the Chickahominy as soon as they learned that Jackson was within range. The crossing was to be accomplished in sequence. A. P. Hill would post a brigade at Half Sink, four miles upstream from his position at Meadow Bridge. Informed of Jackson's approach, this brigade would cross to the left bank and move down it, driving Porter's outposts eastward until they uncovered Meadow Bridge, which Hill would cross to advance on Mechanicsville. This in turn would uncover the turnpike bridge, permitting a crossing by D. H. Hill and Longstreet at that point and in that order. The former would move past his namesake's rear and swing wide around Beaver Dam Creek in support of Jackson. The latter would form on A. P. Hill's right for the advance through Porter's abandoned intrenchments. All four commands would then be in line — in echelon, from left to right: Jackson, D. H. Hill, A. P. Hill, and Longstreet — for the sweep down the left bank of the Chickahominy. Once they cleared New Bridge, four miles below Mechanicsville, they would be in touch with Magruder and Huger, who would have been maneuvering Prince-John-style all this time to discourage an attack on their thin line by the Federal main body in their front. With contact reëstablished between the two Confederate wings, the danger of such an attack would have passed; as Lee said, they would "be on the enemy's heels" in case he tried it. The advance beyond the river would continue, slashing McClellan's communications and coming between him and his base of supplies at White House.

There were objections. Harvey Hill had expressed the opinion that an attack on the Federal left would be more rewarding; McClellan might respond to the assault on his right by changing his base to the James, beyond reach of the attackers. Lee had pointed out, however, that this would involve the army in the bogs of White Oak Swamp and rob it of the mobility which was its principal asset. Besides, Stuart's reconnaissance had shown that the Union base was still at White House, and Lee did not believe the Federals would attempt to make the shift while under attack. Longstreet, too, had indicated what he thought were disadvantages, the main one being the great natural strength of Porter's position along Beaver Dam Creek. However, this objection would be nullified by Jackson, whose approach would maneuver Porter out of his intrenchments by menacing his rear, and if he fell back to another creek-bank stronghold — there were several such in his rear, at more or less regular intervals along the north bank of the Chickahominy — the same tactics could be applied, with the same result. Thus were Hill and Longstreet answered. Stonewall made no comment, being a stranger to the scene, and A. P. Hill, the junior officer present, held his tongue. After the brief discussion, Lee retired to give the quartet of generals a chance to talk his plan over among themselves.

They were young men, all four of them, though they disguised the fact with beards. Longstreet was the oldest, forty-one, A. P. Hill the youngest, thirty-seven; D. H. Hill was forty, Jackson thirty-eight; they had been at West Point together, twenty years ago. Longstreet spoke first, asking Jackson to set the date for the attack, since his was the only command not on the scene. The 25th, Jackson replied without hesitation. Longstreet demurred, advising him to take an extra day to allow for poor roads and possible enemy interference. All right, Jackson said, the 26th. Presently Lee returned and approved their decision. Today was Monday; the attack would be made on Thursday, at the earliest possible hour. He would send them written orders tomorrow.

The council broke up about nightfall. Jackson had spent most of the previous night in the saddle, but he would take no rest until he rejoined his men on the march. Mounting, he rode through the darkness, accompanied as before by a single aide, whom he had instructed to call him Colonel as a precaution against being recognized before he got his army into position to come booming down along McClellan's flank.

★ ★ ★ *W*hile Stonewall clattered north along unfamiliar roads to rejoin the Valley soldiers moving to meet him, McClellan sat alone in his tent, winding up a long day's work by writing to his wife. For various reasons, some definite, some vague, but all disturbing, he felt uneasy. Intelligence reports showed that his army was badly outnumbered, and Stuart's circumferential raid had not only afforded hostile journalists much amusement at the Young Napoleon's expense, it had also emphasized the danger to his extended flank and to his main supply base, both of which lay on the far side of what he still called "the confounded Chickahominy." He had protested, for McDowell's sake as well as his own, against the instructions requiring that general's overland advance and "an extension of my right wing to meet him." Such dispositions, he warned Stanton, "may involve serious hazard to my flank and line of communications and may not suffice to rescue [him] from any peril in which a strong movement of the enemy may involve him."

Nothing having come of this, he was obliged to keep Porter where he was. The danger to his base was another matter, one in which he could act on his own, and that was what he did. On the day Stuart returned to his lines and reported to Lee, McClellan ordered a reconnaissance toward James River, intending to look into the possibility of establishing a new base in that direction. Three days later, June 18, he began sending transports loaded with food and ammunition from White House down the Pamunkey and the York, up the James to Harrison's Landing. Gunboats, stationed there to protect them, would also protect his army in case it was thrown back as a result of an overwhelming assault on its present all-too-vulnerable position astride the Chickahominy. Meanwhile he continued to reconnoiter southward, sending cavalry and topographical engineers beyond White Oak Swamp to study the largely unknown country through which the army would have to pass in order to reach the James.

He had the satisfaction of knowing that he was doing what he could to meet such threats as he could see. However, there were others, vague but real, invisible but felt, against which he could take no action, since all he could feel was their presence, not their shape. He felt them tonight, writing the last lines of the bedtime letter to his wife: "I have a kind of presentiment that tomorrow will bring forth *something* — *what*, I do not know. We will see when the time arrives."

What tomorrow brought was a rebel deserter who gave his captors information confirming McClellan's presentiment of possible disaster. Picked up by Federal scouts near Hanover Court House, the man identified himself as one of Jackson's Valley soldiers; Stonewall now had three divisions, he said, and was moving rapidly south and east for an all-out attack on the Union flank and rear. It would come, he added, on June 28: four days away. McClellan alerted Porter and passed the news along to the War Department, asking for "the most exact information you have as to the position and movements of Jackson." Stanton replied next day, June 25, that Jackson's army, with an estimated strength of 40,000, was variously reported at Gordonsville, at Port Republic, at Harrisonburg, and at Luray. He might be moving to join Lee in front of Richmond; other reports had him marching on Washington or Baltimore. Any one of them might be true. All of them might be false. At any rate, the Secretary concluded, the deserter's information "could not safely be disregarded."

George B. McClellan repeatedly asked Washington for reinforcements to resume his advance on Richmond.

McClellan scarcely knew what to believe, though as always he was ready to believe the worst: in which case only the stump of a fuze remained before the explosion. He opened at once with all his artillery, north and south of the river, and sent Heintzelman's corps out the Williamsburg road to readjust its picket lines and test the enemy strength in that direction. The result was a confused and savage fight, the first in a sequence to be known as the Seven Days. He lost 626 men and inflicted 541 casualties on Huger, whose troops finally halted the advance and convinced the attackers that the front had not been weakened in

★

that direction. McClellan's spirits rose with the sound of firing — he shucked off his coat and climbed a tree for a better view of the fighting — but declined again as the firing died away. Though his line south of the river was now within four miles of the enemy capital, he could not clear his mind of the picture of imminent ruin on the opposite flank, drawn by the deserter the day before.

Returning to headquarters at sundown he wired Stanton: "I incline to think that Jackson will attack my right and rear. The rebel force is stated at 200,000. . . . I regret my great inferiority in numbers, but feel that I am in no way responsible for it, as I have not failed to represent repeatedly the necessity of reinforcements; that this was the decisive point, and that all the available means of the Government should be concentrated here. I will do all that a general can do with the splendid army I have the honor to command, and if it is destroyed by overwhelming numbers, can at least die with it and share its fate. But if the result of the action which will probably occur tomorrow, or within a short time, is a disaster, the responsibility cannot be thrown on my shoulders; it must rest where it belongs."

★ ★ ★ *R*iding toward the sound of heaviest firing, Lee had arrived in time to see Huger's men stop Heintzelman's assault before it reached their main line of resistance. The attack had been savage, however, and it had the look of at least the beginning of a major push. A fine rain was falling, the first in a week, but not hard enough to affect the roads, which had dried out considerably during the hot spell: McClellan might be starting his "battle of posts," advancing his infantry to cover the arrival of his siege guns. Or he might have attacked to beat Lee to the punch, having learned somehow that the line to his front had been weakened to mount the offensive against his flank. In either case, the safest thing for the Confederates to do was call off the north-bank assault and concentrate here for a last-ditch defense of the capital.

These things were in Lee's mind as he rode back through the camps where the men of Longstreet and D. H. Hill were cooking three days' rations in preparation for their march to get in position under cover of darkness for the attack across the Chickahominy next morning. He weighed the odds and made his decision, confirming the opinion one of his officers had given lately in answer to doubts expressed by another as to the new commander's capacity for boldness: "His name might be Audacity. He will take more desperate chances, and take them quicker, than any other general in this country, North or South. And you will live to see it, too." The plan would stand; the Richmond lines would be stripped; McClellan's flank would be assaulted, whatever the risk. And as Lee rode to his headquarters, people drawn to the capital hills by the rumble of guns looked out and saw what they took to be an omen. The sun broke through the

*M*cClellan and his staff watch as Federal artillery duels
with Confederate guns near Mechanicsville. McClellan hoped
to link up with Irvin McDowell's forces north of Richmond.

mist and smoke and a rainbow arched across the vault, broad and clear above the camps of their defenders.

It held and then it faded; they went home. Presently, for those in the northeast suburbs unable to sleep despite the assurance of the spectral omen, there came a muffled sound, as if something enormous was moving on padded feet in the predawn darkness. Hill and Longstreet were in motion, leaving their campfires burning brightly behind them as they marched up the Mechanicsville turnpike and filed into masked positions, where they crouched for the leap across the river as soon as the other Hill's advance uncovered the bridges to their front. By sunup Lee himself had occupied an observation post on the crest of the low ridge overlooking the Chickahominy. The day was clear and pleasant, giving a promise of heat and a good view of the Federal outposts on the opposite bank. The bluecoats took their ease on the porches and in the yards of the houses that made up the crossroads hamlet. Others lolled about their newly dug

★

gun emplacements and under the trees that dotted the landscape. They seemed unworried; but Lee was not. He had received unwelcome news from Jackson, whose foot cavalry was three hours behind schedule as a result of encountering poor roads and hostile opposition.

This last increased the cumulative evidence that McClellan suspected the combination Lee had designed for his destruction. At any moment the uproar of the Union assault feared by Davis might break out along the four-mile line where Magruder, his men spread thin, was attempting to repeat the theatrical performance he had staged with such success at Yorktown, back in April. By 8 o'clock all the units were in position along the near bank of the river, awaiting the sound of Stonewall's guns or a courier informing them that he too was in position. But there was only silence from that direction. A. P. Hill sent a message to the brigade posted upstream at Half Sink: "Wait for Jackson's notification before you move unless I send you other orders." Time wore on. 9 o'clock: 10 o'clock. The three-hour margin was used up, and still the only word from Jackson was a note written an hour ago, informing the commander of Hill's detached brigade that the head of his column was crossing the Virginia Central — six hours behind schedule.

President Davis came riding out and joined the commanding general at his post of observation. Their staffs sat talking, comparing watches. 11 o'clock: Lee might have remembered Cheat Mountain, nine months ago in West Virginia, where he had attempted a similar complex convergence once before, with similar results. High noon. The six-hour margin was used up, and still no sound of gunfire from the north. 1 o'clock: 2 o'clock: 3 o'clock. Where was Jackson?

McClellan knew the answer to that. His scouts had confirmed his suspicions and kept him informed of Stonewall's whereabouts. But he had another question: Why didn't he come on?

After the dramatic and bad-tempered telegram sent at sundown of the day before, he had ridden across the river to check on Porter's dispositions, and finding them judicious — one division posted behind Beaver Dam Creek, the other two thrown forward — had returned in better spirits, despite a touch of neuralgia. "Every possible precaution is being taken," he informed the authorities in Washington before turning in for the night. "If I had another good division I could laugh at Jackson. . . . Nothing but overwhelming forces can defeat us." This morning he had returned for another look, and once more he had come back reassured. Now, however, as the long hours wore away in silence and the sun climbed up the sky, apprehension began to alternate with hope. At noon he wired Stanton: "All things very quiet on this bank of the Chickahominy. I would prefer more noise."

★ ★ ★

★

Shelby Foote

*Federal wounded from Seven
Pines await evacuation on a
flatbed car near a field hospital at
Savage Station, a stop on the
Richmond & York River Railroad.*

FOUR

The Seven Days; Hezekiah

1862 ★ ★ ★ ★ ★ ★

If noise was what he wanted, he was about to get it — in full measure — from a man who had plenty of reasons, personal as well as temperamental, for wanting to give it to him. Before the war, A. P. Hill had sued for the hand of Ellen Marcy. The girl was willing, apparently, but her father, a regular army career officer, disapproved; Hill's assets were $10,000, a Virginia background, and a commission as a Coast Survey lieutenant, and Colonel Marcy aimed a good deal higher for his daughter than that. Ellen obeyed her father, whose judgment was rewarded shortly thereafter when George McClellan, already a railroad president at thirty-three, with an annual income amounting to more than the rejected lieutenant's total holdings, made a similar suit and was accepted, thereby assuring the daughter's freedom from possible future want and the father's position, within a year, as chief of staff to the commander of the Army of the Potomac. Hill meanwhile had gone his way and married the beautiful sister of John Hunt Morgan of Kentucky, redhaired like himself and so devoted to her husband that it sometimes required a direct order from the commander of the Army of Northern Virginia to remove her from the lines when a battle was impending. Hill, then, had in fact more cause to feel gratitude than resentment toward the enemy chief of staff and commander

★

for rejecting and supplanting him. However, he was a hard fighter, with a high-strung intensity and a great fondness for the offensive; so that in time McClellan's soldiers, familiar with the history of the tandem courtships, became convinced that the Virginian's combativeness was a highly personal matter, provoked by a burning determination to square a grudge. Once at least, as Hill's graybacks came swarming over the landscape at them, giving that high-throated fiendish yell, one of McClellan's veterans, who had been through this sort of thing before, shook his head fervently and groaned in disgust: "God's sake, Nelly — why didn't you marry him?"

A narrow-chested man of average height, thin-faced and pale, with flowing hair, a chiseled nose, and cheekbones jutting high above the auburn bush of beard, Hill had a quick, impulsive manner and a taste that ran to the picturesque in clothes. Today, for instance — as always, when fighting was scheduled — he wore a red wool deer-hunter's shirt; his battle shirt, he called it, and his men, knowing the sign, would pass the word, "Little Powell's got on his battle shirt!" More and more, however, as the long hours wore away in front of Meadow Bridge, they began to think he had put it on for nothing. The detached brigade had crossed at Half Sink soon after 10 o'clock, when Jackson sent word that he had reached the railroad. Since then, nothing had been heard from that direction; five hours had passed, and barely that many still remained of daylight. Hill chafed and fretted until he could take no more. At 3 o'clock, "rather than hazard the failure of the whole plan by longer deferring it," as he subsequently reported, "I determined to cross at once."

From his post on the heights overlooking the river Lee heard a sudden popping of musketry from upstream. As it swelled to a clatter he saw bluecoats trickling eastward from a screen of woods to the northwest, followed presently by the gray line of skirmishers who had flushed them. Then came the main body in heavy columns, their bayonets and regimental colors glinting and gleaming silver and scarlet in the sunlight. The Yankees were falling back on Mechanicsville, where tiny figures on horseback gestured theatrically with sabers, forming a line of battle. East of the village, the darker foliage along Beaver Dam Creek began to leak smoke as the Union artillery took up the challenge. Far to the north, directly on Jackson's expected line of advance, another smoke cloud rose in answer; Stonewall's guns were booming. As Little Powell's men swept eastward, the troops of D. H. Hill and Longstreet advanced from their masked positions along the turnpike and prepared to cross the Chickahominy in support. Late as it was — past 4 now, with the sun already halfway down the sky — the plan was working. All the jigsaw pieces were being jockeyed into their assigned positions to form Lee's pattern of destruction for the invaders of Virginia.

As usual, there were delays. The turnpike bridge had to be repaired before Harvey Hill and Longstreet could go to the assistance of A. P. Hill, who was fighting alone on the north bank, prodding the makeshift Yankee line back through Mechanicsville. Lee sent him word not to press too close to the guns massed along Beaver Dam Creek until support arrived and Jackson had had time to outflank the fortified position. While the repairmen were still at work on the bridge, a cavalcade of civilians, mostly congressmen and cabinet members, clattered across in the wake of President Davis, who was riding as always toward the sound of firing. D. H. Hill and Longstreet followed, and at 5 o'clock Lee came down off the heights and crossed with them.

The plain ahead was dotted with bursting shells and the disjointed rag-doll shapes of fallen men. A. P. Hill had taken the village, and by now there were no armed Federals west of Beaver Dam

A narrow-chested man of average height, thin-faced and pale, with flowing hair, a chiseled nose, and cheekbones jutting high above the auburn bush of beard, Hill had a quick, impulsive manner and a taste that ran to the picturesque in clothes.

Creek. But there were plenty of them along it, supporting the guns creating havoc on the plain. Unable to remain out in the open, in clear view of the Union gunners, Hill's men had pushed eastward, against Lee's orders, to find cover along the near bank of the creek. Here they came under infantry fire as well, taking additional losses, but fortunately the artillery was firing a little too high; otherwise they would have been slaughtered. Several attempts to storm the ridge beyond the creek had been bloodily repulsed. The position was far too strong and Porter had too many men up there — almost as many, in fact, as Longstreet and both Hills combined. Everything depended on Jackson, who should have been rounding their flank by now, forcing them to withdraw in order to cover their rear. However, there was no sign of this; the Federals stood firm on the ridge, apparently unconcerned about anything except killing the Confederates to their front. The question still obtained: Where was Stonewall? And now Lee learned for the first time that Little Powell had crossed the

Chickahominy with no more knowledge of Jackson's whereabouts than Lee himself had, which was none at all.

To add to his worries, there on the plain where Union shells were knocking men and horses about and wrecking what few guns A. P. Hill had been able to bring within range, Lee saw Davis and his cavalcade, including the Secretaries of State and War, sitting their horses among the shellbursts as they watched the progress of the battle. A single burst might topple them like tenpins any minute. Lee rode over and gave Davis a cold salute. "Mr President, who is all this army and what is it doing here?" Unaccustomed to being addressed in this style, especially by the gentle-mannered Lee, Davis was taken aback. "It is not my army, General," he replied evasively. Lee said icily, "It is certainly not *my* army, Mr President, and this is no place for it." Davis shifted his weight uneasily in the saddle. "Well, General," he replied, "if I withdraw, perhaps they will follow." He lifted his wide-brim planter's hat and rode away, trailing a kite-tail of crestfallen politicians. Once he was out of sight, however, he turned back toward the battle, though he took a path that would not bring him within range of Lee. He did not mind the shells, but he wanted no more encounters such as the one he had just experienced.

This minor problem attended to, Lee returned to the major one at hand: the unequal battle raging along Beaver Dam Creek, where he had not expected to have to fight at all. Jackson's delay seemed to indicate that McClellan, having learned in advance of the attempt to envelop his flank, had intercepted Stonewall's march along the Totopotomoy ridge. Still worse, he might be mounting an overwhelming assault on the thinly held intrenchments in front of Richmond before Lee could get in position to "be on his heels." Immediately, the southern commander sent messages ordering Magruder to hold his lines at all costs and instructing Huger to test McClellan's left with a cavalry demonstration. Daylight was going fast. Until Lee reached New Bridge, two miles beyond the contested ridge, both wings of his army would be fighting in isolation: McClellan well might do to him what he had planned to do to McClellan. If the Federals were not dislodged from Beaver Dam today, they might take the offensive in the morning with reinforcements brought up during the night. In desperation, Lee decided to attempt what he had been opposed to until now. He would storm the ridge beyond the creek.

All of A. P. Hill's men had been committed, but Harvey Hill's were just arriving. Lee ordered the lead brigade to charge on the right, near the river, and flank the Federals off the ridge. They went in with a yell, surging down the slope to the creek, but the high ground across the way exploded in their faces as the Union guns took up the challenge. Shattered, the graycoats fell back over their dead and wounded, losing more men as they went. The sun went down at 7.15 and the small-arms fire continued to pop and sputter along the dusky front. By 9 o'clock it had stopped. The enemy artillery fired blind for another hour, as if in

*M*en of Truman Seymour's brigade pelt attacking
Confederates with musket fire from their position near Ellison's
Mill during the Battle of Mechanicsville.

mockery of the attackers. Then it too died away, and the cries of the wounded were heard along the creek bank. The Army of Northern Virginia's first battle was over.

It was over and it was lost, primarily because of the absence of the 18,500 troops whose arrival had been intended to unhinge the Federal line along the ridge. The persistent daylong question, Where was Jackson? still obtained. In a way, that was just as well; for in this case, disturbing as the question was, the answer was even more so. Finding his advance expected and contested by enemy cavalry, Stonewall had moved cautiously after crossing the Central Railroad six hours late. At 4.30 that afternoon, after a southward march of seven miles in seven hours — he was now ten hours behind schedule — he reached his objective, Hundley's Corner. From there he could hear the roar of guns along Beaver Dam, three air-line miles away. However, with better than three hours of daylight still remaining, he neither marched toward the sound of firing nor sent a courier to inform Lee of his arrival. Instead, he went into bivouac, apparently satisfied that he had reached his assigned position, however late. His men were much fatigued, being unaccustomed to the sandy roads and dripping heat of the lowlands, and so was their commander, who had had a total of ten hours' sleep in the past four nights. If Lee wanted him to fight the Yankees, let him drive them across his front as had been arranged.

★

While Stonewall's veterans took their rest, A. P. Hill's green troops were fighting and losing their first battle. Lee's ambitious plan for a sweep down the north bank of the river, cutting the enemy off from his base and forcing him to choose between flight and destruction, had begun with a total and bloody repulse that left McClellan a choice of two opportunities, both golden. He could reinforce his right and take the offensive here tomorrow, or he could hold the river crossings and bull straight through for Richmond on the south, depending on which he wanted first, Virginia's army or Virginia's capital. Such was the result of Lee's first battle. Hill's impetuosity and Jackson's lethargy were to blame, but the final responsibility was the army commander's; he had planned the battle and he had been present to direct it. Comparatively speaking, though there was little time for assessment, it had been fought in such a disjointed fashion as to make even Seven Pines seem a masterpiece of precision. Of the 56,000 men supposedly available on this bank of the Chickahominy, Lee had got barely one fourth into action, and even these 14,000 went in piecemeal. Mercifully, the casualty figures were hidden in the darkness and confusion, but time would disclose that the Confederates had lost 1350 soldiers, the Federals 361. In short, it was the worst fiasco either army had staged since Ball's Bluff, back in October, when the figures were approximately reversed.

★ ★ ★ *M*cClellan was elated. Though he left all the tactical dispositions to Porter, he had recrossed the river in time to watch the battle from start to finish. At 9 o'clock, with the guns still intermittently booming defiance, he wired Stanton: "The firing has nearly ceased. . . . Victory of today complete and against great odds. I almost begin to think we are invincible."

However, he was by no means ready to take advantage of either of the golden opportunities afforded by Lee's repulse. Believing himself as heavily outnumbered on the left as on the right, he did not consider a shift to the offensive on either bank of the Chickahominy. He was proud in fact to be holding his own, and he restrained his elation somewhat short of rashness. Nor did he consider reinforcing the embattled Porter with troops from Sumner, Heintzelman, Keyes, or Franklin, who reported the rebels unusually active on their front. Convinced as he was that Lee had at least 180,000 men, McClellan saw all sorts of possible combinations being designed for his destruction. The attack on Mechanicsville, for example, might be a feint, intended to distract his attention while troops were massed for overrunning the four-mile line that covered Seven Pines and Fair Oaks. Such considerations weighed him down. In point of fact, his elation and his talk of being invincible were purely tactical, so to speak. Strategically, he was already preparing to retreat.

Ever since the beginning of the action he had been shifting Porter's

★

wagons and heavy equipment to the south bank — "impediments," he called them — in preparation for a withdrawal as soon as the pressure grew too great. Jackson's late-afternoon arrival within striking distance of Porter's flank and rear, though his attitude when he got there was anything but menacing, had the effect Lee had intended. As soon as the Beaver Dam fight was broken off, McClellan instructed Porter to fall back down the Chickahominy, out of reach of Stonewall, who had brought not only his Valley army, but also his Valley reputation with him. After crossing Powhite Creek, three miles in his rear, Porter was to dig in along the east bank of Boatswain Swamp, a stream inclosing a horseshoe-shaped position of great natural strength, just opposite the northern end of the four-mile line beyond the river.

At daybreak Porter carried out the movement with such skill that McClellan, who had already crossed, wired Stanton in delight: "This change of position was beautifully executed under a sharp fire, with but little loss. The troops on the other side are now well in hand, and the whole army so concentrated that it can take advantage of the first mistake made by the enemy."

★ ★ ★ *L*ee's safest course, after yesterday's repulse, would have been to recross the Chickahominy at Mechanicsville Bridge and concentrate for a defense of his capital by occupying, in all possible strength, the line of intrenchments now thinly held by Huger and Magruder. But he no more considered turning back, apparently, than McClellan had considered moving forward. After sending a staff officer to locate Jackson and instruct him to continue his march eastward beyond the Union flank, Lee ordered a renewal of the assault on the ridge overlooking Beaver Dam, which the bluecoats seemed to be holding as strongly as ever. He intended to force its evacuation by a double turning movement, right and left; but before it could be organized, the Federals pulled back. They were only a rear guard, after all. Lee sent A. P. Hill and Longstreet in direct pursuit, with instructions to attack the enemy wherever they found him, while Harvey Hill swung wide around the left to reinforce Jackson in accordance with the original plan. Though the element of surprise was lost and there were no guarantees against breakdowns such as the one that had occurred the day before, the machine was back in gear at last.

About 9.30 Lee rode forward, doubling Longstreet's column, and mounted the ridge beyond the creek, where burning stores and abandoned equipment showed the haste with which the enemy had departed. Two miles eastward he came upon Jackson and A. P. Hill standing together in a country

*For seven days General Robert E. Lee launched his army in
a series of hammer blows that drove McClellan's Federals from
the gates of Richmond to the banks of the James River.*

★

churchyard. Hill soon left, but Lee dismounted and sat on a cedar stump to confer with Stonewall. The two were a study in contrast, the immaculate Lee and the dusty Jackson, and so were their staffs, who stood behind them, looking each other over. Any advantage the former group had in grooming was more than offset by the knowledge that the latter had worn out their clothes in fighting. Now that D. H. Hill had joined him, Stonewall had fourteen brigades under his command: two more than Longstreet and the other Hill combined. Lee expected the enemy to make a stand at Powhite Creek, just over a mile ahead, and his instructions were for Jackson to continue his march to Cold Harbor, three and a half miles east. There he would be well in rear of the Federals and could cut them off or tear their flank as they came past him, driven by A. P. Hill and Longstreet. Jackson nodded approval, then mounted and rode away.

Lee overtook the head of A. P. Hill's column as it approached Powhite Creek. It was now about noon, and the gravest danger of the original plan was past. Hill's advance had uncovered New Bridge; the two wings of the army were again in contact; Magruder could be reinforced from across the Chickahominy if McClellan lunged for Richmond on that side. Ahead, as Lee had expected, enemy riflemen held the high ground beyond the creek. Determined to force a crossing without delay, Little Powell sent his lead brigade forward unsupported. After a short fire-fight, centered around a brick and timber structure known as Gaines Mill — there was a dam there with a spillway and a sizeable pond above it, placid, shaded by oaks; a cool, unwarlike place of refuge on a hot day in any June but this — the Federals withdrew. Hill's men followed, crossing the creek and occupying the high ground without further opposition. Unlike yesterday, rashness had paid off.

It had been easy: too easy, Lee thought as he mounted the slope and reached the seized position. Then he found out why. Ahead there was a sudden, tearing clatter of musketry, and the men of Hill's lead brigade came stumbling wild-eyed out of the wooded valley into which they had pursued the fleeing bluecoats. "Gentleman, we must rally those men," Lee told his staff, riding forward. Now he knew. Not here along the Powhite as he had expected, but somewhere down in that swale, or just beyond it, the enemy was at bay. While the panicked troops were being rallied — a good many more of them had gone in than had come back out — Hill brought up three additional brigades, and at 2.30, with Longstreet just arriving on the right, sent them forward. Again that sudden clatter erupted, now with the boom of guns mixed in, and again the men came stumbling back, as wild-eyed as before.

Penetrating deeper into the swampy woods, they had come face to face with the death-producing thing itself: three separate lines of Federal infantry, dug one above another into the face of a long, convex hill crowned with guns. McClellan, with his engineer's skill, had chosen a position of enormous strength, moated along its front by the boggy stream called Boatswain Swamp. Rising below Cold Harbor, two miles east of Gaines Mill, it flowed southwest, then turned back east and south around the face of Turkey Hill, affording a clear field of fire for Porter's three successive lines and the batteries massed on the dominant plateau. None of this was shown on the crude map Lee was using, not even Boatswain Swamp; Hill had had to find it for him, groping blind and paying in blood for discouraging information. Now he knew the worst. Yesterday's Union position, overlooking Beaver Dam, had been strong enough to shatter everything he had been able to throw against it; but today's was infinitely stronger. McClellan had found himself a fortress, ready-made.

Lee's hope was that Jackson, threatening the Federal right from the direction of Cold Harbor, would cause Porter to weaken his left by shifting troops to meet him. Until that happened, to continue the assault would be suicidal. In fact, the shaken condition of Hill's men made it doubtful whether they would be able to hold their ground if the enemy counterattacked. Sending word for Longstreet to discourage this with a demonstration on the right, Lee set out for the left to find the answer to yesterday's question, which applied again today: Where was Jackson? On the way, he met Ewell and found out. Harvey Hill had reached Cold Harbor, but Stonewall had been delayed by taking a wrong road. Riding ahead, he had found Hill deploying for attack — precisely what Lee, across the way, was hoping for — and had stopped him; Lee's instructions were for him to strike the Federals after they had been dislodged, not before. To stave off disaster while he digested this bad news, Lee told Ewell to go in on A. P. Hill's left, supporting him, while he himself rode on to talk with Jackson.

Ewell's veterans started forward with a shout. "You need not go in!" Little Powell's troops called out when they saw them coming. "We are whipped; you can't do anything!" The Valley men did not falter. "Get out of our way," they growled as they went by. "We'll show you how to do it." Yelling, they went in on the double. Again there was that uproarious clatter, as if a switch had been tripped, and that triple line of fire ripping back and forth across the face of Turkey Hill, and the roar of guns from the crest. Still on the double, the Valley soldiers came back out again. It was more than they had bargained for, despite the warning, and they were considerably fewer now than when they started forward. Roberdeau Wheat was lying dead in there, along with hundreds of others who had been through Kernstown, Winchester, Cross Keys, and Port Republic. Dick Taylor was not; he had been confined to an ambulance with a mysterious ailment that paralyzed his legs. Missing his firm grip, the gaitered Louisianians broke within sight of the fuming hill and had to be withdrawn. The rest of Ewell's survivors hung on, deep in the swampy woods alongside Hill's, while concentrations of shell and canister flailed the brush around them. Their aim distracted by a constant shower of broken twigs and branches, they kept up a blind long-range fire across Boatswain Swamp.

Riding toward the left, Lee heard a welcome sound from that direction: the popping of muskets and the quaver of the rebel yell. Jackson at last had realized the changed situation and had unleashed Harvey Hill against the Union right, meanwhile sending word to his other division commanders: "This affair must hang in suspense no longer. Sweep the field with the bayonet!" He sounded like himself again, and presently Lee saw him approaching, horse and rider covered with dust, the dingy cadet cap pulled so far down over his face that the bill almost touched the lemon he was sucking.

"Ah, General," Lee said as he rode up, "I am very glad to see you. I had hoped to be with you before." Stonewall jerked his head at the implied rebuke and muttered something indistinguishable in the din. Ewell's attack was reaching its climax; Jackson's division, under Winder, would go in on Ewell's right, filling a widening gap between him and A. P. Hill. "That fire is very heavy," Lee said. "Do you think your men can stand it?" Jackson listened, then replied, raising his voice to be heard above the racket: "They can stand almost anything! They can stand that."

It was now past 5 o'clock, but Lee at last had all of his troops within reach or in position. Far on the right, Longstreet had examined the enemy line with deliberate care and found it too strong to be affected by a feint; only an all-out attack would serve, he said, and he was preparing to deliver one. Lee approved, having reached the same conclusion everywhere along the front. The sun was near the landline; time was running out. At this late hour, no matter what it cost in blood, nothing less than a general assault, all down the line — D. H. Hill and Ewell on the left, Jackson in the center, A. P. Hill and Longstreet on the right — could possibly convert defeat into victory by sweeping the Federals off the face of Turkey Hill and back across the plateau where their massed guns boomed defiance.

★ ★ ★ Fitz-John Porter was holding his own, and he intended to go on holding it, whatever the rebels brought against him. His three divisions had been reinforced by a fourth from Franklin, sent him by McClellan along with a message expressing his pride in the fighting qualities of the men on the north bank: "Send word to all your troops that their general thanks them for their heroism, and says to them that he is now sure that nothing can resist them. Their conduct and your own have been magnificent, and another name is added to their banners. . . . I look upon today as decisive of the war. Try to drive the rascals and take some prisoners and guns."

Much of the credit was due to the division on the right. Its members were U.S. regulars to a man, all 6000 of them, and they fought with the same steady determination they had shown at Bull Run, where they had been fewer than 1000. Their commander, now as then, was George Sykes, then a major but now a major general. He was from Delaware, forty years old, and he held his lines today with a special doggedness, knowing the attacks were launched by Harvey Hill, who had been his roommate at West Point. Porter left the defense of that flank to Sykes and gave his main attention to the left and center of his convex line, supporting his two divisions in that direction with the fourth, which came up soon after 4 o'clock. His 35,000 soldiers were outnumbered three to two, but they gained confidence from every repulse they administered to the screaming graybacks who came charging through the swamp just under their rifles. It was shooting-gallery work, with an excitement out of proportion to the danger involved. Meanwhile they were improving their hillside position, piling dirt and logs, stacking rocks and even knapsacks to thicken and raise the breastworks along their triple line. Dead rebels lay in windrows at the base of the slope, but the defenders had suffered comparatively little. Wherever Porter checked — a handsome man with a neatly barbered, lustrous dark-brown beard, clean linen, and a calm, unruffled manner that matched his clothes — he found his men in excellent spirits, elated over their success and ready to continue it as long as he required.

It would not be much longer now; McClellan had made it clear from the start that this was primarily a holding action. The sun was already red beyond the trees along the Chickahominy when a follow-up message arrived from the army commander, setting a definite limit to their stay: "I am ordering up more troops. Do your best to hold your own . . . until dark."

★ ★ ★ **B**ut the blow was about to fall. Except for two brigades that were coming up now in rear of A. P. Hill, Lee had all his men in position along a nearly semicircular three-mile arc. He planned to use these late arrivers for a breakthrough at the point where Little Powell had tried and failed. One of the two was the Texas Brigade, under John B. Hood, which had shown an aptitude for this kind of work at Eltham Landing. Lee rode back, met Hood at the head of the column, and — omitting none of the difficulties the previous attackers had encountered — told him what he wanted.

"This must be done," he said. "Can you break his line?" Hood did not know whether he could or not; but he said he was willing to try. That was enough for Lee. As he turned to ride away he raised his hat. "May God be with you," he said.

Hood formed along the line of departure, a Georgia regiment on the right, Hampton's Legion on the left, and three Texas regiments in the center. Beyond the Legion, the other brigade commander, Colonel E. M. Law, aligned his four regiments, two from Mississippi and one each from

Brigadier General George Sykes' division included well-drilled battalions of U.S. regular infantry and the colorful 5th New York Zouaves.

Alabama and North Carolina. Longstreet and Jackson had already gone into action on the right and left when these men from the Deep South started forward. The sun was down behind the ridge, twilight gathering in the valley, as Hood and Law passed through the shattered ranks of A. P. Hill and beyond into a clearing, in full view of the blue tiers on the hillside and the batteries massed on the crest, which went into a rapid-fire frenzy at the sight, stabbing the dusk with spits of flame as fast as men could pull triggers and lanyards, then load and pull again. Still the gray-clad attackers came on, through the tempest of iron and lead, not pausing to fire, not even yelling, but moving with long strides down the slope, their rifles at right shoulder lift, closing ranks as they took their losses, which were heavy. If they had looked back they would have seen the ground behind them strewn with their dead and wounded; nearly a thousand had fallen before they reached the near bank of Boatswain Swamp, where they paused to fix bayonets and dress their line. But they did not look back; they looked forward, moving now at the double, across the creek and up the slope on the enemy side, yelling as they came on. Not a shot had been fired by the charging men, but their rifles were now at a carry, the bayonets glinting: twenty yards from the Union line, then ten . . . and the bluecoats scattered in unison, scrabbling uphill and swamping the second line, which joined them in flight, overrunning the third. In the lead, the Texans fired their first volley at a range where every bullet lodged in flesh, then surged over the crest and onto the plateau, where they fired again into a heaving mass of horses and men as the cannoneers tried to limber for a withdrawal. Too late:

★

Hood was out front, tall and blond, gesturing with his sword. Fourteen guns were taken here, while two full regiments from Pennsylvania and New Jersey threw down their arms in surrender, along with other large detachments. Lee now had the breakthrough he had asked for.

Longstreet and Jackson widened the breach in both directions, pumping additional volleys into the wreckage and turning back a desperate cavalry charge, delivered Balaklava-style, which accomplished nothing except the addition of pain-crazed, riderless horses to the turmoil. Ewell, moving forward beyond Jackson, outflanked Sykes and forced him to fall back under pressure from D. H. Hill. Eight more guns were taken and several hundred more prisoners were rounded up in the gathering dusk. However, there was too much confusion and too little daylight for the final concerted push that might have swept the Federals off the sloped plateau and into the boggy flats of the Chickahominy. Besides, in retreat as in resistance, the signs were clear that McClellan's was a very different army from the one that had broken and scattered in the twilight at Manassas; whereas the Confederates, now as then, were too disrupted for pursuit. Not only did Sykes' regulars maintain their reputation by retiring in good order, but as the frightened survivors of the other three divisions broke for the bridges leading south to safety, they met two brigades coming up from Sumner, reinforcements ordered north by Mc-Clellan while the battle racket was swelling toward its climax. The fugitives cheered and rallied. Porter saved his reserve artillery and got his soldiers across the river in the darkness, using these fresh troops and the unshaken regulars to cover the withdrawal.

The 9th Massachusetts Infantry, a Union Irish American regiment whose flag celebrated its Celtic heritage, was heavily engaged at the battle of Gaines's Mill.

★

"Profoundly grateful to Almighty God," Lee sent a dispatch informing Davis that the Army of Northern Virginia had won its first victory. Twenty-two guns and more than 2000 prisoners had been taken, together with a great deal of excellent equipment and a clear road leading eastward to the Union base at White House. But it had been accomplished at a fearful price. Lee had lost 8500 fighting men, the bravest and best the South could ever give him; Porter had lost 6837. Numerically, here at the critical point of contact, the odds were growing longer every day. Its right wing drawn in, shaken but uncrushed, McClellan's army was now assembled as a unit for the struggle that lay ahead, while the southern army was still divided.

"We sleep on the field," Lee closed his dispatch to the President, "and shall renew the contest in the morning."

★ ★ ★ McClellan met that night with his corps commanders at Savage Station, a point on the York River Railroad about midway between Fair Oaks and the Chickahominy crossing. They were not there to help him arrive at a decision, but rather to receive instructions for carrying out a decision already reached. Early that afternoon, before Porter had completed his occupation of the position overlooking Boatswain Swamp, McClellan notified Flag Officer Goldsborough of his desire "that you will forthwith instruct the gunboats in the James River to cover the left flank of this army. . . . I am obliged to fall back." And at 8 o'clock — as the uproar died away beyond the Chickahominy, but before he knew the results of the fighting there — he wired Stanton from his south-bank headquarters: "Have had a terrible contest. Attacked by greatly superior numbers in all directions on this side. . . . The odds have been immense. We hold our own very nearly."

The decision to retreat — or, as McClellan preferred to express it, the decision to "change his base" — was supported by dispatches he had been receiving all day from troop commanders along the four-mile line that ran from Grapevine Bridge down into the near fringe of White Oak Swamp. Here Prince John Magruder had repeated his Yorktown performance with such remarkable success, marching and countermarching his men, demonstrating noisily and retiring stealthily to threaten or seem to threaten other points along the front, thundering aggressively all the while with his guns — "They have it in mind to advance," Joseph Hooker of Heintzelman's corps reported; "I can be whipped before the reserve will get up" — that all four of the south-bank corps commanders were apprehensive that they were about to be swamped, individually and collectively, by overwhelming numbers. Late in the day, when McClellan asked what additional troops they could spare to help Porter, they replied that they needed all they had in order to hold their ground. In fact, they said, if any more reinforcing was being considered, it had better be done in their direction.

By nightfall, having combined these tactical reports with information received from Pinkerton, McClellan was convinced that Lee was jabbing with his left in preparation for throwing a knockout right. The thing to do, if time permitted, was to step back before it landed; or if not back, then sideways. Porter's withdrawal across the Chickahominy had given the Confederates access to the York River supply line and a clear shot at the left flank of McClellan's moving column if he attempted a retreat back down the Peninsula. The only way to go was south to the James, where his foresight had provided a sanctuary under the guns of the fleet and a landing place for the reinforcements Lincoln would be obliged to send, now that a near-disaster had proved the need for them.

Accordingly, at the Savage Station conference he issued instructions for a withdrawal in that direction. Keyes, being farthest south, would cross White Oak Swamp in the morning, followed by Porter as soon as he completed the retirement now in progress. Together they would guard the flank against an attack below the swamp, while Franklin, Sumner, and Heintzelman held the present lines above it and the Chickahominy crossings to the north, covering the passage of the army train with its 25,000 tons of food, ammunition, and medical supplies. Once the train was across the swamp with its 3600 wagons, 700 ambulances, and a herd of 2500 beeves, the remaining corps would follow, guarding the rear on the way to Harrison's Landing.

It was well conceived, well thought out: McClellan took pride in the foresight and coolness which had enabled him to improvise the details under pressure. He did not consider the movement a retreat. It was a readjustment, a change of base required by a change in conditions. However, once the conference was over and the corps commanders had gone out into the night with their instructions for tomorrow, he began to consider the adverse reaction that might follow: not among his soldiers — they would understand — but among the members of the body politic, the public at large, and especially among the molders of popular opinion: the editors, and later the historians. The record would speak for itself in time. He was confident that it would show how Lincoln and Stanton had thwarted him, diverting his troops when his back was turned and ignoring his pleas for reinforcements, in spite of documentary evidence that he was facing an army twice the size of his own. Meanwhile, though, he was not only in danger of being condemned and ridiculed; about to undertake one of the most difficult maneuvers in the art of war, the transfer of an army from one base to another across a fighting front, he was in danger of being physically destroyed. In that event, the record would indeed have to speak for itself, since he would not be there to supplement it before the bar of judgment. Therefore it had better be supplemented in advance, bolstered so as to present the strongest possible case in the strongest possible language. Shortly after midnight, before retiring to sleep for what he knew would be a grinding day tomorrow, he got off a wire to Stanton.

"I now know the full history of the day," it began. After saying flatly, "I have lost this battle because my force was too small," he got down to cases: "I again repeat that I am not responsible for this, and I say it with the earnestness of a general who feels in his heart the loss of every brave man who has been needlessly sacrificed today. . . . If, at this instant, I could dispose of 10,000 fresh men, I could gain a victory tomorrow. I know that a few thousand more men would have changed this battle from a defeat to a victory. As it is, the Government must not and cannot hold me responsible for the result." The clincher came at the end: "I feel too earnestly tonight. I have seen too many dead and wounded comrades to feel otherwise than that the Government has not sustained this army. If you do not do so now the game is lost. If I save this army now, I tell you plainly that I owe no thanks to you or to any other persons in Washington. You have done your best to sacrifice this army."

Having thus unburdened his troubled mind, and bolstered the record in the process, he took to his bed. "Of course they will never forgive me for that," he subsequently told his wife. "I knew it when I wrote it; but as I thought it possible that it might be the last I ever wrote, it seemed better to have it exactly true."

★ ★ ★ *S*aturday's dawn, June 28, showed Confederate ambulances moving about the field where thousands of wounded soldiers from both armies had suffered through the night. Lee was there before sunrise. Presently couriers began to arrive from Longstreet and Jackson, informing him that Porter had pulled out. They had pushed down toward the Chickahominy without encountering any live Federals except the injured and stragglers, including one of McCall's brigade commanders, Brigadier General John F. Reynolds, who had slept too long in the woods and was captured. The bridges had been burned, they said, and guns were massed on the ridge beyond to challenge any attempt to rebuild them.

Lee did not mind the watchful guns or the wrecked bridges; he had no intention of crossing the river here. However, the original plan for marching in force down the left bank to get astride McClellan's communications could not be followed until he knew for certain in which direction the Federals were retreating — toward White House, toward Williamsburg, or, conceivably, toward the James — or whether, indeed, they might not be massing on the right bank for a drive on Richmond, slicing between the divided wings of the Confederate army to get there. A move in the wrong direction would throw Lee out of position for interfering with either of McClellan's remaining alternatives. Until he knew, he was

Retreating Union troops pass a column of smoke from fires at Savage Station. Federal quartermasters torched stocks of supplies and ammunition to keep them out of rebel hands.

stymied. For the present all he could do was order Stuart to press on down the left bank, supported by Ewell's division, and cut the railroad at or near Dispatch Station, the advance Union supply base just east of the river. McClellan's reaction to that would tell him much. Meanwhile, there was little to do but attend the wounded, bury the dead, and take such rest as fretfulness would permit.

A sort of wanderlust came over the army in its idleness. Too much had happened too fast these past two days, apparently, for the troops to sit still now. As the sun climbed up the sky, giving promise of much heat, they began to roam the field, singly or in groups, mingling with the burial squads in their search for missing friends and relatives. Even Stonewall was infected. Examining the terrain where Hood and Law had made their breakthrough, the dead still lying thick to mark the path of their assault, he shook his head and exclaimed in admiration: "The men who carried this position were soldiers indeed." Lee too took time to ride in search of his youngest son Robert, an eighteen-year-old cannoneer in a Virginia battery. At first the boy could not be found, but a comrade finally spotted him sleeping under a caisson, unresponsive to the shouts.

★

Prodded with a sponge staff, he came out into the sunlight, grimy and blinking. Lee spoke to him and rode on, and nobody seemed to think it strange that the son of the army commander should be serving in the ranks.

Information began to trickle in. Shortly before midday one of Ewell's brigadiers reported that a man he had sent up a tree with a spyglass had seen the Federals moving south in heavy columns. As if in confirmation, a widening cloud of dust began to darken the sky beyond the river, rising over the treetops. Then came flashes, followed by the crump and rumble of distant explosions and pillars of smoke standing tall along the horizon. Magazines were being fired; McClellan was unquestionably on the march. But where to? Lee did not know, though presently he learned at least that it was not toward White House. A courier arrived from Stuart. He had cut the railroad at Dispatch Station, encountering only token resistance, and the Federal horsemen, falling back, had burned the Chickahominy trestle. Definitely, then, McClellan was abandoning his base on the Pamunkey.

Three alternatives were left to him: a retreat down the Peninsula, a change of base to the James, or a lunge at Richmond. Without anything resembling definite evidence — any one of the three, for instance, might be preceeded by a movement south — Lee now began to consider the second of these choices the most likely. This belief was arrived at by a process of elimination, rejecting those movements which did not seem to him to be in keeping with the character of his opponent. He did not think McClellan had the boldness to adopt the third course, nor did he think he would willingly risk the damage to his prestige that would result from adopting the first. If this logic was correct, then he was making for the James: in which case there was a need for haste if Lee was to cut him off before he reached the shelter of his gunboats. But the stakes were too great and the odds too long for a gamble based on logic. Confederate guns, shelling the wooded ridge beyond the Chickahominy, were receiving return fire. The Federals were still there, and as long as that was so, Lee could not afford to risk throwing three fourths of his army out of position by sending it off on what might turn out to be an empty chase. Sunset came, then nightfall. The long day was over, and all Lee knew for certain was that McClellan was not reacting as he had expected him to do.

★ ★ ★ **E**arly Sunday morning two of Longstreet's engineers **made a reconnaissance across the river,** and soon after sunrise Lee received a message from them which added considerable weight to yesterday's logic. The extensive fortifications covering the key Federal position opposite the mouth of Powhite Creek had been abandoned.

This meant that McClellan had no intention of making a lunge at Richmond. He was retreating, and almost certainly he was retreating in the direction of the James, since neither Stuart nor Ewell had reported any movement toward the lower crossings of the Chickahominy. It was not conclusive evidence; the Federals' nonarrival at Bottom's Bridge or Long Bridge, another five miles downstream, might have been caused by a bungled march or a late start; but it shortened the odds at least enough for Lee to risk a gamble. His original plan had been designed to force the enemy to fall back from in front of Richmond or else come out from behind his intrenchments, where he could be hit. McClellan had obliged by doing both. In doing so, however, he had moved in an unexpected direction and had gained a full day's head start in the process. Lee's

Scantily spanned and badly swollen, impenetrable along most of its length, the stream disguised its quicksand deadliness behind a mazy screen of vines and creepers . . .

problem now was to devise a new plan: one that would take advantage of the opportunities created by the old one, now outmoded, and at the same time overcome the advantage his opponent had made for himself. In brief, Lee wanted a plan by which he could overtake McClellan and destroy him.

Before he could be overtaken, however, he would have to be impeded, and Lee's principal asset in this regard was White Oak Swamp. A sort of miniature Chickahominy, it rose southwest of Seven Pines, in the angle between the Williamsburg and Charles City roads, and flowed in a slow crescent across the Federal line of march, emptying into the parent river midway between Bottom's Bridge and Long Bridge. Scantily spanned and badly swollen, impenetrable along most of its length, the stream disguised its quicksand deadliness behind a mazy screen of vines and creepers, luring the northern commander toward an excellent possibility of destruction. If this army could be caught with its head south and its tail north of this boggy stretch, it might be slaughtered like a hamstrung ox, more or less with impunity. McClellan might or might not be aware of this; Lee was. Before the sun was midmorning high, he had begun to compose and issue orders which, if carried out, would place his troops in position to begin the butchery.

Magruder, moving east along the railroad and the Williamsburg road, was to attack the tail, supported on the left by Jackson, who was to repair and cross Grapevine Bridge with his own and D. H. Hill's divisions. Huger, moving southeast along the Charles City road, was to attack the head, supported on the right by Longstreet, who was to cross New Bridge with his own and A. P. Hill's divisions, marching across Huger's rear to get in position south of the swamp. Meanwhile, on the off chance that McClellan might veer east and try for a getaway down the Peninsula, Ewell was to hold his present position at Bottom's Bridge, supported by Stuart farther down. The assault on the head, below the swamp, could not be made today; Longstreet and Little Powell had fifteen dusty miles to go before they would be in position; their attack would have to be launched on Monday. However, the assault on McClellan's hindquarters could and should be made without delay, since it would impede him further by causing him to have to turn in mid-career and fight a rear-guard action north of White Oak Swamp.

Once more then, with his orders issued, Lee had to wait for the execution of another ambitious convergence. If this one worked, McClellan's oxhide would hang dripping on the Confederacy's barn door before tomorrow's sun went down. Now as before, however, the first move was up to Stonewall — and Magruder.

★ ★ ★ *P*rince John had been having his troubles all along. In fact, so wholly had he flung himself into the part he was playing — his "method" presaged that of Stanislavsky, who would not be born till the following year, five thousand miles away — his theatrical exertions had been as hard on his own nervous system as on those of the blue-coated spectators out front. This intensity had infected his supporting players, too. Yesterday, for example, one of his brigadiers — fiery, slack-mouthed Robert Toombs, Georgia statesman turned Georgia troop commander — had got so carried away that he converted a demonstration into a full-scale assault on the heavily manned Federal intrenchments. The result, of course, was a bloody repulse and, Magruder believed, a decided increase in the likelihood that the enemy would discover the true weakness behind the ferocious mask. Ever since then, like an actor with the illusion lost and the audience turned irate, he had been expecting to be booed and overrun.

This morning, after dosing himself with medicine in an attempt to ease the pangs of indigestion, he decided to stage an attack. The enemy guns had slacked their fire and then had fallen silent in the fortifications to his immediate left front. Mindful of his instructions to keep pressure on the Union lines, he was determined to develop the situation in strength. However, when he sent word to Lee of his intention, the army commander replied facetiously that a forward movement was indeed in order, but that in storming the works he was to exercise care not to injure Longstreet's two engineers, who had already occupied them. Chagrined, Magruder advanced and was relieved to find it true. Not that there was any lessening of the general tension. Whatever victories had been scored on the far side of the Chickahominy, the peril here on the south bank, now that all five of the Federal corps were united in his front, seemed to him even greater today than yesterday or the day before. Presently, with the arrival of Lee's orders for overhauling and destroying McClellan, Prince John's alarm increased at once to the point of horror and unbelief. Except for the doubtful assistance of that unpredictable eccentric, Stonewall Jackson — who had yet to arrive anywhere on time — it seemed to Magruder that he was being required to assault the whole 100,000-man Yankee army with his one frazzled 13,000-man division.

Lee rode over before midday and explained in person just what it was he wanted. Magruder was to push eastward along the railroad, making contact with Jackson south of Grapevine Bridge, and together they would assail the Union rear. Magruder listened and nodded distractedly; Lee rode on, convinced that his orders were understood. However, Prince John's misgivings were by no means allayed. He got his men into assault formation, straddling the tracks so that Lee's big railway gun protected his center, and started forward. At Fair Oaks, surrounded by piles of smoldering equipment abandoned by the Federals in haste, he came under long-range artillery fire; whereupon he halted and called for help from

*Curious Federal soldiers examine General
Magruder's armored railway gun after
its capture at the war's end.*

Huger, who was advancing down the Charles City road. Huger countermarched with two brigades, stayed with him briefly, then went his way, unable to see that he was needed. Magruder went forward again, but with mounting misgivings.

Sure enough, just short of Savage Station, two miles down the track, he came under heavy close-up fire and saw bluecoats clustered thickly in his front, supported by batteries massed in their rear. It was 5 o'clock; Magruder was where Lee wanted him, due south of Grapevine Bridge, in position to press the Federals when Jackson came slamming down on their flank. But now it was his turn to ask the question others had been asking for the past two days: Where was Jackson? There was no sign of him off to the left, no sound of his guns, not even any dust in that direction. Nettled, Prince John went on without him; or anyhow he tried, probing tentatively at the Union line and banging away with the "Land Merrimac."

None of it did any good at all. The Federals repulsed every advance and concentrated so much counterbattery fire on the railway gun that it was forced to backtrack and take shelter in a cut. Night came on, and the cannon kept up their long-range quarrel. Then at 9 o'clock a thunderstorm broke and ended the Battle of Savage Station, in which about 500 men had fallen on each side. Magruder had advanced five miles in the course of the day, but the Federals had not yielded a single unwilling inch. Fighting stubbornly, they had preserved the integrity of their line wherever challenged. More important, they had covered the retreat of the slow-grinding wagon train, which wound southward unmolested. In effect, McClellan had gained another day in his race against time and Lee.

The one person most responsible for this success was not the Union commander or any of his lieutenants, however stubbornly they had fought. Nor was it Magruder, who had fumbled his way forward and then had fought without conviction. It was Jackson, who had not fought at all. Thursday and Friday he had had reasons for failing to strike or threaten the Federal flank on schedule: not good ones, but anyhow reasons. He had been delayed on the march. He had gotten lost. Today, as the sound of Magruder's guns rolled up from the south, he replied to a request for help by saying that he had "other important duties to perform." Presumably this was the repairing of Grapevine Bridge, so listlessly attempted that it turned out to be an all-day job. At any rate, he had kept his men on the north bank of the Chickahominy while Magruder's were fighting and dying at Savage Station.

Consequently, there were some who recalled an early rumor as to how he won his battle name on the field of Manassas. According to this version, Bee had called him Stonewall, not in admiration of his staunchness, but in anger at his refusal to come to his assistance there on the forward slope of Henry Hill. What the South Carolinian had really said, men whispered now about the camps, was: "There stands Jackson — like a damned stone wall!"

* * * *Lee now knew the results of the day, and mostly they were worse than disappointing.* North of the swamp, where Magruder had faltered and Jackson had stood stock still, the limited attack had probably done more to assist than to impede McClellan's withdrawal. Southward, the situation was not much better. Delayed by a countermarch which had served no purpose, Huger had moved a scant half-dozen miles down the Charles City road and had gone into camp without making contact with the enemy. But even this poor showing put him well in advance of Longstreet and A. P. Hill, who had been stopped by darkness and the thunderstorm, six miles short of tomorrow's objective. Such encouragement as there was came from Stuart, and it was more of a negative than of a positive nature: McClellan had destroyed his base at White House and severed all connections with the Pamunkey and the York.

Thus assured that there was now not even an outside chance that his opponent had it in mind to veer off down the Peninsula, Lee could withdraw Ewell's division from its post at Bottom's Bridge and add its weight to the attempted strike at McClellan's flank and rear. Also, he learned from Richmond, Holmes' division had crossed from Drewry's Bluff, so that it too would be available when — and if — the retreating Federal host was brought to bay.

To effect this end, while thunder pealed and lightning described its garish zigzag patterns against the outer darkness where the men of his scattered divisions took such rest as they could manage in the rain-lashed woods and fields, Lee gave his attention to the map, once more studying ways and means to correct a plan that had gone awry. For all its sorry showing today, the army was approximately in position for the destructive work he had assigned it for tomorrow. Three roads led southeast below White Oak Swamp, roughly parallel to each other and perpendicular to the Federal line of retreat: the Charles City road, the Darbytown road, and the New Market road. Huger was on the former, nearest the swamp; Holmes was on the latter, nearest the James; Longstreet and A. P. Hill were in the center. Advancing, all three columns would enter the Long Bridge road, which led east-northeast to the Chickahominy crossing that gave it its name, and encounter McClellan's southbound column in the vicinity of Glendale, a crossroads hamlet located at the intersection of the Charles City and the Long Bridge roads. These four divisions, reinforced by Magruder — who would countermarch on the Williamsburg road, then swing south and take position as a general reserve well down the Darbytown road — would constitute the striking force. Its mission was to intercept and assail the head and flank of the enemy column, while Jackson and Harvey Hill, rejoined by Ewell, would continue (or rather, begin) to press the Federal rear, to and beyond White Oak Swamp. Caught in the resultant squeeze, with 45,000 graybacks on his flank and another 25,000 in his rear — so that, observed from above, his predicament somewhat resembled that of a thick-bodied snake pursued by hornets — McClellan would be forced to stop and fight, strung out in the open as he was, thereby affording Lee the best chance so far to destroy him.

His orders written and given to couriers who rode out into the slackening storm, Lee could sleep at last for what he hoped would be a happier tomorrow. Seeking to avoid delay — the main cause of disappointment up to now — he had instructed his troop commanders to move at dawn. Huger, being nearest the enemy, was to signal the opening of the battle by firing his guns as soon as he made contact, whereupon the others were to close in for the destruction according to plan. Unless today's ragged performance was improved, however, that goal would never be attained. Lee knew this, of course, and the knowledge made him edgy: so much so, in fact, that in his concern he rebuked not Jackson — the principal offender — but Magruder, the only one of his generals who had struck a blow in the past two days.

"I regret very much that you have made so little progress today in the pursuit of the enemy," he informed him by courier. "In order to reap the fruits of our victory the pursuit should be most vigorous. . . . We must lose no more time, or he will escape us entirely."

★ ★ ★ Always, up to now, when McClellan spoke to them of tests and hardships — Yorktown, Williamsburg, Fair Oaks: the victory hill got steeper with every step — the men had cheered him and kept climbing, reinforcing their belief in their commander, Little Mac, with an increasing belief in themselves. Now there was this sterner downhill test.

In some ways, the past four days had been harder on the Federals south of the Chickahominy than on those who were fighting for their lives on the opposite bank. Thursday and Friday there had been a boiling cloud of smoke obscuring the northern sky, and conflicting reports of battles won or lost as the boom and rumble of guns swelled or sank in that direction. Saturday the smoke and noise subsided, then rose again in the afternoon, farther east and of a different intensity, more deliberate than frantic: supply and ammunition dumps were burning and exploding. Also, there was a constant movement of men and wagons across the rear: Porter's troops were over the river, slogging south in the wake of Keyes', who had pulled out on the left. The men of Franklin and Sumner and Heintzelman, left behind, looked at one another and passed the word along: "It's a big skedaddle."

Sunday they themselves had backtracked, fighting a series of rear-guard skirmishes as they moved eastward down the railroad. Then at Savage Station they called a halt and rocked the pursuers back on their heels, "Land Merrimac" and all. It was a victory, and they felt considerably better: especially Sumner, whose battle blood was up. The old man could scarcely believe his ears when he got orders to continue the retrograde movement. "I never leave a victorious field," he sputtered. "Why, if I had 20,000 more men I would crush this rebellion!" When someone finally found a candle, struck a light, and showed him the written order, he still protested. "General McClellan did not know the circumstances when he wrote that note. He did not know that we would fight a battle and gain a victory." Finally, though, he acquiesced; orders were orders. Heintzelman had already left, and Franklin and Sumner followed, crossing White Oak Swamp in the darkness. By 10 o'clock next morning the last man was safely across and the bridge had been burned to discourage pursuit.

It had not been accomplished without losses. A hospital camp of 2500 sick and wounded was abandoned at Savage Station, together with an ample supply of medicines and surgeons who volunteered to stay behind with their charges. At the Chickahominy railroad crossing, loaded ammunition trains were set afire and run full tilt off the wrecked bridge, with spectacular results. Sunday's landscape was smudged with the acrid smoke of burning cloth and leather, relieved from time to time by the more pleasant aroma of coffee and bacon given to the flames instead of to the rebels. The price, in fact, had been heavy; but so was the gain. Whatever else might be in store, McClellan's army was not going to be caught astride the only natural obstacle that lay athwart its line of march to the James.

★ ★ ★ *M*onday was Lee's last, best chance for the Cannae he had been seeking all along, and as usual he was early on the scene. The main blow, as he designed it, would be delivered by Longstreet and A. P. Hill just south of Glendale. If successful, this would sever the Union column, interrupt its retreat, and expose its disjointed segments to destruction in detail. But much depended also on the commanders of the various other columns of attack: on Huger, who would open the action on the left: on Jackson, who would force a crossing of White Oak Swamp and press the Federal rear: on Magruder, who would come up in support of the center: and on Holmes, who would advance on the right so as to bring the disorganized bluecoat survivors under his guns as they fled past him, reeling from the effect of the multiple blows.

Since Magruder had the longest march, Lee rode over to Savage Station before sunrise to make certain he understood the orders and started promptly. The first commander he encountered there was not Prince John, however, but Jackson, who had finally repaired Grapevine Bridge and started his men across it before dawn. Both generals dismounted and advanced for a hand-shake, Lee removing his gauntlet as he came forward. According to a young artillery officer who observed the meeting, Stonewall "appeared worn down to the lowest point of flesh consistent with active service. His hair, skin, eyes and clothes were all one neutral dust tint, and his badges of rank so dulled and tar-nished as to be scarcely perceptible." Yesterday's strange lethargy had left him, along with his accustomed reticence. He "began talking in a jerky, impetuous way, meanwhile drawing a diagram on the ground with the toe of his right boot.

> *"General McClellan did not know the circumstances when he wrote that note. He did not know that we would fight a battle and gain a victory."*
>
> — Edwin V. Sumner

He traced two sides of a triangle with promptness and decision; then, starting at the end of the second line, began to draw a third projected toward the first. This third line he traced slowly and with hesitation, alternately looking up at Lee's face and down at the diagram, meanwhile talking earnestly." Suddenly, as the third line intersected the first, he stamped his foot, apparently indicating the point at which McClellan would be wrecked beyond repair. "We've got him," he said decisively, and signaled for his horse.

Lee watched him go, that strange man in another of his strange guises, then mounted too and continued his search for Magruder. Presently he found him. After making certain that Prince John understood today's orders as well as Stonewall did, Lee hurried down the Darbytown road to establish army head-quarters in rear of the proposed center of the impending battle.

As events turned out, however, there was no need for haste: at any rate, not on his part. Longstreet's men were going forward, supported by Hill's, but it was noon by the time they formed their line near the junction with the Long Bridge road, facing eastward to await the already overdue boom of Huger's guns signaling contact on the left. What came instead was a message: the South Carolinian's progress was "obstructed" — whatever that meant. Lee was left wondering. Southward, Holmes was silent too; nor was there any indi-cation that Jackson was pressing down from the north against the enemy rear. Somewhere out beyond the screening pines and oaks, east of where Lee stood waiting for his lost columns to converge, the Federals were hurrying southward past the point where he had intended to stage his Cannae. He might still stage it — seven hours of daylight still remained — if he could find the answer to certain questions: What had delayed Huger? What had happened to Holmes? And again, as so often before: Where was Jackson?

Huger had the shortest march of all, and what was more he had made an early start. But he went slowly, fearing ambush, for which the terrain was particularly suited. This had been tobacco country in the old days, checkerboard-neat for the most part, but in time the soil had leached out; neglected, it had gone back to second-growth scrub timber, broken here and there by clearings where men still tried to scratch a living from it. The general's natural caution was further increased by the presence of White Oak Swamp, which afforded a covered approach to his left flank. Presently, to make matters worse, word came back

Placid in the midst of all this uproar — bursting projectiles, screaming men and horses, hoarse and futile shouts of command by rattled captains — Holmes emerged from the roadside house, suspiciously cupping one ear. "I thought I heard firing," he said.

that the road ahead was obstructed, the Yankees having chopped down trees that fell across it as they retreated. Instead of leaving his artillery behind or trying to clear the fallen timber from his path, Huger ordered a new road cut through the woods, parallel to the old one. Progress was slowed to even more of a snail's pace than before. And while he chopped, Longstreet and Hill, having formed for battle, waited. At 2.30, detecting signs of the enemy ahead, Huger brought up a couple of light fieldpieces and shelled the brush.

Holmes too was involved in a nightmare this day — a far bloodier and noisier one than Huger's contest of axes, though in point of fact the noise was not a very disturbing element for the fifty-seven-year-old North Carolinian, who was deaf. After waiting most of the afternoon at the junction of the New Market and Long Bridge roads, he received word that the bluecoats were streaming in thousands across Malvern Hill, a tall ridge three miles ahead, in the

★

final stage of deliverance from the unsprung trap Lee had contrived for their destruction around Glendale. His 6000 men were too few for a successful infantry attack on the heavy column of Federals, but Holmes decided to do what he could with his artillery to frustrate their escape. Accordingly he rode forward, found a position well within range of the hill, then brought up six rifled pieces, supported by a regiment of infantry, and prepared to open fire.

While the guns were being laid he stepped into a house by the side of the road. Just then a single large-caliber projectile broke with a clap like sudden blue-sky thunder over the heads of his startled men, followed promptly by what one of them called "a perfect shower of shells of tremendous proportion and hideous sound." The result was instantaneous pandemonium. Infantry and artillery alike, the green troops clustered and scattered and milled aimlessly about in search of cover, which was scarce. Some in their greenness took shelter from the ten-inch shells by crouching behind two-inch saplings; others simply knelt in their tracks and clasped their hands, palms down, on the tops of their heads. Placid in the midst of all this uproar — bursting projectiles, screaming men and horses, hoarse and futile shouts of command by rattled captains — Holmes emerged from the roadside house, suspiciously cupping one ear. "I thought I heard firing," he said.

The big shells, called "lamp posts," came from gunboats on James River, which looped northward within half a mile of the Confederate position. Soon Malvern Hill was wreathed in smoke as siege guns on its crest added canister to the weight of metal already falling on Holmes' demoralized soldiers. He pulled them back out of range. It was nearly sunset, and like Huger — whose daylong two-mile march left him a full mile short of contact with the Federal main body hastening south across his front — Holmes had taken no appreciable part in the day's fighting. Nor had Magruder, who came up in rear of Longstreet just as the uproar exploded on the far right, near the James, and was sent in that direction to help stem what sounded like a full-scale counterattack up the River road. Nor had Jackson, with better than one third of the whole army under his command.

After the early morning Savage Station conference with Lee, Stonewall had pushed on down toward White Oak Swamp, gleaning in the woods and fields a bumper harvest of abandoned U.S. equipment and prisoners as he went. This was always a pleasant task for the "wagon hunter," and today it gave him particular satisfaction, affording as it did an outlet for his apparent superabundance of nervous energy. When a companion protested that the captives would be of considerable expense to the government, Jackson shook his head. "It is cheaper to feed them than to fight them," he said. He pressed on, encountering no opposition. There was time, even, to stop and write the usual Monday letter to his wife. "An ever-kind Providence has greatly blessed our efforts," it began. About noon, approaching the sodden jungle of the swamp, he found that the Federals had already crossed it, burning the bridge behind them, and had emplaced their artillery on a commanding southside ridge, supported by heavy columns of infantry. Promptly he brought up his own guns under cover, opened suddenly on the enemy batteries, and saw them displace in frantic haste, abandoning three pieces in their confusion. Delighted, Jackson ordered his cavalry to ford the stream at once, intending for them to harry the fleeing bluecoats, and — in accordance with Lee's instructions — put a crew to work without delay, rebuilding the bridge in order to take up the pursuit with his infantry.

So far it had gone well: Stonewall seemed to have recovered his identity. But now, quite abruptly, it stopped cold. The cavalry, having crossed, was repulsed by the Federal batteries, which had not fled, as had been thought, but had simply moved to a new position, where they outgunned their smooth-bore rivals north of the swamp. Worse still, the ring of sharpshooter's rifles, accompanied from time to time by the sickening thwack of a bullet striking flesh, drove the bridgebuilders from their work almost as soon as they got started. Worst of all, however, was Jackson's reaction, which was rather as if the mainspring of some tightly wound-up mechanism had suddenly lost its resilience or run down. Formerly alert and energetic, he grew taciturn and drowsy, even sullen. Recalling his troops from exposure to danger, he lay down under a tree and went to sleep.

That was about 3 o'clock. When he woke an hour later — or halfwoke, rather, sitting slump-shouldered on a log, the bill of his dingy cadet cap pulled down over his sleep-puffed eyes — he heard sounds of heavy firing from the south. It made little impression on him, though. Nor did the suggestions of his lieutenants, who had been reconnoitering for a way around the impasse while he slept. A cavalry colonel sent word that he had located a useable ford nearby, but Jackson ignored the message. Wade Hampton, commanding an infantry brigade, went off on his own and presently returned to report in person that he had found an excellent downstream crossing that would bring his men in position to strike the unsuspecting Federal flank. Jackson stirred. Could Hampton build a bridge there? Yes, the South Carolinian said, but the noise might alert the enemy. Build the bridge, Jackson told him. Hampton left. Soon he was back, reporting that the work had been done without alarming the Union troops. Stonewall gave no sign that he had heard him. For a long time he sat there on the log, silent, collapsed like a jointed doll whose spinal string had snapped. Then abruptly he rose, still without replying, and walked away.

Hampton's bridge went unused — as did Jackson's third of Lee's army, which remained north of White Oak Swamp, out of touch with the enemy all day. At supper, soon after dark, Stonewall went to sleep with a piece of unchewed biscuit between his teeth. Jarred awake by his own nodding, he looked blankly about, then got up from the table. "Now, gentlemen," he told his staff, "let us at once to bed . . . and see if tomorrow we cannot do something."

★ ★ ★ Of all the days in the eventful month since that last night in May when the President tendered him command of the leaderless army as they rode back from the confused and gloomy field of Seven Pines, this final day of June had been for Lee the longest and the saddest. None had promised more at the outset, or yielded less in the end, than this in which better than two thirds of his soldiers were withheld from contact with the fleeing enemy by the inabilities and eccentricities of the commanders of three out of his four intended columns of attack.

Davis was with him, now as then. At 2.30, mistaking the boom of Huger's guns, shelling the brush on the Charles City road, for the prearranged signal that the battle had opened on the left, Lee hurried north on the Long Bridge road in search of Longstreet and found him talking with the President in a little clearing of stunted pines and broomstraw. As Lee rode up, Davis greeted him with a question designed to forestall a repetition of the repulse he had suffered at the Virginian's hands four days ago at Mechanicsville: "Why, General, what are you doing here? You are in too dangerous a position for the commander of the army."

"I'm trying to find out something about the movements and plans of those people," Lee replied. (For him, the Federals were invariably "those people.") Then, attempting to recover the initiative, he added: "But you must excuse me, Mr President, for asking what *you* are doing here, and for suggesting that this is no place for the Commander in Chief of all our armies."

"Oh," Davis told him with a smile, airy but determined, "I am here on the same mission that you are."

Lee had to let it go at that, though presently the danger was considerably heightened. When Longstreet rode away and had some nearby batteries open fire in acknowledgment of what he thought was Huger's signal, the reply came not from the Confederates to the north, but from the Federals to the east. Suddenly the clearing was dotted with bursting shells. Concerned with the peril to Davis and Lee, A. P. Hill came dashing up and addressed them sternly: "This is no place for either of you, and as commander of this part of the field I order you both to the rear!" The two moved off — "We will obey your orders," Davis said — but when they drew rein, still within the zone of fire, red-bearded Little Powell overtook them and spoke with the same mock harshness as before: "Did I not tell you to go away from here, and did you not promise to obey my orders? Why, one shot from that battery over yonder may presently deprive the Confederacy of its President and the Army of Northern Virginia of its commander." Abashed, the two withdrew beyond range of the exploding shells and the explosive Hill.

It was then that Lee received unwelcome news that McClellan was closer to safety than he had supposed. A cavalry commander, patrolling ahead of Holmes on the River road, informed him by courier that the enemy, undamaged and unhindered, was crossing Malvern Hill within gunshot of the James. Lee at once rode down and saw for himself the truth of the report. The bulk of the Union supply train, accompanied by heavy columns of infantry, was making its escape. If the Confederate attack was delayed much longer, it would strike not the enemy flank, but the enemy rear: which meant that the chance for a Cannae would be gone. In fact, it might be gone already. Having approved Holmes' intention to disrupt the retreat as much as possible with his guns, Lee turned back toward Glendale. He still had heard nothing from Jackson, and nothing from Huger except that his route was "obstructed." But time was running out. Concentrated or not, he would throw what he had at the Federal flank before the tail of the blue column cleared the junction near which Hill and Longstreet had been waiting all this time.

Encountering Davis, who reproached him again for rashly exposing himself, Lee replied quite truly — it was, in fact, the crux of the problem, what with the inadequate communications and the lack of an adequate staff — that all he could learn of the situation was what he saw with his own eyes. As he rode northward, the uproar of the naval bombardment exploded behind him. What it meant he did not know, but when he returned to the broomstraw clearing, still under fire from the batteries ahead, he found that Magruder, arriving at last, had been ordered south by Longstreet, who interpreted the heavy-caliber uproar as a counterattack by the Federals near the James. For all Lee knew, that was what it was. Besides, there was no time for recalling Magruder. If the assault was to be delivered before the bluecoats cleared the junction, it would have to be launched at once by the troops at hand; that is, by the divisions of Longstreet and A. P. Hill. He told them to go forward — which they did. The result was the Battle of Glendale; or Frayser's Farm, it was sometimes called, since much of the hottest fighting occurred on this two-hundred-acre property south of the junction.

Not that it wasn't hot enough all over. In sending two divisions against an enemy force of undetermined strength, Lee's hope was that they would find the Federals strung out on the roads and unprepared. As it turned out, however, he was hoping for a good deal more of an advantage than his opponent was willing to grant. McClellan had disposed his eleven divisions with several eventualities in mind, and in fact was readier for this than for any other. Keyes' two divisions, along with two of Porter's, were already in position on Malvern Hill; two more — one from Sumner and one from Franklin — were on

The 60th Virginia Infantry Regiment was awarded the crossed bayonets on its battle flag for engaging in fierce hand-to-hand fighting during the battle at Frayser's Farm.

rear-guard duty, observing the quiescent Jackson across White Oak Swamp; Franklin's other division was astride the Charles City road, blocking Huger. The remaining four — Heintzelman's two and one each from Sumner and Porter — were in front of Glendale, ready for whatever came their way. The result was a savage, stand-up fight, beginning two hours before sundown and continuing through twilight into darkness.

Longstreet went in, driving hard and capturing guns in the rush, but presently, encountering stiffer resistance as the blue mass absorbed the blow, called for help. Hill's men charged with a yell on the left and right, their backs to the setting sun. Again the Federals yielded; again they rallied. The fighting now was hand to hand. Bayonets crossed and musket butts cracked skulls. More guns were taken, lost, and retaken as the lines surged back and forth in the dusk, across clearings and through woods. Longstreet remained calm, feeding men into the holocaust and matching his skill against the odds. When a group of jubilant Virginians brought him a captured brigadier, he recognized an old army comrade, George McCall, commander of Porter's third division. About to extend his hand in greeting, he saw that the prisoner was in no mood for the amenities, however, and directed instead that he be taken at once to Richmond as a trophy.

Gradually the battle racket died away in the darkness: the Confederates held the field. Having paid for it with the blood of 3300 men, they received by way of dividend eighteen Yankee guns and one Yankee general. But these were the only substantial results. The real objective — McClellan's supply train and reserve artillery, for which he would have had to turn and fight without the

Federal artillery duels with Stonewall Jackson's rebel batteries across the marshy low ground at White Oak Swamp. Confederate counterbattery fire eventually forced the Federal gunners to withdraw.

alternative of an orderly retreat — was not obtained, and in fact had been unobtainable since midday, five hours before the battle started. Under cover of night, the Federals continued their withdrawal toward the James.

McClellan himself was there already, having gone aboard the ironclad *Galena* to confer with the gunboat commander and arrange for support while Keyes and Porter were filing into position on Malvern Hill. A telegram from Lincoln, sent two days ago and rerouted through Fortress Monroe, showed something of the official reaction up to the time the White House line was cut. "Save your army at all events," the President urged him. "Will send reinforcements as fast as we can. . . . If you have had a drawn battle or a repulse it is the price we pay for the enemy not being in Washington. . . . It is the nature of the case, and neither you nor the Government are to blame."

Though he agreed with no more than half of the final sentence, McClellan was too worn down by exertion and anxiety to press the point just yet. At sundown, proud but gloomy, he replied: "My army has behaved superbly, and have done all that men can do. If none of us escape, we shall at least have done honor to the country. I shall do my best to save the army. Send more gunboats."

★

Tuesday's dawn, July 1, showed the Union lines abandoned around Glendale, and though there was no longer a
chance for interception, Lee ordered his army to concentrate
for pursuit. He had no real way of knowing what effect the past six days of
fighting — and the past five days of falling back — might have had on the
Federals. Up to now they had fought stubbornly and hard; but last night's
fierce encounter, followed by still another retreat, might have tipped the scale
toward panic. If they were in fact demoralized, the slightest tap on this seventh day of combat might cause the blue host to fly apart, like an overstrained
machine, and thus expose it to destruction in detail. At any rate, Lee was determined to take advantage of any opening McClellan might afford him for
striking a crippling blow.

Magruder was already on hand, having countermarched in the
night to relieve the battle-weary men of Hill and Longstreet. The southern
commander joined these three while awaiting the arrival of Jackson and Huger,

whose advance was unopposed. He bore himself calmly, but it was obviously with considerable effort. The cumulative strain of watching his combinations fail and his plans go awry because of fumbling had upset his digestion and shortened his temper. Longstreet, on the other hand, seemed as confident as ever, if not more so. When a Union surgeon came to request protection and supplies for the wounded he had stayed behind to tend, Longstreet asked him what division he belonged to. McCall's, the doctor said. "Well, McCall is safe in Richmond," Longstreet told him, adding that if it had not been for the Pennsylvanian's stubborn resistance along this road the day before, "we would

The Seven Days — one gigantic twenty-mile-long conflict, with bewildering intermissions, not for resting, but for groping spastically in the general direction of an enemy who fought so savagely when cornered that the whole thing had been rather like playing blindman's buff with a buzz saw.

have captured your whole army. Never mind," he said. "We will do it yet."

Lee said nothing. But Harvey Hill, whom they presently encountered, did not agree with the burly, eupeptic Georgian. One of Hill's chaplains, a native of the region, had given him a description of the terrain ahead. It was well adapted for defense, he said: particularly Malvern Hill, which the bluecoats were reported to have occupied already. "If General McClellan is there in strength, we had better let him alone," the saturnine Hill declared.

"Don't get scared, now that we have got him whipped," Longstreet broke in with a laugh.

Hill made no reply to this. Nor did Lee, who apparently had all he could do to maintain his composure. In this he was not entirely successful, however. When a newly arrived brigadier came up to the group and expressed concern lest McClellan escape, the gray-bearded commander's patience snapped. "Yes, he will get away," Lee said bitterly, "because I cannot have my orders carried out!"

Events coming hard on the heels of this uncharacteristic outburst did not improve the general's disposition. Malvern Hill was less than three miles away, no more than a normal one-hour march, but with seven divisions crowding a single southward road, the result was confusion and delay. (A parallel road,

★

half a mile to the east, which Keyes had taken with his whole corps the previous night, went unused because it was not shown on Lee's crude map.) On top of all this, a mix-up in Magruder's orders sent his division swinging off on a tangent; time was lost before he was missed, and still more before he could be found and put back on the track. It soon developed that today, as on every other of what was to be known as the Seven Days — one gigantic twenty-mile-long conflict, with bewildering intermissions, not for resting, but for groping spastically in the general direction of an enemy who fought so savagely when cornered that the whole thing had been rather like playing blindman's buff with a buzz saw — Lee's army would not be within striking distance of the day's objective until well past noon. In fact, it was 1.30 before six of the eight Confederate divisions — Magruder was still off on his tangent, and Holmes was still licking yesterday's wounds, down on the River road — had filed into position facing the 150-foot height, which bristled with guns parked hub-to-hub to the front and rear of long blue stalwart-looking lines of Federal infantry.

Bad as it looked at first glance from the attacker's point of view, closer inspection of the position McClellan had chosen produced even stronger confirmation of D. H. Hill's long-range opinion that "we had better let him alone." Porter, who was in tactical command, was obviously ready for anything Lee might throw at him there on the undulating plateau, a mile and a half long and half as wide. He and Keyes, with two divisions each, held a line about midway up the slope; Heintzelman was in immediate reserve with two more, while Sumner and Franklin remained on call, in case their four were needed; which seemed unlikely, considering the narrow front, the apparently unassailable flanks, and the direct support of more than one hundred guns. These last were what made the position especially forbidding, and it was on them that Porter seemingly placed his chief reliance. First, in advance of the heavy ranks of infantry on the left and center, fieldpieces were massed in a long crescent so as to sweep the open ground across which the graybacks would have to charge if they were to come within musket range of the defenders. Other batteries were in support, all the way back to the brow of the hill, where siege guns were emplaced. Still farther back, on the James itself, naval gunners stood to their pieces, ready to arch their heavy-caliber shells into the ranks of the attackers.

In full view of all those cannon frowning down, attack seemed outright suicide. But this was Lee's last chance to destroy McClellan before he reached the safety of the river, rested and refitted his army under cover of the gunboats, then launched another drive on Richmond, giving the Confederates the bloody task of driving him back again. This first repulse had been hard enough to manage; a second, with the Federal host enlarged by reinforcements and based securely on the James, might be impossible. With this in mind — and also the thought that the stalwart look of the Union troops, near the end of their long retreat, might be no more than a veneer that covered profound despair — Lee ordered his men to take up assault positions while he searched for a way to get at "those people" and administer the rap which he hoped would cause them to come apart at the seams. Huger was on the right, D. H. Hill in the center; Magruder would form between them when he arrived. Jackson and Ewell were on the left. Longstreet and A. P. Hill, still weary from yesterday's fight, were in reserve; Holmes, around on the River road, would coöperate as developments permitted. This arrangement left much to be desired, but it would have to do until a better could be evolved. What that would be Lee did not know until he was on his way to reconnoiter Jackson's front, which seemed to offer the best chance for success.

As he set out, a message came from Longstreet, who reported that he had found a good artillery position on the right, a terraced knoll with a direct line of fire to the Union batteries. From there, he added, he could see on the Confederate left an open field which also afforded an excellent position. If guns were massed at these two points, Longstreet said — forty on the right, say, and twice that many on the left — a converging fire would throw the northern batteries into confusion and open the way for an attack by the southern infantry. Lee saw in this the opportunity he was seeking: a charge in the style of the one across Boatswain's Swamp four days ago, with even greater rewards to follow success. Accordingly, he ordered the guns to occupy the two positions and notified his front-line commanders of the plan. One of Huger's brigades, posted closest to the enemy, would be able to judge best the effect of the bombardment. If it was successful, the brigade would go forward with a yell, which in turn would be the signal for an end-to-end assault by the whole gray line, the object being to close with the blue army and destroy it there on the rolling slopes of Malvern Hill.

It was not going to be easy; it might even be impossible; but as a last chance Lee thought it worth a try. In any case, if the bombardment failed in its purpose, the infantry need not advance. Already they were taking punishment from the siege guns on the brow of the hill as they filed through the wooded and swampy lowlands to get in position for the jump-off. The heavy-caliber fire was deliberate and deadly: as Harvey Hill could testify. While his troops were forming under a rain of metal and splintered branches, the North Carolinian sat at a camp table on the exposed side of a large tree, drafting orders for the attack. When one of his officers urged him at least to put the trunk between him and the roaring guns: "Don't worry about me," Hill said. "Look after the men. I am not going to be killed until my time comes." With that, a shell crashed into the earth alongside him, the concussion lifting the predestinarian from his chair and rolling him over and over on the ground. Hill got up, shook the dirt from his coat, the breast of which had been torn by a splinter of iron, and resumed

If guns were massed at these two points, Longstreet said — forty on the right, say, and twice that many on the left — a converging fire would throw the northern batteries into confusion and open the way for an attack by the southern infantry.

Anchored in the James River, the Union gunboats Galena (left) and Mahaska lob shells at Confederates beyond Malvern Hill. The Rebels dubbed the huge projectiles "lamp posts."

his seat — on the far side of the tree. This and what followed were perhaps the basis for his later statement that, with Confederate infantry and Yankee artillery, he believed he could whip any army in the world.

What followed was a frustrating demonstration that southern gunners were no match for their northern counterparts: not here and now, at any rate. On the right and left, batteries came up piecemeal, no more than twenty guns in all — less than a fifth the number Longstreet had recommended — and piecemeal they were bludgeoned by counterbattery fire. Nowhere in this war would Federal artillerists have a greater advantage, and they did not neglect it. Sometimes concentrating as many as fifty guns on a single rebel battery, they pounded it to pulp and wreckage before changing deflection to repeat the treatment on the next one down the line. Half an hour was all they needed. By 2.30, with the whole Union position still billowing smoke and coughing flame — one six-gun battery near the center, for example, fired 1300 rounds in the course of the afternoon — not a single Confederate piece with a direct line of fire remained in action. What had been intended as a preliminary bombardment, paving the way for the infantry, had been reduced to a bloody farce. If Lee's soldiers were to come to grips with the bluecoats on that gun-jarred slope, they would have to do it some other way than this.

The southern commander resumed his reconnaissance on the left, hoping to find an opening for an attack that would flank the Federals off the hill. Far on the right, Huger's lead brigade was working its way forward. In its front was a large field of wheat, lately gleaned, with sharpshooters lurking behind the gathered sheaves of grain. Little would be gained by taking the wheatfield — on its far side, just beyond musket range, the crescent of guns standing hub to hub could clip the stubble as close as the scythe had lately done — but Huger's men, bitterly conscious that theirs was the only division which had done no real fighting since the opening attack six days ago, were determined to have a share in the bloody work of driving the invaders. Taking their losses, they surged ahead and finally took cover in a gully at the near edge of the wheatfield, well in advance of the rest of the army, while the sharpshooters fell back on their guns. Magruder, arriving about 4 o'clock to assume command of the right, notified Lee that he was on hand at last and that Huger's men had driven the enemy and made a substantial lodgment.

Lee meanwhile had found what he thought might be an opening on the left, and had sent word for the men of Longstreet and A. P. Hill to come forward and exploit it. Weary though they were, they were all he had. Just then, however, as Lee rode back toward the center, the message arrived from Magruder, together with one from the left reporting signs of a Federal withdrawal. That changed everything. This first advantage, if followed up, might throw McClellan's army into panic and open the way for an all-out flank-to-flank assault.

★

Quickly he gave verbal orders, which the messenger took down for delivery to Magruder: "General Lee expects you to advance rapidly. He says it is reported the enemy is getting off. Press forward your whole command."

By now Prince John had had a chance to look into the situation a bit more carefully on the right, and as a result he was feeling considerably less sanguine. However, Lee's three-hour-old order, calling for a general advance if the preliminary bombardment was successful, reached him soon after he arrived. Since it bore no time of dispatch, Magruder assumed that it was current: an assumption presently strengthened by the prompt arrival of the message directing him to "press forward your whole command." That was what he did, and he did it without delay, despite the unpromising aspect which a hasty examination had revealed on this shell-torn quarter of the field. Quickly he formed his men and sent them forward on the right of Huger's lead brigade, which cheered at the sight of this unexpected support, leaped eagerly out of the gully, and joined the charge across the wheatfield. On the far side of the cropped plain, the long crescent of guns began to buck and jump with redoubled fury, licking the stubble with tongues of flame.

After the failure of the preliminary bombardment and the encounter with the shell that had seemed to have his name written on it, D. H. Hill had decided that no large-scale attack would be delivered. All the same, since Lee had never countermanded the tentative order for an advance if Huger's troops raised a yell, he kept his brigade commanders with him, ready to give them time-saving verbal instructions in case the unexpected signal came. Near sundown, just as he was advising them to return to their men and prepare to bed them down for the night, the firing rose suddenly to crescendo on the smoky hill and the sound of cheering broke out on the right. "That must be the general advance!" Hill exclaimed. "Bring up your brigades as soon as possible and join it." Quickly they rejoined their commands and led them forward through the woods. By the time they came out into the open, however, a fair proportion of the troops who had attacked on the right were lying dead or dying in the wheatfield, and the rest were either hugging what little defilade they could find or else were running pell-mell toward the rear. The flaming crescent of Union guns shifted east in time to catch the new arrivers at the start of their advance up the long slope. "It was not war, it was murder," Hill said later.

That was what it was, all right: mass murder. Hill and Magruder and Huger gave it all they had, despite the hurricane of shells, only to see charge after charge break in blood and flow back from the defiant line of guns. Dusk put an end to the fighting — none of it had been hand to hand, and much of it had been done beyond musket range — though the cannon sustained the one-sided argument past dark. By that time, 5590 Confederates had fallen, as compared with less than a third that many Federals, and all for nothing. The Seven Days were over; Lee had failed in his final effort to keep McClellan from reaching the James.

Now that he had examined the ground over which the useless attack had been launched, he saw that it had clearly been foredoomed, and he could not understand how any commander, there on the scene, with all those guns staring down his throat, could not have known better than to undertake it in the first place. So he went looking for Magruder. At Savage Station, two days ago,

---

After a while the sun came out, and when it burned the mist away he saw a thing he would never forget, and never remember except with a shudder. Down there on the lower slope, the bodies of five thousand gray-clad soldiers were woven into a carpet of cold or agonized flesh.

---

he had reproached him by messenger; this time he intended to do it in person, or at any rate demand an explanation. At last he found him. "General Magruder, why did you attack?" he said. Prince John had remained silent under the previous rebuke; but this time he had an answer, and he gave it. "In obedience to your orders, twice repeated," he told Lee.

Jackson's men, at the far end of the line of battle, had spent another non-fighting day — their sixth out of the seven. Only the artillery had been engaged on the left. The infantry, moving forward through the swampy underbrush, had not been able to come up in time to take part in the assault, though as Stonewall rode through the gathering dusk he found one of Ewell's brigadiers forming his troops under cover of the woods, their faces reflecting the eerie red flicker of muzzle-flashes out on the slope ahead. Jackson drew rein.

"What are you going to do?" he asked.

"I am going to charge those batteries, sir!"

"I guess you had better not try it," Stonewall told him. "General D. H. Hill has just tried it with his whole division and been repulsed; I guess you had better not try it, sir."

Presently the firing died to a rumble. About 10 o'clock it stopped, and out of the moonless darkness came the agonized cries of the wounded, beyond reach on the uptilted, blood-soaked plain. Jackson lay down on a blanket and went to sleep. Three hours later he was wakened by Ewell and Harvey Hill, who believed that McClellan was preparing to launch a dawn

★

attack and had come to ask if Stonewall wanted them to make any special dispositions to meet it. One sleepy officer, seeing the three men squatting in a circle, thought they resembled a triumvirate of frogs. "No," Jackson said quietly, "I believe he will clear out in the morning."

———————— ✦ ————————

★ ★ ★   *H*e was right; McClellan did clear out, but not without having to override the protests of several high-ranking subordinates. Even Porter, who was his friend and generally favored all his actions, opposed this one, saying that he believed a determined advance from Malvern Hill would throw Lee into retreat through the streets of his capital. Phil Kearny, the hardest fighter among the brigade commanders — a spike-bearded New Jersey professional whose thirst for combat had not been slaked by the loss of an arm while leading a cavalry charge in Mexico — was the most vociferous of all. When the retirement order reached him at the close of the battle, he rose in the presence of his staff and cried out in anger: "I, Philip Kearny, an old soldier, enter my solemn protest against this order for retreat. We ought instead of retreating to follow up the enemy and take Richmond. And in full view of the responsibility of such a declaration, I say to you all, such an order can only be prompted by cowardice or treason."

McClellan either ignored this protest, or else he never heard it. In any case, his reply to Kearny would have been the same as the one he had made three days ago, when a cavalry colonel suggested a dash on the southern capital while Lee still had most of his men on the north bank of the Chickahominy: "If an army can save this country it will be the Army of the Potomac, and it must be saved for that purpose." He was taking no chances. If Lee would let him alone for the present, he was more than willing to return the favor.

And so it was that the same cavalry colonel found himself and his regiment alone on the hilltop next morning at dawn, with only a skirmish line of infantry left for show, while the rest of the army followed the road to Harrison's Landing. A mizzling rain had fallen before daylight, and mist blotted the lower slope from view. He could see nothing down there, but out of the mist came a babble of cries and wails and groans from the wounded who had managed to live through the night. After a while the sun came out, and when it burned the mist away he saw a thing he would never forget, and never remember except with a shudder. Down there on the lower slope, the bodies of five thousand gray-clad soldiers were woven into a carpet of cold or agonized flesh. "A third of them were dead or dying," he later wrote, "but enough of them were alive and moving to give the field a singular crawling effect."

★

Disposing his troops in a pretense of strength, the colonel presently agreed with feigned reluctance to an informal truce, and while rebel ambulance details came out of the woods and moved among the sufferers on the hillside, he withdrew under cover of a drenching rain and joined the rear of the retreating column, the van of which was led by the army commander. "My men are completely exhausted," McClellan wired Washington, "and I dread the result if we are attacked today by fresh troops. . . . I now pray for time. My men have proved themselves the equals of any troops in the world, but they are worn out. . . . We have failed to win only because overpowered by superior numbers."

He had not lost: he had "failed to win." Nor had he been outfought: he had been "overpowered." So he said. And if his words were unrealistic, it might be added in extenuation that all the events of the past week had occurred in an atmosphere of unreality. Watching the week-long twenty-mile-wide conflict had been something like watching a small man beat a large one, not by nimble footwork or artful dodging or even boxing skill, but rather by brute force, driving headlong, never relinquishing the offensive, and taking a good deal more punishment than he inflicted. This last was confirmed by the casualty lists, which were beginning to be compiled now that the two armies were out of contact.

Three months ago the news of Shiloh had arrived from the West with a dreadful shock; 23,741 American fighting men had been killed, wounded, or captured in that battle. Now the East's turn had come. The best, and the worst, that could be said of the battle known as the Seven Days was that this grim western figure had been exceeded by more than half; 36,463 was the total. And though in the earlier conflict most of the casualties had been Union, here it was the other way around; 15,849 Federals and 20,614 Confederates were on the list. In killed and wounded, moreover, the advantage increased from almost three to four to better than one to two. Nearly 10,000 Federals had fallen, 1734 killed and 8062 wounded, as opposed to nearly 20,000 Confederates, 3478 and 16,261. However, this preponderance was considerably reduced by the 6053 Federals missing in action; only 875 Confederates were in that category. In the end, since approximately half of the uncaptured wounded would return in time to the ranks of their respective armies, this made the actual loss of fighting men somewhat lower for the Confederates, 8000 of whom would be returning, whereas half of the Federal wounded had been captured, leaving only half of the remainder to return — about 2000 — so that the actual loss in combat strength, after recuperation of the injured, would be 14,000 Federals and 12,500 Confederates.

Knowing as he did that the South could not afford a swapping game on anything like a man-for-man basis of exchange, Lee found little solace in such figures. When Jackson and Longstreet came by headquarters, seeking refuge from the storm while the aid men and the burial squads worked among

★

the wounded and the dead on the rain-swept hillside, he asked Longstreet for his impression of the fighting. "I think you hurt them about as much as they hurt you," the forthright Georgian told him. Lee winced at this, for he knew how badly his army had suffered, and there was a touch of irony in his reply: "Then I am glad we punished them well, at any rate."

Longstreet left. Soon afterward, unexpectedly, President Davis walked in, taking Lee so much by surprise that he omitted the Mister from his salutation. "President," he said, "I am delighted to see you." They shook hands. Across the room, Jackson had risen and was standing at attention beside his chair. Lee saw Davis looking at him. "Why, President, don't you know General Jackson? This is our Stonewall Jackson." They were acquainted, of course, but the relationship had been strained by the Romney controversy, in which the Mississippian had supported Benjamin and the Virginian had submitted his resignation. The result, in this first meeting since then, was a curious exchange. Observing the Valley general's bristling manner, Davis did not offer his hand. Instead he bowed, and Jackson replied with a rigid salute. Neither of them said anything to the other.

Their last encounter had been under similar circumstances, after the victory at Manassas, and here again the question was how or whether to pursue a driven foe. Stonewall felt the same way about it as he had felt a year ago, but Lee and Davis agreed that the disorganized condition of the southern army precluded any chance to overcome the Federals' substantial head start down the muddy road, which would be under gunboat fire at several points. Asked for his opinion, Jackson said dourly: "They have not all got away if we go immediately after them." Lee shook his head. For the present at least, pursuit would have to be left to the cavalry, which had arrived the night before. The rest of the army would spend what was left of the day attending the wounded, burying the dead, and preparing to resume the chase tomorrow.

For today, then — as well as for a good part of tomorrow, since Harrison's Landing was eight muddy miles from Malvern Hill — Jeb Stuart had McClellan to himself. And the truth was, he preferred it so. Except for an encounter with a gunboat on the Pamunkey, three days ago — he reported with pride that he had repulsed it with a single howitzer, forcing the monster to close its ports and slink off, full-speed-astern; "What do you think of that?" he wrote his wife — outpost duty along the lower Chickahominy had kept his troopers out of the main channel of events during the past momentous week, affording them little chance for a share in the glory of driving the Yankees away from the gates of Richmond. All that was behind them at last, however, and now that they were back in the limelight — stage center, so to speak — their plumed commander intended to make the most of whatever opportunities came his way. Today there were few, the pursuit being mainly a matter of gathering up the

Federal sentries gaze across their earthworks and fallen timber abatis toward the mouth of Kimmidges Creek, the left flank of McClellan's fortified camp at Harrison's Landing.

stragglers and equipment which the blue host dribbled in its wake on the River road. Night fell before he found what he was seeking.

Next morning, though — July 3; the rain had slacked and stopped in the night; the day was bright and sunny — he came within sight of the answer to his prayers. The northern army had gone into camp beside the James, and Stuart, mounting a low ridge called Evelington Heights, looked down and saw the quarry spread out before him, close-packed and apparently ripe for destruction. McClellan had chosen the position with care. The creeks on his flanks, one of which curved along his front as well, and the gunboats anchored in his rear, their big guns trained across the meadows, gave him excellent protection from attack by infantry. But in failing to occupy Evelington Heights he had left his soldiers open to terrible punishment from the plunging fire of any guns the Confederates might bring up. Stuart saw this at once, and quickly got off a message informing Lee of the opportunity. Unwilling to wait, however, and with no regard for the long odds or concern for the consequences of alerting the Federals to the danger of leaving the dominant ridge unoccupied, he brought up the little howitzer that had peppered a gunboat into retreat four days ago, and at 9 o'clock opened fire on the bluecoats huddled on the mudflats down below.

The effect was instantaneous and spectacular, a moil of startled men and rearing horses thrown abruptly into milling consternation. Stuart was delighted. Informed by Lee that Longstreet, Jackson, and A. P. Hill were on the march to join him, he kept the little fieldpiece barking terrier-like to sustain the confusion until they arrived to compound it. But it was a case of too little too soon. Spotting the trouble at last, the Federals moved to get rid of it by advancing a six-gun battery and a regiment of infantry. Stuart held his position until he was down to his last two rounds, still hoping for the arrival of support. At 2 o'clock, with hostile guns approaching his front and infantry probing around his flanks, he fired his two last shells and pulled back off the ridge. He had done no appreciable damage, but he was pleased that he had found this chance to give McClellan one last prod. Moreover, he wrote home next day, "If the army had been up with me we would have finished his business."

As it was, however, the lead elements of Longstreet's division, moving in front of the other two, did not arrive until sunset, too late to undertake an attack even if the heights had still been naked of guns, which they were not; McClellan had been shown his mistake and had moved to rectify it. Next morning the ridge was crowned with batteries, supported by heavy columns of infantry. Hill and Jackson had come up by then, and Longstreet, who assumed command by seniority, put them in line for an all-out assault, holding his own division in reserve. Lee arrived to find Jackson protesting that his men were too weary and the heights too strong for the attack to be anything but a fiasco. After looking the situation over, Lee was obliged to agree regretfully with Stonewall; the assault was canceled, and the troops went into camp. The campaign was over.

Certain regiments were left on picket duty to observe the enemy, and one among them was stationed in a clump of woods overlooking an open field, beyond which there was another clump of woods where a Federal regiment was posted. All in all, the situation indicated a sudden renewal of bloodshed. This was the Fourth of July, however, and what was more the field was full of ripe blackberries; "so," as one rebel private later remembered, "our boys and the Yanks made a bargain not to fire at each other, and went out in the field, leaving one man on each post with the arms, and gathered berries together and talked over the fight, traded tobacco and coffee and exchanged newspapers as peacefully and kindly as if they had not been engaged for the last seven days in butchering one another."

★ ★ ★

★

Shelby Foote

*Officers of the 3d Pennsylvania
Cavalry pose for photographer
Alexander Gardner in their camp
near Harrison's Landing
on the banks of the James River.*

FIVE

Lincoln Reappraisal; Emancipation?

1862 ★ ★ ★ ★ ★ **N**apoleon was taking the waters at Vichy when news of the Seven Days reached him in mid-July. Hard on its heels came John Slidell, with an offer of one hundred thousand bales of cotton if France would denounce the Federal blockade. Unable to act alone in the matter, however eager he might be to feed his country's looms, the Emperor — called "Napoleon the Little" to distinguish him from his illustrious uncle — promptly telegraphed his Foreign Minister: "Demandez au gouvernement anglais s'il ne croit pas le moment venu de reconnaître le Sud."

Across the channel the mills were hungry too, and though Mason was somewhat handicapped by the impracticality of offering an Englishman anything so indelicate as a bribe, the time was propitious from the Confederate point of view. "There is an all but unanimous belief that you *cannot* subject the South to the Union," an influential partisan of northern interests was informing a friend across the ocean. "I feel quite convinced that unless cotton comes in considerable quantities before the end of the year, the governments of Europe will be knocking at your door." Moreover, even as he wrote, a pro-Confederate member was introducing a motion before Parliament for British-French mediation in the American Civil War, which in effect amounted to recognition of the

★

infant nation as a reward for throwing the blue invader off its doorstep. Fortu-nately, however — from the Federal point of view — the long vacation was under way, and before the issue could be forced the Cabinet was scattered from Scotland to Germany, in pursuit of grouse and relaxation. Action was deferred.

Distracting as these transatlantic dangers were, or might have been, the truth was Lincoln had more than enough material for full-time worry here at home. Hedged in by cares, blamed alike by critics right and left of the hostile center, he later said of the period under question: "I was as nearly inconsolable as I could be and live." In contrast to the adulation heaped on Davis, whose critics had been muzzled by the apparent vindication of his policies and whose countrymen now hailed him as a second Hezekiah, the northern leader heard

---

"The simple truth is, there was never such a shambling half-and-half set of incapables collected in one government since the world began."

— Francis Fessenden

---

himself likened unto Sennacherib, the author and director of a ponderous fiasco. Henry Ward Beecher was saying of him from a pulpit in Brooklyn, "Not a spark of genius has he; not an element for leadership. Not one particle of heroic en-thusiasm." Wendell Phillips thought him something worse, and said so from a Boston lecture platform: "He may be honest — nobody cares whether the tortoise is honest or not. He has neither insight, nor prevision, nor decision. . . . As long as you keep the present turtle at the head of the government, you make a pit with one hand and fill it with the other."

The politicians were in full bay, particularly those of his own party who had been urging, without success, his support of antislavery legislation which he feared would lose him the border states, held to the Union so far by his promise that no such laws would be passed. It also seemed to these Republicans that entirely too many Democrats were seated in high places, specifically in the cabinet and the army; and now their anger was increased by apprehension. About to open their campaigns for reëlection in November, they had counted on battle-field victories to increase their prospects for victory at the polls. Instead, the main eastern army, under the Democrat McClellan — "McNapoleon," they called him — had held back, as if on purpose, and then retreated to the James, complaining within hearing of the voters that the Administration was to blame. Privately,

★

many of the Jacobins agreed with the charge, though for different reasons, the main one being that Lincoln, irresolute by nature, had surrounded himself with weak-spined members of the opposition party. Fessenden of Maine put it plainest: "The simple truth is, there was never such a shambling half-and-half set of incapables collected in one government since the world began."

The people themselves were disconsolate. "Give me a victory and I will give you a poem," James Russell Lowell wrote his publisher; "but I am now clear down in the bottom of the well, where I see the Truth too near to make verses of." Apparently the people shared his gloom. Their present reaction was nothing like the short-lived panic they had staged five weeks ago, when Stonewall Jackson broke through to the line of the Potomac. Nor was it characterized by aroused determination, as in the period following Bull Run the year before. It was in fact strangely apathetic and difficult to measure, even for a man who had spent a lifetime with one hand on the public pulse, matching the tempo of his actions to its beat. Lincoln watched and wondered. One indication was the stock market, which broke badly under the impact of the news from the Peninsula; another was the premium on the gold in the Union dollar, which had stood at three and one-half percent a month ago, but since then had risen to seventeen. He watched and wondered, unable to catch the beat.

In response to McClellan's call for reinforcements on the day of Malvern Hill — "I need 50,000 more men, and with them I will retrieve our fortunes" — Lincoln told him: "Maintain your ground if you can, but save the army at all events, even if you fall back to Fort Monroe. We still have strength enough in the country, and will bring it out." Well, McClellan had "saved the army," and the "strength enough" was there; but Lincoln was uncertain as to how to "bring it out." The present apathy might be a lull before the storm that would be brought on by another call for troops. As he phrased it, "I would publicly appeal to the country for this new force were it not that I fear a general panic and stampede would follow, so hard is it to have a thing understood as it really is."

As usual, he found a way. To call for troops was one thing; to receive them was another. Seward was sent to New York to confer with men of political and financial power, explain the situation, and arrange for the northern governors to "urge" the President to issue a call for volunteers to follow up "the recent successes of the Federal arms." Lest there be any doubt as to whether the Administration intended to fight this war through to a finish, Seward took with him a letter: "I expect to maintain this contest until successful, or till I die, or am conquered, or my term expires, or Congress or the country forsake me. . . . Yours, very truly, A. Lincoln."

Seventeen governors, plus the president of the Military Board of Kentucky, responded promptly by affixing their signatures to a communication written by Seward, addressed to the Chief Executive, and saying in part: "We

★

respectfully request, if it meets with your entire approval, that you at once call upon the several States for such number of men as may be required . . . to garrison and hold all of the numerous cities and military positions that have been captured by our armies, and to speedily crush the rebellion that still exists in several of the Southern States, thus practically restoring to the civilized world our great and good Government." Being thus urged, Lincoln took his cue and in early July — "fully concurring in the wisdom of the views expressed to me in so patriotic a manner" — issued a call for 300,000 volunteers. In fact, so entirely did the request meet with his approval, he followed this first call with another, one month later, for 300,000 more.

Lowell, "clear down in the bottom of the well," had said he could produce no poem unless he received a victory as payment in advance; but lesser talents apparently required a lesser fee. J. S. Gibbons found in this second call a subject fit for his muse, and Stephen Foster set the result to music:

> *If you look up all our valleys where the growing harvests shine*
>
> *You may see our sturdy farmer boys fast forming into line,*
>
> *And children from their mothers' knees are pulling at the weeds*
>
> *And learning how to reap and sow against their country's needs,*
>
> *And a farewell group stands weeping at every cottage door:*
>
> *We are coming, Father Abraham, three hundred thousand more!*

Reinforcements would be welcome all along the line; there was scarcely a mile of it that did not have some general calling plaintively or angrily for more soldiers. But more soldiers, even half a million of them, would not solve the basic problem, which was one of high command. For four months now, ever since the abrupt relief of McClellan back in March, the overall conduct of the war had been directed by Lincoln and Stanton — a sort of two-headed, four-thumbed amateur — with results just short of disastrous in the theater which had received their main attention. Stonewall Jackson, for example, had frightened Stanton and decoyed Lincoln into breaking up the combinations McClellan had designed for taking Richmond: so that Davis and Lee, professionals both, had been able to turn the tables on the Army of the Potomac, effecting countercombinations that drove it headlong to the James. Part of the fault could be assigned to flaws that developed in subordinate commanders — on the one hand, Frémont's ineptness; on the other, McClellan's lack of aggressive instincts — but most of it lay with the overall direction, which had permitted the enemy to bring pressure on those flaws.

★

Lincoln could see this now in retrospect, much of it at any rate, and in fact he had begun to suspect it soon after the failure of his chessboard combinations in the Valley. In his distress, before the blow fell on the Peninsula, his mind turned back to Winfield Scott, the one general who had shown thus far that he really knew what war was all about. The old man was in retirement up the Hudson at West Point, too infirm for travel. So on June 23 — a Monday; the first of the Seven Days was two days off — Lincoln boarded a special train and rode north to see him. What they talked about was a secret, and it remained so. But when McClellan wired the War Department on June 27, while Porter was under attack on Turkey Hill: "I will beg that you put some one general in command of the Shenandoah and of all troops in front of Washington for the sake of the country. Secure unity of action and bring the best men forward," Lincoln, who had returned two days before, had already done what he suggested, even before his visit up the Hudson. That is, he had united the troops under one commander. Whether he had brought the best man forward remained to be seen.

John Pope was the man: Halleck had praised him so highly he had lost him. Indeed, for months now the news from that direction had seemed to indicate that the formula for victory, so elusive here on the seaboard, had been discovered by the generals in the West — in which case, as Lincoln and Stanton saw it, the thing to do was bring one of them East and give him a chance to apply it. Grant's record having been tarnished by Shiloh and the subsequent rumors of negligence and whiskey, Pope was the more or less obvious choice, not only because of Island Ten and Halleck's praise of his aggressiveness during the campaign against Corinth, but also because Lincoln, as a prairie lawyer pleading cases in Pope's father's district court, had known him back in Illinois. There were objections. Montgomery Blair, for instance, warned that old Judge Pope "was a flatterer, a deceiver, a liar and a trickster; all the Popes are so." But the President could not see that these were necessarily drawback characteristics in a military man. While admitting the general's "infirmity" when it came to walking the chalk-line of truth, he protested that "a liar might be brave and have skill as an officer." Also, perhaps as a result of a belief in the Westerner's ability to combine effectively the several family traits Blair had warned of, he credited him with "great cunning," a quality Lincoln had learned to prize highly as a result of his brush with Stonewall Jackson in the Valley. So Pope was sent for.

Arriving while Lincoln was up the country seeing Scott, he made at once an excellent impression on Stanton and the members of the Committee on the Conduct of the War, who saw in him the antithesis of McClellan. For one thing, there was nothing of caution about him; he was a talker, and his favorite words were "I" and "forward." (If he had been placed in charge of the West in the early spring, he said, nothing could have stopped his march on New Orleans;

by now he would have split the South in two and gone to work on the crippled halves.) For another, he was sound on the slavery question, assuring the committee that he and it saw eye to eye on the matter. Wade and the others were delighted, not only with his opinions, civil as well as military, but also with his appearance, which they found as reassuring as his beliefs. He had shaved his cheeks and his upper lip, retaining a spade-shaped chin beard that bobbed and wagged decisively as he spoke, lending weight and point to his utterances and increasing the overall impression of forcefulness and vigor. Lincoln, when he returned from the visit with Scott, was pleased to see the confidence Pope had managed to invite within so brief a span, and gave him at once his orders and his assignment to the command of an army expressly created for his use.

John Pope alienated many subordinates with the overconfident tone of his general orders to the army.

The Army of Virginia, it was called. Its strength was 56,000 men and its mission was to move in general down the line of the Orange & Alexandria Railroad, just east of the Blue Ridge Mountains, so as to close in on the Confederate capital from the west and north, while McClellan's Army of the Potomac applied pressure from the east; thus Richmond would be crushed in a giant nutcracker, with Pope as the upper jaw. His army was created by consolidating the commands of McDowell, Banks, and Frémont. All three of these generals outranked him — an unusual arrangement, to say the least — but only one of them took official umbrage. This was Frémont: which solved another problem. His protest resignation was accepted, and Lincoln replaced him with Franz Sigel, whose appointment, though it involved a thousand-mile transfer, was considered especially felicitous since so many of the troops involved were of German extraction.

Pope's instructions, issued June 26 as part of the order creating his army, required him to operate so as to protect Washington from "danger or insult" and to "render the most effective aid to relieve General McClellan and capture Richmond." It was a large order, but Pope only laid down one condition: McClellan must be given peremptory orders to attack the minute he heard that Pope was engaged. This was necessary, Pope said, because of the known timidity and irresolution of his partner in the squeeze play.

★

For the present, however — as he learned all too soon — the stipulation was unnecessary. On the day the Army of Virginia came officially into being, McClellan no longer had any choice in the matter; the Seven Days had opened, and the Army of the Potomac found itself engaged in a tremendous struggle for survival, trying first to fend off Lee's assault down the north bank of the Chickahominy and then to reach the gunboat sanctuary of the James. When news of the attack reached Washington, Pope showed that there were elements of caution in his make-up after all. He advised Lincoln not to let McClellan fall back southward, since this would unhinge the jaws of the nutcracker, but to order him to retire in the direction of the York. That way, Pope said, he could eventually go to his assistance — and vice versa, in case the Army of Virginia ran into similar trouble moving south. But there was nothing Lincoln could do about it, even if he had wanted to; the wires were cut and the Army of the Potomac was already in motion for the James. Pope began to see the handwriting on the wall. It warned him plainly that there was an excellent chance that he would be entirely on his own as he moved down the road that led to Richmond.

Discouraging as this prospect was to the newly arrived commander, a look into the backgrounds of the three groups he was expected to weld into an effective striking force proved equally discouraging, if not more so. Two of the three (Banks' and Sigel's) had traditions of defeat, and the third (McDowell's) had slogged all over northern Virginia, seemingly without profit to anyone, least of all to itself. Unquestionably, even in their own eyes — "Milroy's weary boys" were a case in point — this was the second team, restricted to an occasional scrimmage which served primarily to emphasize its lack of style, while the first team got the cheers and glory on the Peninsula. For all his bluster, Pope saw one thing clearly. However second-rate his material might be in some respects, he had here the makings of a first-class disaster, unless he could somehow restore or establish confidence in the breasts of his downhearted charges. Accordingly, as a first step before he took the field, he issued an address "To the Officers and Soldiers of the Army of Virginia," giving them, along with much else in the way of advice, a chance to see what manner of man was about to lead them against the rebel force that had just finished mauling the first team and flinging it back from the goal-post gates of Richmond.

"Let us understand each other," he told them. "I have come to you from the West, where we have always seen the backs of our enemies; from an army whose business it has been to seek the adversary and to beat him when he was found; whose policy has been attack and not defense. . . . I presume that I have been called here to pursue the same system and to lead you against the enemy. It is my purpose to do so, and that speedily." He supposed they longed for distinction in the jar and shock of battle, and he was prepared to show them how to win it. In any event, he said, "I desire you to dismiss from your minds certain phrases, which I am sorry to find so much in vogue amongst you. I hear constantly of 'taking strong positions and holding them,' of 'lines of retreat,' and of 'bases of supplies.' Let us discard such ideas. The strongest position a soldier should desire to occupy is one from which he can most easily advance against the enemy. Let us study the probable lines of retreat of our opponents, and leave our own to take care of themselves. Let us look before us, and not behind. Success and glory are in the advance, disaster and shame lurk in the rear."

The words had a Stantonian ring, which Pope explained long afterwards by identifying the Secretary himself as their author. At any rate, whoever wrote them, the effect was something other than the one that had been intended: particularly among the men the undersigned general addressed. They found the comparison odious, and they resented the boasting tone in which it was made. "Five Cent Pope," they dubbed their new commander, while old-time regulars recalled a parody that had made the army rounds some years ago, when he issued oversanguine reports of success in boring for artesian water on the bone-dry plains of Texas:

Pope told a flattering tale

Which proved to be bravado

About the streams which spout like ale

On the Llano Estacado.

McClellan's supporters of course resented him, too: Fitz-John Porter for example, who declared that Pope had "written himself down [as] what the military world has long known, an ass. . . . If the theory he proclaims is practiced you may look for disaster."

Beyond the lines, where the address enjoyed wide circulation, the Confederate reaction combined contempt and amusement. Reports that this new spread-eagle opponent was heading his dispatches "Headquarters in the Saddle" prompted a revival of the old army jibe that he had his headquarters where his hindquarters ought to be.

★ ★ ★ *B*y the time Pope's flamboyant address was issued in mid-July, Lincoln had been down to the Peninsula and back. Between the two boat-rides, going and coming, he not only made a personal inspection of the Army of the Potomac and questioned its chief and subordinate generals, but he also made up his mind about a matter he had been pondering ever since his visit to Winfield Scott three weeks ago — a command decision, involving this and all the other armies of the Union.

Within two days of his July 1 plea for 50,000 men, with which to

★

"retrieve our fortunes" after the blood-letting of the Seven Days, McClellan doubled the ante; 100,000 would now be needed, he declared. Lincoln replied on the 4th that any such figure "within a month, or even six weeks, is impossible. . . . Under these circumstances the defensive for the present must be your only care. Save the army — first, where you are, if you can; secondly, by removal, if you must." He added, perhaps ironically: "P.S. If at any time you feel able to take the offensive, you are not restrained from doing so." Once more he was losing patience fast. Sending troops to McClellan, he said, was like trying to shovel fleas across a barnlot; so few seemed to get there. Also there were alarming rumors as to the condition of the men the general already had. Lincoln decided to see for himself. Boarding a steamer on the night of July 7, he reached Harrison's Landing late the following afternoon and rode out at once with the army commander for a sundown inspection of the camps.

Apparently to his surprise he found the men in good condition and high spirits — though the latter could be accounted for, at least in part, as a reaction to seeing the President on horseback. For one thing, an observer wrote home, there was the imminent danger that his long legs "would become entangled with those of the horse . . . and both come down together." Occupied as he was in the attempt to control his mount, which seemed equally nervous, he had trouble tipping his tall hat in response to cheers that were redoubled when the difficulty was seen. "That arm with which he drew the rein, in its angles and position resembled the hind leg of a grasshopper — the hand before, the elbow away back over the horse's tail. . . . But the boys liked him," the soldier-observer added. "In fact his popularity with the army is and has been universal. Most of our rulers and leaders fall into odium, but all have faith in Lincoln. 'When he finds out,' they say, 'it will be stopped.' . . . God bless the man and give answer to the prayers for guidance I am sure he offers."

If guidance was what he was seeking he could find it right there alongside him, astride Dan Webster. Less than three weeks ago McClellan had requested permission to present his views on the state of military affairs throughout the country; Lincoln had replied that he would be glad to have them — preferably in a letter, he said — if their presentation would not divert too much of the general's time and attention from his immediate duties. So tonight, when they returned to headquarters, McClellan handed the President a letter "covering the whole ground of our national trouble" and setting forth the conditions under which he believed the struggle could be won.

The rebellion, he said, had now "assumed the character of a war," and "as such . . . it should be conducted upon the highest principles known to Christian civilization. It should not be a war looking to the subjugation of the people of any State in any event. It should not be at all a war upon population, but against armed forces and political organizations. Neither confiscation of property, political executions of persons, territorial organization of States, or forcible abolition of slavery should be contemplated for a moment." This last was a point he emphasized, since "a declaration of radical views" in this direction would "rapidly disintegrate our present armies." More strictly within the military province, he advised concentration as the guiding rule. "The national force should not be dispersed in expeditions, posts of occupation, and numerous armies, but should be mainly collected into masses, and brought to bear upon the armies of the Confederate States. Those armies thoroughly defeated, the political structure which they support would soon cease to exist," and the southern people, unembittered by depredations, would turn against the willful men who had misled them out of the Union and sue at once for peace and reëntry. So he saw it. However, no matter what "system of policy" was adopted, he strongly urged the appointment of a general-in-chief, "one who possesses your confidence, understands your views, and who is competent to execute your orders." He did not ask that post for himself, he said; but he made it clear that he would not decline the reappointment, since he was "willing to serve you in such position as you may assign me," including this one. In closing he added a final explanation and disclaimer: "I may be on the brink of eternity, and as I hope forgiveness from my Maker I have written this letter with sincerity toward you and from love for my country."

Lincoln took it and read it through, with McClellan standing by. "All right," he said, and put it in his pocket. That was all. Apparently he had not come down here in search of guidance.

What he had come for, it developed, was a look at the present condition of the army and some specific answers to a specific question which he put the following day to the five corps commanders: "If it were desired to get the army away from here, could it be safely effected?" Keyes and Franklin replied that it could and should be done. The other three thought otherwise. "It would be ruinous to the country," Heintzelman said; "We give up the cause if we do it," Sumner said; "Move the army and ruin the country," Porter said. Once the questioning was over, Lincoln and the generals took a glass of wine together and the President got ready to go back to Washington.

McClellan was upset: particularly by the evidence that the Administration might order him to evacuate the Peninsula. After seeing Lincoln off next morning, he wrote his wife that he feared the President had some "paltry trick" up his sleeve; his manner, he said, "seemed that of a man about to do something of which he was ashamed." For a week the general brooded and delivered himself of judgments. Lincoln was "an old stick, and of pretty poor timber at that," while Stanton was "the most unmitigated scoundrel I ever knew, heard, or read of." He believed he saw which way the wind was blowing: "Their game seems to be to withhold reinforcements, and then to relieve me for not advancing, well knowing that I have not the means to do so." Accordingly, in mid-July he wrote

★

AFTER HIS LAST RUN.

Doctor Lincoln:—" WELL, M'CLELLAN, AND HOW ARE YOUR POOR FEET?"

A concerned "Doctor" Lincoln attends an "in-hot-water" General McClellan after the army's retreat from Richmond in this 1862 political cartoon. McClellan's failure led to calls for his replacement.

to his friend William H. Aspinwall, asking the New York transportation tycoon to be on the lookout for a job for him.

Lincoln meanwhile had made up his mind to act on the command decision which he had been considering for weeks. All through the previous autumn, old General Scott had held out in Washington for as long as he could, putting up with McClellan's snubs and digs for the sake of Halleck, who was on his way from California. It was Scott's hope that Old Brains would be there to take his place when he retired as general-in-chief. But the way was long and the digs were sharp; the old man gave up before Halleck got there, and McClellan got the job. Since then, the contrast in accomplishments East and West seemed to reinforce Scott's original opinion, which he repeated when the President came to West Point on the eve of the Seven Days. Lincoln saw merit in the recommendation, but he thought he would have a talk with Halleck before he acted on it. Back in Washington in time for the outbreak of the Seven Days, he wired the western commander: "Please tell me, could you make me a flying visit for a consultation without endangering the service in your department?"

Halleck did not want to come, and said so. Even if he did, he added, "I could advise but one thing: to place all the [eastern] forces . . . under one head, and hold that head responsible."

Refusal was always provocative for Lincoln; in the course of the war, several men were to learn that the surest way to get something from him was to pretend they did not want it. He almost made up his mind, then and there.

★

Down on the Peninsula, however, the matter was more or less cinched by McClellan himself. His Harrison's Landing letter, an exegesis of the conservative position, was the strongest possible proof that its author was not the kind of man to fight the kind of war Lincoln was rapidly coming to believe the country was going to have to fight if it was going to win. Returning to Washington on the night of July 10, he had Stanton send a wire to Corinth next morning, which left the recipient no choice in the matter: "*Ordered,* that Maj. Gen. Henry W. Halleck be assigned to command the whole land forces of the United States as General-in-Chief, and that he repair to this capital as soon as he can with safety to the positions and operations within the department under his charge."

There were delays; Halleck did not arrive for nearly two weeks, being occupied with the incidentals of transferring his command. The delay was hard on Lincoln; "I am very anxious — almost impatient — to have you here," he wired. Down on the Peninsula, McClellan was spared for nine days the shock of hearing that his old post had gone to a rival. Then he read of it in a newspaper. "In all these things," he wrote his wife, "the President and those around him have acted so as to make the matter as offensive as possible. He has not shown the slightest gentlemanly or friendly feeling, and I cannot regard him as in any respect my friend. I am confident that he would relieve me tomorrow if he dared to do so. His cowardice alone prevents it. I can never regard him with other feelings than those of contempt."

★ ★ ★   *T*his was going to be a harder war from here on out, and Lincoln knew it. He knew it because he was going to make it so. In fact, he was going to make it just as hard as he had to, and he said as much quite frankly to anyone who asked him. Most particularly, despite conflicting advice from McClellan and men like him, it was going to be harder on civilians. Of the four actions which the general had said "should [not] be contemplated for a moment" — 1) confiscation of property, 2) political execution of persons, 3) territorial organization of states, and 4) forcible abolition of slavery — the first and second had already been carried out with governmental sanction, the third was in the legislative works, and the fourth was under urgent consideration.

The second of these was the most obviously harsh, and for that reason should be the most obviously effective in securing obedience to occupation rule. So Benjamin Butler reasoned, at any rate, when he reached New Orleans and found that the national ensign, prematurely raised over the Mint, had been ripped from its staff by the mob. "They have insulted our flag — torn it down

★

with indignity," he notified the War Department. "This outrage will be punished in such manner as in my judgment will caution both the perpetrators and abettors of the act, so that they shall fear the stripes if they do not reverence the stars in our banner." As good as his word, Butler found a man still wearing a tatter of the outraged bunting in his buttonhole, brought him before a drum-head court, and carried out the resultant sentence by hanging him in public from a window of the building where the crime had been committed.

It worked about as well as he had expected. The sight of one man dangling by his neck from the eaves of the Mint sobered the others considerably. Fear, not reverence, was what Butler had wanted, and he got it — at least from the men. The women were another matter. In them he saw no signs of fear, and certainly none of reverence. In fact, they missed no chance to show their contempt for the blue-clad invaders. Passing them on the street, they drew their skirts aside to escape contamination, or else they walked straight ahead, taking their half of the sidewalk out of the middle, and forced oncoming Yankees to step off into the mud. The climax came when one of them, taking careful aim from an upstairs window, emptied a slopjar onto the head of Farragut himself. Butler retaliated with a general order, directing "that hereafter when any Female shall, by word, gesture, or movement, insult or show contempt for any officer or soldier of the United States, she shall be regarded and held liable to be treated as a woman of the town plying her avocation."

At home and abroad, the reaction was uproarious. Beauregard made Butler's order the subject of one of his own: "Men of the South! shall our mothers, our wives, our daughters and our sisters be thus outraged by the ruffianly soldiers of the North, to whom is given the right to treat, at their pleasure, the ladies of the South as common harlots? Arouse, friends, and drive back from our soil those infamous invaders of our homes and disturbers of our family ties!" Overseas, Lord Palmerston remarked: "Any Englishman must blush to think that such an act has been committed by one belonging to the Anglo-Saxon race." In Richmond, before the year was out, Davis branded Butler a felon, an outlaw, an enemy of mankind, and ordered that in the event of his capture "the officer in command of the capturing force do cause him to be immediately executed by hanging."

Southerners and their blushful friends abroad were not the only ones offended by the cock-eyed general's zeal. Pro-Union men of the region he controlled found that they too came under his strictures, particularly in economic matters such as the seizure of cotton and the freezing of foreign funds, and they were equally vociferous in protest. But Lincoln had little use or sympathy for them. If these riders on the ship of state thought they were "to touch neither a sail nor a pump, but to be merely passengers — deadheads at that — to be carried snug and dry throughout the storm, and safely landed right side up," they were mistaken. He gave them a midsummer warning that the voyage was about to get rougher.

★

"The true remedy," he said, switching metaphors, "does not lie in rounding the rough angles of the war, but in removing the necessity for war." This they could accomplish, he replied to one protestant, by bringing Louisiana back into the Union. Otherwise, "it is for them to consider whether it is probable I will surrender the government to save them from losing all. If they decline what I suggest, you scarcely need to ask what I will do. What would you do in my position? Would you drop the war where it is? Or would you prosecute it in future with elder-stalk squirts charged with rosewater? Would you deal lighter blows rather than heavier ones? Would you give up the contest, leaving any available means unapplied?" The questions were rhetorical, and he closed by answering them: "I am in no boastful mood. I shall do no more than I can, and I shall do all I can, to save the government, which is my sworn duty as well as my personal inclination. I shall do nothing in malice. What I deal with is too vast for malicious dealing."

Already he had sent an official observer, a Maryland senator, down to New Orleans to look into the situation. But when the senator reported that there was indeed much harshness and irregularity (Butler's brother was getting

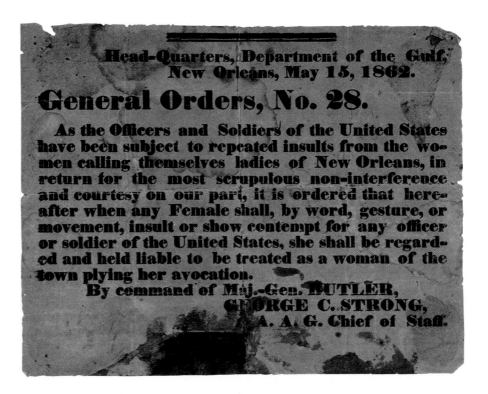

Benjamin Butler's order stating that women of New Orleans who insulted Federal soldiers were liable to be treated as prostitutes caused general outrage throughout the South.

★

rich on confiscated cotton, and the general himself had been given the nickname "Spoons," implying considerable deftness in the execution of his duties) as well as much disturbance of the master-slave relationship by the enlistment of Negroes in labor battalions, Lincoln was even more forthright in his statement of conditions and intentions: "The people of Louisiana — all intelligent people everywhere — know full well that I never had a wish to touch the foundations of their society or any right of theirs. With perfect knowledge of this they forced a necessity upon me to send armies among them, and it is their own fault, not mine, that they are annoyed." Here again the remedy was reëntry into the Union. "And might it not be well for them to consider whether they have not already had time enough to do this? If they can conceive of anything worse . . . within my power, would they not better be looking out for it?. . . I am a patient man, always willing to forgive on the Christian terms of repentance. Still, I must save this Government if possible. What I cannot do, of course, I will not do; but it may as well be understood, once for all, that I shall not surrender this game leaving any available card unplayed."

★ ★ ★ **T**he unplayed card was emancipation. Mindful, so far, of his inaugural statement: "I have no purpose, directly or indirectly, to interfere with the institution of slavery in the states where it exists. I believe I have no lawful right to do so, and I have no inclination to do so," Lincoln had resisted all efforts to persuade him to repudiate his words. He resisted mainly on practical grounds, considering the probable reaction in the border states; "We should lose more than we should gain," he told one Jacobin delegation. Not only had he refused to issue such a proclamation as they were urging on him, he had revoked three separate pronouncements or proclamations issued by subordinates: one by Frémont, one by Cameron, and recently a third by Hunter in South Carolina. In the instance of the latter revocation, however, he had shown which way his mind was turning in mid-May: "Whether it be competent for me, as Commander in Chief of the army and navy, to declare the slaves of any state or states free, and whether, at any time, in any case, it shall have become a necessity indispensable to the maintenance of the government to exercise such supposed power, are questions which, under my responsibility, I reserve to myself."

This was putting a new face on the matter. What a President had no right or inclination to do in peacetime, Lincoln was saying, might become an indispensable necessity for a wartime Commander in Chief. Besides, he had done some ciphering back in March, and had come up with a simple dollars-and-cents solution to the problem. Figuring the cost of the war at two million dollars a day, and the cost of slaves at four hundred dollars a head, he had found the value of Delaware's 1798 slaves to be less than the cost of half a day of fighting. Extending his computations on this basis, he found that the total value of the 432,622 slaves in the District of Columbia and the four border states — Delaware, Maryland, Kentucky, Missouri — amounted to less than the cost of three months of warfare. Accordingly, he laid these figures before Congress in support of a resolution proposing compensated emancipation. In early April it was adopted, despite the objections of abolitionists who considered it highly immoral to traffic thus in souls; but nothing practical came of it, because the slave-state legislatures would not avail themselves of the offer. Lincoln was saddened by this failure, and on revoking Hunter's proclamation the following month addressed a special plea to the people of the border region: "I do not argue — I beseech you to make arguments for yourselves. You cannot, if you would, be blind to the signs of the times. I beg of you a calm and enlarged consideration of them, ranging, if it may be, far above personal and partisan politics. This proposal makes common cause for a common object, casting no reproaches upon any. It acts not the Pharisee. The change it contemplates would come gently as the dews of heaven, not rending or wrecking anything. Will you not embrace it? So much good has not been done, by one effort, in all past time, as in the providence of God it is now your high privilege to do. May the vast future not have to lament that you have neglected it."

The signs of the times were indeed plain to read; they had in fact the glistening clarity of wet paint, most of them having been posted about the legislative landscape during the current session of Congress. In March, subscribing to the opinion that the Dred Scott decision did not constitute law, the members fulfilled a Republican campaign promise by-passing an act prohibiting slavery in all present or future national territories. The following month, the "peculiar institution" was abolished in the District of Columbia, with compensation for the owners and provisions for colonization of the freedmen, which Lincoln considered the best practical solution to the problem. "There has never been in my mind any question upon the subject," he declared as he signed the bill, "except the one of expediency, arising in view of all the circumstances." In May, the United States and Britain agreed by treaty to coöperate in suppressing the slave trade: a diplomatic move that gave much pleasure to the Jacobins, whom Lincoln had been at pains to please whenever he could. For their sake he had proposed that the country give formal recognition to the Negro republics of Haiti and Liberia, which Congress gladly did, and back in February — despite the known leniency of his nature in such matters — he sustained the sentence of execution brought against Nathaniel Gordon of Portland, Maine, the first and only slave trader ever hanged in accordance with Federal law.

Gratifying as all this was, including the hanging, the Jacobins were by no means satisfied. They wanted more, much more, and they never stopped letting Lincoln know it. "The pressure in this direction is still upon me and

*Abraham Lincoln struggled with himself
and with factions in Congress over when
and how to emancipate the slaves.*

★

increasing," he said on July 12 when he called twenty border-state congressmen into his office for a final appeal before next week's adjournment sent them scattering for their homes. He spoke of the continuing attempts by the seceded states to persuade their sister slave communities farther north to join them in revolt — attempts which, incidentally, if successful would deprive these representatives of their jobs. The pull was strong, Lincoln admitted, and he wanted these men to help him weaken it. "You and I know what the lever of their power is. Break that lever before their faces and they can shake you no more forever." Besides, he said, slavery was failing fast already. "If the war continues long . . . the institution in your states will be extinguished by mere friction and abrasion. . . . How much better for you and for your people to take the step which at once shortens the war and secures substantial compensation for that which is sure to be wholly lost in any other event."

They heard him out, and then they shook their heads. The adopted resolution not only seemed to them a violation of State Rights, but they also questioned the constitutional power of Congress to appropriate funds for such a purpose. What was more, they doubted the sincerity of their fellow congressmen; the offer, one of the callers said, "was but the enunciation of a sentiment which could not or was not likely to be reduced to an actual tangible proposition." If Congress really meant it, let the money be put in the President's hands, and then they would consider acceptance. Then too — though this objection went unspoken — the plan entailed payment in government bonds, and though slave property was admittedly precarious and declining fast in value, the national credit was declining even faster. In short, they wanted no part of the offer as things now stood. Respectfully they bowed and took their leave, and Lincoln was left saddened and alone.

Left alone, he would act alone. He knew well enough the arguments against what McClellan, four days before, had called "a declaration of radical views" on the slavery issue: possible loss of the border states, possible loss of large segments of the army through desertion, possible loss of the fall elections. He knew, too, of currents that ran deeper — of Archbishop John Hughes of New York, for example, who had warned in a widely reprinted official declaration: "We, Catholics, and a vast majority of our brave troops in the field, have not the slightest idea of carrying on a war that costs so much blood and treasure just to gratify a clique of Abolitionists in the North." A Westerner, Lincoln knew the rabid division on the subject in the West, where candidates were tagged "charcoal" and "snowflake" in anger and derision, regardless of party. Such considerations, the concrete along with the nebulous, had weight. But he also knew the arguments in favor of positive action. First, it would allay the danger of foreign intervention by engaging the sympathy and arousing the enthusiasm of the rank and file of Europe, against which not even the most avid of the

During an 1861 visit to Washington, abolitionist Julia Ward Howe penned The Battle Hymn of the Republic by putting new words to the popular marching song "John Brown's Body."

pro-Confederate rulers and ministers would dare to act. Second, whatever it did to the Democrats here at home, it would heal the split in his own party, which was rapidly getting out of hand.

Beyond if not above all these, and entirely aside from his promises to those who claimed to have removed themselves from his authority, there was the question of personal ethics, of whether the considered step was consonant with honor. He had called the nation to arms in support of a single issue, the preservation of the Union; could he now adopt a second — superimpose it, so to speak — without being guilty of chicanery or worse? He believed he could, and he based his persuasion on necessity. "Things had gone on from bad to worse," he later explained, "until I felt that we had reached the end of our rope on the plan of operations we had been pursuing; that we had about played our last card, and must change our tactics or lose the game." The truth was, the war had already outlasted the heady burst of enthusiasm that had flared up after Sumter. What was needed was a new cause, not to supplant, but to supplement the old; and this was it. Having appealed at the outset to reason, he now would appeal to conscience. He would translate the conflict into the terms of a holy war — a crusade — for which Julia Ward Howe had already composed the anthem:

> *In the beauty of the lilies Christ was born across the sea . . .*
>
> *As he died to make men holy, let us die to make men free,*
>
> *While God is marching on.*

★

Before the night was over, though the details were still to be worked out, he had completed his decision. He would do it. And next afternoon — much to their surprise, since always before, as one of them said, "he had been prompt and emphatic in denouncing any interference by the general government with the subject" — he spoke of it to two members of his cabinet.

The occasion was a funeral; the Stantons had lost a newborn child, and Lincoln rode to the burial in a carriage with Welles and Seward. According to Welles, the President "dwelt earnestly on the gravity, importance, and delicacy" of the slavery question and the advisability of issuing an emancipation proclamation "in case the rebels did not cease to persist in their war on the government . . . of which he saw no evidence." He said he "had about come to the conclusion that it was a military necessity absolutely essential for the salvation of

Newly freed slaves, dubbed contrabands, await distribution of rations in a square in Baton Rouge, Louisiana. An 1862 act of Congress provided that slaves held by persons in rebellion against the government could be seized and freed as "contraband of war."

the Union, that we must free the slaves or be ourselves subdued." Asked for their opinions on the matter, both men were at first too taken aback by what Welles called "this new departure" to say anything at all. Seward, recovering first, replied that "his present opinion inclined to the measure as justifiable," but he would rather think the matter through before giving a final answer. Welles said he felt the same way about it. Lincoln let it go at that, though he made it clear that he was "earnest in the conviction that something must be done."

Four days later, July 17, Congress came very close to stealing his thunder. In August of the previous year, this body had passed a Confiscation Act endorsing Butler's contention that the slaves of disloyal masters were "contraband," liable to seizure and eligible for freedom on entering Union lines. Now, in the final hours before adjournment of the current session, a second such Act was passed. Considerably sharper-toothed than the one that had gone before, it provided "That every person who shall hereafter commit the crime of treason against the United States, and shall be adjudged guilty thereof, shall suffer death, and all his slaves, if any, shall be declared and made free." Discretion was left to the courts as to whether a prison term and/or a fine should be substituted in lieu of the death penalty, but no leeway was allowed as to the disposition of a traitor's slaves, who were automatically freed upon his conviction. At first glance, with nearly the whole slave region in rebellion, this

> *"It may be viewed as the last measure of an exhausted government, a cry for help; the government stretching forth its hands to Ethiopia, instead of Ethiopia stretching forth her hands to the government."*
>
> — William Seward

appeared to be the very proclamation Lincoln was considering. However, closer reading showed it to be no such thing. No slave was to be freed by it until his master had been convicted of treason in a federal court. There was the rub. Secession — or rebellion, as the Jacobins preferred to call it — might be treason, but no court had ever said so (or ever would say so) no matter what opinion the radicals had on the matter. All the Acts really did was provide a sanctuary for such slaves as crossed the Federal lines: with the result that the U.S. government became, in effect, the greatest slaveholder the world had ever known, not excepting the Pharaohs of Egypt.

Lincoln doubted the legality of the Act; "It is startling to say that Congress can free a slave within a State," he declared in a veto message which he had prepared against its passage. All the same, he signed it as soon as it reached his desk; but in doing so he forwarded the proposed veto message in order to make his objections part of the record when the legislation was tested in the courts. Read in both houses as a prelude to adjournment, the message was greeted with sneers and laughter by the radicals, who took it as an admission that when the chips were down he did not dare to oppose them with anything but words.

In this they were much mistaken, though words were very much a part of what he had in mind. On July 22, to the surprise of all but Welles and Seward, who had been prepared for something of the sort by his remarks in the funeral carriage nine days back, he read to the assembled cabinet an emancipation proclamation which he proposed to issue without delay. Unlike the Confiscation Act, which required that individuals be convicted of treason before their slaves were freed, Lincoln's edict left no burden of proof upon the government. He intended it as a military pronouncement, designed to help win the war, and that was all. He was not concerned with "legality," as such, since he did not deal with individuals as such; all he required was that they live within an area where the authorities, after a specified date, continued to defy the federal government. The object of the war, he repeated, was the preservation of the Union; "And as a fit and necessary military measure for effecting this object, I, as Commander in Chief of the Army and Navy of the United States, do order and declare that on the first day of January, in the year of our Lord one thousand eight hundred and sixty-three, all persons held as slaves within any State or States wherein the constituted authority of the United States shall not then be practically recognized, submitted to, and maintained, shall then, thenceforward, and forever be free."

Reactions varied. Chase and Stanton approved, but wanted it stronger; Bates wanted it as it was; Welles wanted it weaker; Blair and Smith did not want it at all, or at least not before the fall elections. Then Seward spoke, having turned the matter over in his mind. "Mr President," he said, "I approve of the proclamation, but I question the expediency of its issue at this juncture. The depression of the public mind, consequent upon our repeated reverses, is so great that I fear the effect of so important a step. It may be viewed as the last measure of an exhausted government, a cry for help; the government stretching forth its hands to Ethiopia, instead of Ethiopia stretching forth her hands to the government. It will be considered our last *shriek* on the retreat. Now, while I approve the measure, I suggest, sir, that you postpone its issue until you can give it to the country supported by military success, instead of issuing it, as would be the case now, upon the greatest disasters of the war."

Lincoln had not considered this aspect of the question, but now that he did so, he perceived its wisdom and acted in accord with Seward's view. "I put the draft of the proclamation aside," he later told an artist friend, "as you do your sketch for a picture, waiting for a victory." Halleck, the man he counted on to give him one, was on the way at last: would arrive, in fact, tomorrow. Meanwhile, this thunderbolt would keep.

★　★　★

Federals labor to repair the rail bridge across the Elk River in southern Tennessee. The bridge, burned the month before, was vital to Buell's supply line.

SIX

Grant, Farragut, Buell

1862 ★ ★ ★ ★ ★ There was gloom in the West as in the East, but it was of a different nature, proceeding from different causes. Here too the advance had stalled; yet it was precisely in this apparent similarity that the difference obtained. McClellan had been stopped by Lee, but Halleck stopped himself. Curiously enough, or perhaps not curiously at all, the men on the Peninsula who had fought and fallen back, fighting as they went, had developed a fierce pride that burned brighter at the end of their retreat than it had ever burned before; they had fought well and they knew it; whereas Halleck's soldiers felt less elation at the end of their burrowing advance than at the start, not having fought at all. That was the source of a different kind of gloom.

Sherman did not share it, still being happy with the new stars on his shoulders and the sense of having "found" himself in the ordeal of Shiloh. But when he called by army headquarters not long after the fall of Corinth, he heard something that caused him to suspect that his friend Grant was in lower spirits than ever. Halleck happened to remark that Grant had applied for a thirty-day leave; he was going away next morning. Halleck said he did not know why, but Sherman took it to mean that Grant, "chafing under the slights," intended this as a first step in submitting his resignation. Determined to stop him

★

if he could, Sherman rode over and found him sitting in his tent, sorting some letters and tying them into bundles with red tape. Grant said it was true that he was leaving, and when the red-headed general asked him why, he replied: "Sherman, you know. You know I am in the way here. I have stood it as long as I can, and can endure it no longer."

Where was he going? "St Louis," Grant said. Did he have any business there? "Not a bit," Grant said. So Sherman, being then in what he called "high feather," began to argue with him, illustrating Grant's case with his own. Look at him, he said. They had called him crazy as a loon, but he had hung on through Shiloh, and "that single battle had given me new life." Besides, if Grant went away, "events would go right along, and he would be left out; whereas, if he remained, some happy accident might restore him to favor and his true place." This had its effect; Grant promised to wait, or at any rate not to leave without seeing Sherman again or sending him word. Satisfied, Sherman left, and before the week was out received a note from Grant. He had reconsidered; he would stay. Sherman replied that he was glad to hear it; "for you could not be quiet at home for a week when armies were moving."

Armies were moving now, though not in the direction of the Confederates who had fallen back before them. Like a man riding an oversized mettlesome horse, which he feared might take the bit in its teeth and bolt off with him any minute, Halleck kept as close a rein as possible on his 120,000-man army. Even so, the advance had already covered more ground than he had intended. Once he had accomplished what he set out for — in particular, control of a sizeable stretch of the Memphis & Charleston Railroad — he was more than ready to call a halt and consolidate his gains. Four days after the occupation of Corinth, he warned the commander of the pursuit against goading the rebels into rashness. All he wanted, he said, was for them to fall back far enough to be beyond reach of the railroad. And he added: "There is no object in bringing on a battle if this object can be obtained without one. I think by showing a bold front for a day or two the enemy will continue his retreat, which is all that I desire."

Having withheld his army from pursuit, he now proceeded to dismember it. Eastward, westward, even northward he dispersed it: every way, in fact, but southward. On June 9 he instructed Pope — who presently was on his way to Washington, superseded by Rosecrans — to draw back closer to Corinth and take up outpost positions to defend it. And that same day the scattering began: a scattering that divided the Grand Army into four main parts, rather as if the aforementioned timid rider had decided not only to get rid of his mettlesome horse, but to do so by having it drawn and quartered. Buell was ordered east with four divisions to make connection with Ormsby Mitchel, who had encountered so much difficulty in North Alabama; his goal was Chattanooga, which would put him within possible reach of Knoxville or Atlanta. Sherman was sent west; he would garrison Memphis with two divisions, repairing the railroad on the way and doing what he could to restore the wrecked economy by "assur[ing] all country people that they will be permitted to take their cotton freely to market and that the ordinary channels of trade will be immediately reopened." McClernand, with a similar force, was given a similar mission, except that his destination lay fifty miles north at Jackson, Tennessee; he too was to repair the lines of supply and give the "country people" whatever assurance was needed to make them happy. Halleck himself would remain with the force at Corinth, coördinating the efforts of the other three.

With a Union force advancing from Corinth toward Chattanooga and Federal armies in west Tennessee and central Kentucky, the defense of Chattanooga became vital to the Confederates.

★

His main concern in ordering the dispersal, he told Stanton, was the "sanitary condition" of the men. At present it was good, he said, but the question arose: "Can it be kept so during the summer?" He thought it could, provided he steered clear of a southward advance; for "if we follow the enemy into the swamps of Mississippi there can be no doubt that the army will be disabled by disease." (At least one of the general's wool-clad soldiers agreed with him. After being exposed to what Halleck was now avoiding, an Indiana veteran declared: "You load a man down with a sixty-pound knapsack, his gun and forty rounds of ammunition, a haversack full of hardtack and sow belly, and a three-pint canteen full of water, then start him along this narrow roadway with the mercury up to 100 and the dust so thick you could taste it, and you have done the next thing to killing this man outright.") "And yet," Halleck wrote, "to lie still, doing nothing, will not be satisfactory to the country nor conducive to the health of the army." He had therefore "deemed it best" to do as he had done. There was one drawback, one calculated risk: "This plan is based on the supposition that the enemy will not attempt an active campaign during the summer months. Should he do so . . . the present dispositions must be varied to suit the change of circumstances."

One immediate result the shake-up had. George Thomas returned to his old division, which was stationed under Halleck's eye at Corinth, and Grant was restored to the command of his old Army of the Tennessee, which included the divisions under Sherman and McClernand. Receiving permission to establish headquarters at Memphis, he set out on June 21 with a dozen troopers as escort, and after narrowly escaping capture on the way — Confederate horsemen, tipped off that he was coming, missed intercepting him by less than an hour — arrived three days later to find affairs "in rather bad order, secessionists governing much in their own way." He reported that there was even a plot to burn the city, which he thought might "prove partially successful," though he believed that such an action would "operate more against the rebels than ourselves." The main thing he needed, he told Halleck, was more troops.

Old Brains was in no mood just now to give him anything but trouble. By the end of June they had renewed their old-time wrangle. Halleck began it, wiring: "You say 30,000 men are at Shelbyville to attack La Grange. Where is Shelbyville? I can't find it on any map. Don't believe a word about an attack in large force on La Grange or Memphis. Why not send out a strong reconnaissance and ascertain the *facts*? It looks very much like a mere stampede. Floating rumors must never be received as facts. . . . I mean to make somebody responsible for so gross a negligence." Grant replied: "I did not say 30,000 troops at Shelbyville, but at Abbeville, which is south of Holly Springs, on the road to Grenada." Then he too got his back up. "I heed as little of floating rumors about this city as anyone," he protested. He had asked for more troops, he said, "that I might do effectively what you now ask. Stampeding is not my weakness. On the contrary, I will always execute any order to the best of my ability with the means at hand." Halleck drew in his horns at this, replying four days later: "I made no insinuation that there had been the slightest neglect on your part. . . . Nor did I suppose for a moment that you were stampeded; for I know that is not in your nature." Then — as if he had leaned down to stroke Old Rover, only to have Old Rover snap at his hand — he added: "I must confess that I was very much surprised at the tone of your dispatch and the ill-feeling manifested in it, so contrary to your usual style, and especially toward one who has so often befriended you when you were attacked by others."

This was more or less the note on which the other hassle had ended, four months back; Grant was willing to let it go at that. But five days later, July 8, Halleck was at him again: "The Cincinnati *Gazette* contains the substance of your demanding reinforcements and my refusing them. You either have a newspaper correspondent on your staff or your staff is very leaky." Three days later, the Memphis telegraph receiver clacked off a blunt one dozen words from Corinth: "You will immediately repair to this place and report to these headquarters."

Just what have I done now? Grant must have thought. It was not his way to worry, but he apparently had cause. For the past two weeks — and, in-deed, before — Halleck had shown all the earmarks of a commander engaged in the old army game of needling an unwanted subordinate enough to keep him edgy and fatten the record against him, but of holding back from the big pounce until something downright ruinous turned up to head the list of charges and specifications. Whether his sin was one of omission or commission, Grant did not know, though he had three full days for wondering while his horse retraced the steps taken three weeks ago with its head in the opposite direction. At last, July 15, the worried general reached Corinth and was face to face with his tor-mentor. What he was confronted with, however, was not the climax to a series of well-organized reproaches, but rather the accomplishment of the "happy acci-dent" Sherman had persuaded him to wait for. Halleck was ordered to Washing-ton to take over the direction of all the armies, East and West, and Grant was to receive, by seniority, the lion's share of what he left behind. Specifically, this in-cluded command of two armies — his own, now under McClernand and Sher-man, and Pope's, now under Rosecrans — and of the department embracing North Mississippi, West Tennessee, and Kentucky west of the Cumberland River.

He had what he wanted, but not as he preferred it. The fact was, he disapproved of nearly all that had been done since Halleck's arrival from St Louis, later saying: "For myself I am satisfied Corinth could have been captured in a two days' campaign commenced promptly on the arrival of reinforcements after the battle of Shiloh." Most of all he disapproved of what had been done, or left undone, since Beauregard's sly evacuation of Corinth. With the Missis-

★

sippi in Union hands, northward above Baton Rouge and southward below Memphis, "the Confederates at the west were narrowed down for all communication with Richmond to the single line of road running east from Vicksburg." That was the true goal now: that city, that stretch of river, that railroad. "To dispossess them of this . . . would be equal to the amputation of a limb in its weakening effects." As he saw it, "after the capture of Corinth a moveable force of 80,000 men, besides enough to hold all the territory acquired, could have been set in motion for the accomplishment of [this] great campaign for the suppression of the rebellion." Thus Grant, by hindsight. But Halleck could not see it, or else he feared to undertake it, and "the work of depletion commenced."

Even so, when he wound up his paperwork and departed for Washington two days later, he left his successor in immediate command of more than the 80,000 troops which Grant afterwards said would have been enough for the taking of Vicksburg that summer. The trouble was, they were far from "moveable," except when they were needed as reinforcements in adjoining departments. Before he had been at his post a week he was ordered to send a division to

★

Their goods stacked in a wagon drawn by an odd assemblage of oxen, horses, and mules, a southern family, possibly Unionist refugees, stops to register with the provost marshal in Union-occupied Corinth, Mississippi.

strengthen Samuel Curtis, who had marched from Northwest Arkansas to Helena, where the St Francis River flowed into the Mississippi, fifty air-line miles below Memphis. Still, this left Grant with well over 75,000 effectives. Sherman had 16,000 at Memphis, and McClernand had 10,000 around Jackson. Another 7500 were stationed at Columbus, Cairo, and Paducah, while the rest of the Army of the Tennessee, 12,000 men under Major General E. O. C. Ord — a West Point classmate of Halleck's, just arrived from Virginia — were at Corinth. Rosecrans' Army of the Mississippi, 32,000 strong, was spread along a thirty-five-mile front that extended from south of Corinth to Cherokee, Alabama.

It was a sizeable force, but deep in enemy country as he was, charged with the consolidation of all that had been gained since Donelson and Shiloh, Grant found that its very size increased his major immediate problem: which was how to keep it fed and equipped. Just as the foregoing spring had set records for rainfall, so now the summer was breaking records for drouth, and as a result the Tennessee River was all but worthless as a supply line. So was the Memphis & Charleston Railroad, for the rebels had torn up the track between Chewalla and

★

Grand Junction, and west of there the line had had to be abandoned for lack of rolling stock. All that was left him — except in Memphis, which of course could be supplied by river; the Mississippi never got really thirsty — was the slender thread of the Mobile & Ohio, stretching back to Columbus across more than a hundred miles of guerilla-infested West Tennessee, vulnerable throughout its length to attack by bands of regular and irregular cavalry, equally skilled at burning bridges and wrecking culverts, of which there were many. Tactically, too, the problems were not simple. Principal among them was the presence in North Mississippi of a highly mobile Confederate force, reckoned at 35,000 men, under the command of the resourceful and diabolical Earl Van Dorn, who sooner or later was probably going to succeed in one of his hair-trigger schemes. Its strength was less than half Grant's own, but its advantages were large. Van Dorn, for example, did not have to post a single man on guard in his rear, and best of all — or worst — he could choose the point of attack. He could strike the unconnected extremities, Corinth at one end, Memphis at the other, or he could pierce the lightly held center and knife straight through for Bolivar, Jackson, or Brownsville. What was more, he could choose the time.

Grant did not look forward to the coming months. Committed as he was to the defensive — much as he had been while biding his time before Shiloh — this was still not his kind of war. It was true, he had learned from what had happened then; from now on, he would keep in close touch with his field commanders and see to it that they had their men intrench. But he still did not like it, and he declared long afterwards that these midsummer months had been for him "the most anxious period of the war."

Discontent was general — amphibious, so to speak. For the navy, too, the successes of late spring and early summer, up and down the falling river, north and south of Vicksburg, were followed by a hot-weather season of doubts and tribulations. Every victory was accompanied by a setback, and the fruits thereof were bitter, their savor turning to ashes in the mouth. For Flag Officers Farragut and Davis, as for Grant, the midsummer word was *anxious.*

Davis ran into trouble first. As if Plum Run Bend had not been proof enough that his ironclads were vulnerable, it was presently re-proved in backwoods Arkansas, and on one of the resurrected victims of that earlier disaster. In the course of his eastward march from Pea Ridge to Helena, Curtis had to cross White River: a task that was complicated by the presence of a Confederate fort at St Charles, sixty miles from the mouth. Given orders to

Off-duty Federal sailors relax on the deck of the U.S.S. Hartford, Admiral Farragut's flagship, on the Mississippi River. The Hartford's heavy cannon made her a potent force on the river.

reduce it immediately after his Memphis triumph, Davis assigned the mission to four gunboats and an Indiana regiment which went along in transports. Raised, pumped out, and patched, the *Mound City* had the flag; this was her first outing since her encounter with the *Van Dorn*, back in May. When the flotilla came within sight of the fort, June 17, the Hoosier colonel requested permission to assault by land — there were only just over a hundred rebels in the place — but the naval commander refused to yield or even share the honors. Closing with the flagship, he opened fire at point-blank range: whereupon the fort replied with a 42-pound solid that pierced the *Mound City*'s casemate and went right through her steam drum, scalding to death or drowning 125 out of her crew of 175 men, injuring 25 more, and leaving only 25 unhurt. (It was freakish in more ways than one, including arithmetically; for the round-looking casualty figures were exact.) Helpless, the ironclad went with the current and the other gunboats withdrew, leaving the proposed reduction to the Indianians, who encircled the fort and took it without the loss of a man. Davis had himself another victory,

★

though he had it at far from a bargain price and the credit went to the army.

Farragut's troubles, downriver, were at once less bloody and more personal, and having a slopjar emptied onto his head from a French Quarter window was only the least of them. Five days after congratulating him for his "magnificent execution" and "unparalleled achievements" at New Orleans, Assistant Secretary Fox heard that the Tennessee sailor had abandoned the attempt against Vicksburg. "Impossible!" Fox cried. "Sending the fleet up to meet Commodore Davis was the most important part of the whole expedition. The instructions were positive." Quickly he reiterated them in triplicate, dispatching the original and two copies in three different ships to make certain of delivery: "It is of paramount importance that you go up and clear the river with utmost expedition. Mobile, Pensacola, and, in fact, the whole coast sinks into insignificance compared with this." Two days later he repeated the admonition in a sec-

Upper and nether millstones had come together at last, and now there was not even grist between them.

ond dispatch, invoking the support of higher authority: "The President requires you to use your utmost exertions (without a moment's delay, and before any other naval operation shall be permitted to interfere) to open the Mississippi and effect a junction with Flag Officer Davis."

On his previous trip upriver, Farragut had explained to Butler why he did not think a limited expedition against Vicksburg should be undertaken: "As they have so large a force of soldiers here, several thousand in and about the town, and the facility of bringing in 20,000 in an hour by railroad from Jackson, altogether, [I] think it would be useless to bombard it, as we could not hold it if we take it." He still felt that way about the proposition; but the orders from Fox, which presently arrived, left him no choice. He put the fleet in order for the 400-mile ascent, taking part of Porter's mortar flotilla with him this time, as well as 3000 men from Butler, and came within sight of Vicksburg's red clay bluff on the same day the *Mound City* took the solid through her boiler. He was back again, and though he still did not like the task before him, he wrote home that he was putting his trust in the Lord: "If it is His pleasure to take me, may He protect my wife and boy from the rigors of a wicked world."

He spent ten days reëxamining the problem and giving the mortars time to establish ranges. Then on the night of June 27 he made his run. Eleven warships were in the 117-gun column: three heavy sloops, two light sloops, and six gunboats. Skippers of the eight smaller vessels were instructed to hug the western bank while the large ones took the middle, the *Richmond* leading because her chase guns were situated best for high-angle fire, then the flagship *Hartford*, and finally the *Brooklyn*, lending a heavy sting to the tail. Two hours after midnight the attack signal was hoisted, and for the next three hours it was New Orleans all over again — except that this time the rebel gunners, high on their 200-foot bluff, were taking little punishment in return. Down on the river, by contrast, everything was smoke and uproar; the *Brooklyn* and two of the gunboats were knocked back, and all of the others were hit repeatedly. Total casualties were 15 killed and 30 wounded. But when daylight came, eight of the ships were beyond the hairpin turn, and Farragut was farther from salt water than he had been since he first left Tennessee to join the navy, more than fifty years before.

Two days later, July 1, Davis brought his gunboats down from Memphis and the two fleets were joined. There was much visiting back and forth, much splicing of the main brace — and with cause. Upper and nether millstones had come together at last, and now there was not even grist between them.

There, precisely, was the trouble; for now that Farragut was up here, there was nothing left for him to do. The day before the blue-water ships steamed past the batteries, Colonel A. W. Ellet, his brother's successor, took two of his rams up the Yazoo River, which emptied into the Mississippi a dozen miles above Vicksburg, to investigate a report that the rebels had three gunboats lurking there. It turned out to be true, one of them being the *Van Dorn*, only survivor of the Memphis rout; but all three were set afire as soon as the rams hove into view, and Ellet came back out again to report that he had destroyed the fag end of Confederate resistance on the western rivers. Then the Gulf Squadron made its run and the two fleets rode at anchor, midway between Vicksburg and the mouth of the Yazoo. As far as Farragut could see, however, all the exploit had really yielded was more proof that he could take his ships past fortifications: a fact he had never doubted in the first place. "We have done it," he informed the Department, "and can do it again as often as may be required of us." Just now, though, what he mainly wanted was a breath of salt air in his lungs. Requesting permission from Washington to go back downriver again, he emphasized the point that there were now two fleets biding their time in an area where there was not even work enough for one.

While awaiting an answer he did what he could to keep his sailors busy, including having them fire a high-noon 21-gun salute in celebration of the Fourth. The 3000 soldiers were no problem in this respect. With an ingenuity worthy of Butler himself, their commander Brigadier General Thomas Williams had them digging a canal across the narrow tongue of land dividing the shanks of the hairpin bend in front of Vicksburg. When the river rose, the general said, it would widen the ditch and sluice out a passage for the fleet, beyond the range of the batteries on the bluff. But there was the rub. The river was not rising; it was falling. It was falling so fast, in fact, that Farragut had begun to fear that his deep-draft sea-going fleet would be stranded up here all summer. On July 13 he sent a wire which he hoped would jog the Department into action on his request: "In ten days the river will be too low for the ships to go down. Shall they go down, or remain up the rest of the year?"

One problem more there was, though he did not consider it a matter for real concern, never having had much of an ear for rumor. In addition to the three gunboats whose destruction Ellet had effected when he appeared up the Yazoo, there were whispers that the Confederates were building themselves an ironclad up there. Farragut did not give the rumor much credence. Even if it were true, he said, there was small chance that the rebels would ever be able to use such a craft, bottled up as she was, with two powerful Federal fleets standing guard in the Mississippi, just below the only point of exit. "I do not think she will ever come forth," he reported.

Davis was not so sure. Unlike Farragut, he had Plum Run Bend in his memory, which had taught him what havoc a surprise attack could bring. Determined not to suffer such a reverse again, he ordered three warships up the Yazoo to investigate and take up lookout stations. They left immediately after early breakfast, July 15: the ironclad *Carondelet*, the wooden gunboat *Tyler*, and the steam ram *Queen of the West*.

★ ★ ★ *T*he rumors were all too true, as Farragut was about to discover. The mystery ship was the *Arkansas*, floated unfinished down the Mississippi and towed up the Yazoo to Greenwood after the fall of Island Ten exposed her to capture in Memphis. Naval Lieutenant Isaac Newton Brown, a forty-five-year-old Kentuckian who had held the same rank as a Vera Cruz veteran in the old navy, which he had entered from Mississippi nearly thirty years ago, was given command of her in late May, together with orders to "finish and equip that vessel without regard to expenditure of men or money."

He did not realize what a large order this was until he got to Greenwood and saw her. Unfinished was not the word; she was scarcely even begun.

"The vessel was a mere hull, without armor. The engines were apart. Guns without carriages were lying about the deck. A portion of the railroad iron intended as armor was at the bottom of the river, and the other and far greater part was to be sought for in the interior of the country." So he later reported; but now he got to work. After a day spent fishing up the sunken iron, he towed the skeleton *Arkansas* 150 miles downriver to Yazoo City, where the facilities were better, though not much. Scouring the plantations roundabout, he set up fourteen forges on the river bank and kept them going around the clock, rural blacksmiths pounding at the wagonloads of scrap iron brought in from all points of the compass. Two hundred carpenters added to the din, hammering, sawing, swarming over the shield and hull. Perhaps the biggest problem was the construction of carriages for the guns; nothing of the sort had ever been built in Mississippi; but this too was met by letting the contract to "two gentlemen of Jackson," who supplied them from their Canton wagon factory. Other deficiencies could not be overcome, and were let go. Since there was no apparatus for bending the iron around the curve of the vessel's quarter or stern, for example, boiler plate was tacked over these parts — "for appearance' sake," Brown explained. Also, the paint was bad. She was intended to be chocolate brown, the color of the river, but no matter how many coats were applied she kept her original hue, rusty red. Despite all this, the work in the

A steamer hoists a cannon aboard the C.S.S. Arkansas, near Greenwood, Mississippi, on the Yazoo River. The captain of the Arkansas, Isaac N. Brown (inset), was a veteran of the Mexican War.

improvised yard went on. Within five weeks, according to one of her lieu-tenants, "we had a man-of-war (such as she was) from almost nothing."

By July 12 she was as finished as she would ever be. Brown sent the mechanics ashore and dropped down to Sartartia Bar, where, as he later said, "I now gave the executive officer a day to organize and exercise his men." In the crew of about 175, two thirds were from the recently burned gunboats; the rest were infantry volunteers, distributed among the ten guncrews serving weapons of various calibers, three in each broadside, two forward, and two aft. July 14, the descent resumed. Fifteen miles below, at the mouth of the Sunflower River — the guns of the two Union fleets, engaged in target practice out on the Mis-sissippi, were plainly audible from here — it was discovered that steam from the engines and boiler had penetrated the forward magazine. Brown tied up along-side a sawmill clearing, landed the wet powder, and spread it on tarpaulins to dry in the sun. "By constant shaking and turning," he reported, "we got it back to the point of ignition before the sun sank below the trees." Packing what they could of it into the after magazine, the guncrews came back aboard and the *Arkansas* continued on her way, "guns cast loose and men at quarters, expecting every moment to meet the enemy."

At midnight her commander called a rest halt near Haines Bluff; then at 3 a.m. — July 15 — continued down the river. Information received from Vicksburg put the number of enemy warships at thirty-seven, and Brown intended to be among them by daylight, with every possible advantage of surprise. It was not to be. The twin-screw vessel's engines had a habit of stopping on dead center, one at a time, which would throw her abruptly into bank, despite the rudder, and this was what happened now in the predawn darkness. While the rest of the crew was engaged in getting her off again, a lieutenant went ashore in search of infor-mation. He came to a plantation house, but found that the residents had fled at the first sound of a steamer on the river. All that was left was one old Negro woman, and she would tell him nothing, not even the whereabouts of her people. In fact, she would not admit that they had been there in the first place.

"They have but just left," the lieutenant insisted. "The beds are yet warm."

"Don't know 'bout that. And if I did, I wouldn't tell you."

"Do you take me for a Yankee? Don't you see I wear a gray coat?"

"Certain you's a Yankee," the woman said. "Our folks aint got none them gumboats."

It took an hour to get the unwieldy *Arkansas* underweigh again; the lieutenant returned from his profitless excursion with time to spare. Attempting to get back on schedule, Brown called for all the speed the engineers could give him, but it was by no means enough. When daylight filtered through, the iron-clad was still in the Yazoo. The sun came up fiery as she entered Old River, a ten-mile lake formed by a cutoff from the Mississippi, and the lookout spotted three Union warships dead ahead, steaming upstream in line abreast, the *Caron-delet* in the center, flanked by the *Tyler* and the *Queen of the West*. Brown made a brief speech, ending: "Go to your guns!" Stripped to the waist in the early morning heat, with handkerchiefs bound about their heads to keep the sweat from trickling into their eyes, the guncrews stood to their pieces. The officers, too, had removed their coats, and paced the sanded deck in their undershirts — all but Brown, who remained in full uniform, his short, tawny beard catching the breeze as he stood on the shield, directly over the bow guns, which he or-dered not to fire until the action was fully joined, "lest by doing so we should diminish our speed." He and the *Carondelet*'s captain, Henry Walke, had been friends in the old navy, messmates on a voyage around the world, and he wanted nothing to delay this first meeting since they had gone their separate ways.

The Federal skippers reacted variously to their first glimpse of the rust-red vessel bearing down on them out of nowhere. *The Queen of the West*, un-armed and with her speed advantage canceled by the current, turned at once and frankly ran. The *Carondelet* and *Tyler* stayed on course, intending to fire their bow guns, then swing round and make a downstream fight with their stern pieces, hop-ing the noise would bring help from the rest of the fleet. Both fired and missed. By the time they had turned to run for safety, the *Arkansas* was upon them.

She chose the *Carondelet*, the slower of the two, pumping shells into her lightly armored stern, which ate at her vitals and slowed her even more. The return shots glanced off the *Arkansas*' prow, doing no considerable damage ex-cept to one seaman who, more curious than prudent, stuck his head out of a gunport for a better view and had it taken off by a bolt from an 8-inch rifle. The headless body fell back on the deck, and a lieutenant, fearing the sight would demoralize the rest of the guncrew, called upon the nearest man to heave it overboard. "Oh, I can't do it, sir! It's my brother," he replied.

Other casualties followed, one among them being Brown himself. Most of the shots from dead ahead struck the inclined shield and were deflected back and upwards, ricocheting, but presently one did not carom high enough and Brown received what he later called "a severe contusion on the head." He thought he was done for until he drew a handful of clotted blood from the wound and failed to find any particles of brain mixed in. He stayed at his post, continuing to direct both the gunnery and the navigation. Just then, however, the *Tyler* dropped back to help the crippled *Carondelet*, her riflemen firing volleys at Brown, the only live target outside the shield. A minie struck him over the left temple, tumbling him down a hatchway and onto the forward guns. When he re-gained consciousness, the aid men were laying him among the dead and wound-ed below deck. He promptly got up and returned to his place on the shield.

The *Carondelet* was much closer now, he saw, and so was the mouth of the river. Just as she reached it, and just as he was about to ram her stern, she veered into bank, leaking steam and frantic survivors from all her ports. Brown did not stay to complete her destruction or force her surrender. Instead, he took up pursuit of the *Tyler*, which by now had entered the Mississippi and was doing all she could to overtake the *Queen*. Aboard the fleet, the sailors had heard the firing, but had assumed that the boats were shelling snipers in the woods. Now they saw better, though they still did not understand what they saw. Observing the gunboat returning with a strange red vessel close on her heels, one officer remarked: "There comes the *Tyler* with a prize."

They soon learned better. Within range of the fleet — "a forest of masts and smokestacks," Brown called it; "In every direction, except astern, our eyes rested on enemies" — noting that the army rams were anchored behind the bigger ships, in position to dart out through the intervals, the Confederate skipper told his pilot: "Brady, shave that line of men-of-war as close as you can, so that the rams will not have room to gather headway in coming out to strike us." Brady gave him what he asked for, and the second battle opened.

At its beginning, steam down, guns unloaded, not a single Federal vessel was prepared for action; but this was presently so thoroughly corrected that Brown could later say, "I had the most lively realization of having steamed into a real volcano." Guns were flashing, and as he advanced "the line of fire seemed to grow into a circle constantly closing." Even so, he saw one definite advantage to fighting solo from an interior position, and the *Arkansas* was not neglectful of it, "firing rapidly to every point of the circumference, without the fear of hitting a friend or missing an enemy."

Now, though, she was taking about as much punishment as she gave. The big ocean-going sloops had run their guns out, and the Davis ironclads were firing for all they were worth. The *Arkansas* took hits from all directions. An 11-inch solid broke through her casemate armor and laid a sixteen-man gun-crew dead and dying on her deck. A rifle bolt laid out eleven more. Shrapnel quickly gave her stack the look of a nutmeg grater, so that for lack of draft the pressure dropped from 120 pounds to 20, barely enough to turn the engines. The temperature in the fire-room soared to 130°, and the engineers worked fifteen-minute shifts, by the end of which they had to be hauled up, half-roasted, and relieved by men from the guns. Sixty dead and wounded men were in her; her cast-iron snout was broken off; one whole section of plating was ripped from her flank; her boats were shot away and dragging. However, she still was giving as good as she got, or better. Out on the shield, where he had had his spyglass shot from his hands, her captain had never stopped calling orders to the pilot house and guns. A ram broke into the clear at last, driving hard in a final effort to block the way; "Go through him, Brady!" Brown shouted. But one of the bow guns averted the need for a collision by putting a shell through the Federal's boiler. Steam went up like a geyser and the bluejacket crew went overboard.

That was the final round. The *Arkansas* was into the clear, past the outer rim of the volcano. Limping badly, but unpursued, she held her course for Vicksburg, where a crowd had assembled on the bluff to greet her. Soldiers and townspeople alike, they tossed their hats in joy and admiration, but the cheers froze in their throats when they looked down and saw the carnage on her gundeck.

★ ★ ★ **F**arragut was infuriated. He had been sleeping late that morning, and when the cannonade erupted he appeared on the *Hartford*'s deck in his nightshirt. However, the flagship's engines were under repair; there was nothing he could do but watch and fire at the strange vessel as it went by. When the action was over he surveyed the wreckage — which was not only considerable, but was largely self-inflicted by cross fire — then returned to his cabin, muttering as he went: "Damnable neglect, or worse, somewhere!"

The more he thought about it, the madder he got. By the time he came back on deck again, fully dressed, he had made up his mind to steam down to Vicksburg with all his ships and attack the *Arkansas* in broad open daylight, hillside batteries and all. His staff managed to dissuade him from this — at least give the fleet captains time to wash the blood from their scuppers, they said — but, even so, the old man would not be put off any longer than nightfall: Porter's mortar schooners, together with the *Brooklyn* and the two laggard gunboats, were still below the city, where the apparently unsinkable rebel ironclad might engage them any minute. He ordered all guns loaded with solids and suspended his heaviest anchor from the tip of the *Hartford*'s port main-yardarm, intending to drop it through the *Arkansas*' deck and bottom when he got alongside her. The Davis gunboats and the Porter mortars would give covering fire, above and below, while he went in and dragged the upstart monster from its lair. Just before sunset he hoisted the familiar pennant for attack, and the fleet moved downriver.

It did not work out at all the way he intended. For one thing, in the ruddy murk between sunset and dusk, the rust-red boat was almost invisible under the red clay bank. The first each skipper saw of her as the ships came past in single file, taking in turn a pounding from the batteries overhead, was the flash of her guns as he crossed her line of fire. By then it was too late to attempt to check up and grapple; all there was time for was one quick broadside in reply, before the current swept him out of range. Aboard the *Arkansas*, dismay at having to fight the day's third battle, tied to bank and with less than half her crew still functional, gave way to elation as the action progressed. One by one, the ships glided past with their towering spars in silhouette against the glow of the western cloudbank, and one by one they took them under fire, as if in a gigantic shooting gallery. But when the *Hartford* stood in close, groping blindly with the an-

*Flagship of the Mississippi Squadron,
the sloop of war Hartford dries her sails near
the waterfront at Baton Rouge.*

chor swaying pendulous from her yardarm, and they loosed a broadside at her, she thundered back with a tremendous salvo. An 11-inch solid pierced the side of the *Arkansas* just above the waterline, crashed through the engine room, killing and mangling as it went, and lodged in the opposite casemate armor, making what one of her officers called "a bulging protuberance outside." She kept firing until the river stopped sending her targets. Then once more there was silence.

Farragut was where he wanted to be, south of the infernal bluff, and he had made the downstream run with fewer casualties than before — 5 killed, 16 wounded: only a handful more than his adversary had suffered — but he was far from satisfied. He wanted that ram, and he intended to have her, whatever the cost. At daylight he sent an urgent message to Davis, proposing that both fleets go in together at high noon and fight the rebel to a finish. Davis declined the invitation, counseling prudence and self-control. "I have watched eight rams for a month," he replied, "and now find it no hard task to watch one."

He continued to resist the pressure which Farragut kept applying. Five days later, July 21 — the *Arkansas* having ventured out meanwhile on a sortie that was aborted by another engine failure — he agreed to make an attempt next morning with the ironclad *Essex* and the *Queen of the West*. The plan was for the gunboat to shove the rebel vessel hard against bank and hold her there, sitting-duck fashion, so that the ram could butt a hole in her side and send her to the bottom. But this did not work either. Brown had the *Arkansas* moored with her head upstream, and when he saw the *Essex* coming at him he slacked his bow-line and presented his sharp armored prow to the blunt-nosed gunboat, which swerved at the last minute to avoid being sliced in two, taking and giving punishment as she passed. The *Queen*, following close behind, anxious to redeem her performance up the Yazoo the week before, could manage no more than a glancing blow. She worked her way back upstream, rejoining Davis, but the *Essex* went with the current, her engines badly shot up in the melee, and joined the fleet below.

Farragut threw up his hands at this. Fuel was low, and what with the need for keeping up steam in case the *Arkansas* staged another sudden appearance, was getting considerably lower every day. Sanitation was also a problem, as Halleck had foreseen. The swampy Mississippi heat had nearly half of Farragut's sailors on the sick list, along with three quarters of the canal-digging soldiers. The falling river seemed about to make good its threat to strand him up here, out of circulation for the rest of the year. Besides, a message from Welles — sent before the Secretary learned of the rebel ram's emergence — had just arrived: "Go down the river at discretion." That was what Farragut did, and he did it without delay. Starting south on July 26, he dropped the orphaned *Essex* and two of the smaller wooden gunboats off at Baton Rouge, along with Williams' shovel-weary soldiers, and put into New Orleans for repairs that would fit the rest of his salt-water ships for more agreeable blockade duty along the Gulf. Back in his native element at last, able to breathe all the way to the depths of his lungs, he said goodbye to the Mississippi — forever, he hoped.

Davis pulled out northward that same day, transferring his base to Helena, two hundred miles upstream. Vicksburg was delivered, along with a great stretch of the river between Napoleon and Natchez.

Welles was extremely angry when he heard the news. He told Farragut, "It is an absolute necessity that the neglect or apparent neglect of the squadron should be wiped out by the destruction of the *Arkansas*." Nothing came of this as far as Farragut was concerned; he was downstream and he stayed there. But it was an event that rankled in the Secretary's memory ever after — worse than Donelson, worse than Hampton Roads; worse, even, than Head of the Passes or Plum Run Bend. Bitter and chagrined, Welles later wrote: "The most disreputable naval affair of the war was the descent of the steam ram *Arkansas* through both squadrons, until she hauled into the batteries of Vicksburg, and there the two Flag Officers abandoned the place and the ironclad ram, Farragut and his force going down to New Orleans, and Davis proceeding with his flotilla up the river."

On Vicksburg's bluff, conversely, there was rejoicing and there was pride, not only because the naval siege had been raised, but also because of the manner in which the feat had been accomplished. The combined might of two victorious Union fleets had been challenged, sundered, and repulsed by a single homemade ten-gun ironclad, backed by the industry and daring of her builder and commander. Coming as it did, after a season of reverses, this exploit gave the people of the Lower Mississippi Valley a new sense of confidence and elation. They were glad to be alive in a time when such things could happen, and they asked themselves how a nation could ever be conquered when its destiny rested with men like those who served aboard the *Arkansas* under Isaac Newton Brown.

★ ★ ★ *I*n the Transmississippi, too, there was the discomfort of indigestion, proceeding from a difficulty in assimilating all that had been gained.
Sam Curtis was glad to have the Davis rams and gunboats with him: almost as glad as he had been to receive the division from Grant, which reached Helena the week before and brought his total strength to 18,000. This was the largest force he had yet commanded, half again larger than the army with which he had won the Battle of Pea Ridge; but, as he saw it, he had need of every man and gun he could get, ashore or afloat. Looking back on that savage conflict, which involved the repulse of a slashing double envelopment by Price and McCulloch, with Van Dorn hovering wild-eyed in the background and swarms of painted Indians on his flank, he perceived a hundred things that might have spelled defeat if they had gone against instead of for him. It seemed to him now in late July that events were building up to another such encounter, in which the scales — balanced against him, he believed, as they had been in early March — might tip the other way.

For a time it had been otherwise. Through April and May he had occupied a vacuum, so to speak; Van Dorn and Price had crossed the Mississippi and left Arkansas to him. On the final day of May, however, this leisure season ended with the Confederate appointment of Major General Thomas C. Hindman, a Helena lawyer and congressman who had led a division at Shiloh, to command the area including Missouri, Arkansas, Louisiana south to the Red, and Indian Territory. A dapper little man just over five feet tall, addicted to ruffled shirts and patent-leather boots, Hindman — like his predecessor, Earl Van Dorn — made up in activity for what he lacked in size. He had need of all his energy now. The situation on his arrival was about as bad as it could be, the scarcity of volunteers lending support to the postwar tall tale that the entire state of Mon-

Major General Thomas C. Hindman, a former lawyer from Helena, Arkansas, took command of Confederate forces in Missouri, Arkansas, and part of Louisiana.

tana was afterwards populated by rebel fugitives from Elkhorn Tavern; but he went immediately to work, issuing fiery proclamations and enforcing the new conscription law in his native state with troops brought from Texas. Lacking arms and munitions, he set up factories and chemical works to turn them out, operated lead mines and tanyards, and even organized the women of his department into sewing circles to furnish uniforms for all the able-bodied men he could lay hands on. Word of his activity soon spread, and recruits began to trickle in from Missouri, some of whom he sent back home with orders to raise guerilla bands to harass the invader's rear. Before long, Curtis was receiving intelligence reports that put the Confederate strength in midland Arkansas at 25,000 men.

His plan had been to march on Little Rock as soon as his army had recovered from its exertions, thus adding to the southern list of fallen capitals, but the presence of Hindman's newborn army in that direction changed his mind. Instead, after much conferring back and forth with Washington, he moved toward Helena for a possible share in the amphibious descent of the Mississippi. Even that was hard enough. All through June, bridge-burners and irregular cavalrymen, instructed by Hindman to bushwhack Union pickets, destroy all food, and pollute the water "by killing cattle, ripping the carcasses open and throwing them in," harassed his line of march and kept him in almost constant expectation of being swamped by overwhelming numbers. At last he reached the big river — only to find that the descent had been called off; Halleck was busy consolidating his gains. It was just as well, as far as Curtis was concerned. He began to fortify his Helena position, not knowing what all-out mischief Hindman might be plotting in the brush.

★

Even after the arrival of the division from Memphis and the iron-clads from Vicksburg, together with siege guns brought downriver from Birds Point, Columbus, and Fort Pillow, he felt far from easy about his situation. Not only was there danger in front; he now learned of a new danger in his rear. The Missourians who had gone back home with instructions for making trouble were showing a good deal of talent for such work. Brigadier General John M. Schofield, the Federal commander there, reported that he had discovered "a well-devised scheme" for a monster guerilla outbreak involving thirty to fifty thousand men who were assembling now at designated places to await the appointed signal "and, by a sudden *coup de main,* seize the important points in the state, surprise and capture our small detachments guarding railroads, &c., thus securing arms and ammunition, and coöperate with an invading army from Arkansas." He called on Curtis to deal with this invasion force, which had moved into the vacated area around Pea Ridge, while he did his best to deal with the guerillas. "You are aware, General, that I have no force sufficient to drive them back without your assistance," he implored. "Let me ask you to act as quickly as possible."

Curtis could not help him. If it came to the worst, he wasn't even sure he could help himself. He had all sorts of troubles. As a result of trying to encourage trade in cotton, he said, his camp was "infested with Jews, secessionists, and spies." Then too, his health was failing; or, as he put it, "I am not exactly well." At any rate, whatever rebel hosts were gathering in Northwest Arkansas, the last thing he intended was a retracing of his steps on the harried march he had just completed. All he could do was hold what he had, probing occasionally at the country roundabout as the long hot summer wore on toward a close.

Schofield's fears for Missouri were soon fulfilled, though in a less concerted fashion than he had predicted. No less than eighty skirmishes were fought there during July and August, including one that resulted in the capture of Independence by guerillas under Charles Quantrill, who presently was commissioned a Confederate captain as a reward for this exploit. Kansas too was threatened. Jim Lane, the grim Jayhawk chieftain, was raising Negro troops; "Zouaves d'Afrique," they were called, for they drilled in baggy scarlet pantaloons Stanton had purchased, in the emergency, from France. North of there, in the absence of soldiers transferred south and east, the Minnesota Sioux went on the warpath, massacring settlers by the hundreds.

Everywhere Curtis looked he saw trouble, though most of it was fortunately well beyond his reach at Helena. Remaining in the fine big house on a hill overlooking the river — it was Hindman's, or it had been; Curtis had taken it for his headquarters — he improved his fortifications, put his trust in the Mississippi as a supply line, and shook his head disapprovingly at the chaos all around him. "Society is terribly mutilated," he reported.

★

★ ★ ★ *A*t the opposite end of the western line, **Buell was moving eastward;** or he had been, anyhow, until he encountered troubles he would gladly have swapped for those of Curtis and Grant combined, with Schofield's thrown in for good measure. As it turned out, he not only had supply and guerilla problems as acute as theirs; presently it became obvious, too, that his was the column that was to receive the main attention of the main Confederate army in the West — beginning with the twin thunderbolts, Morgan and Forrest, who were thrown at him soon after he got started.

In giving him instructions for the eastward move, ten days after the fall of Corinth, Halleck was heeding the repeated suggestion of Ormsby Mitchel, who for a month had been signaling frantically that he could see the end of the war from where he stood in Northeast Alabama. If he were rein-forced, he said, he could march straight into Chattanooga, then turn south and take Atlanta. From there, he added, the way lay open to Richmond's back door, through a region that was "completely unprotected and very much alarmed." Old Brains could see merit in this — and he also saw a possible vari-ation. Knoxville, too, lay beyond that mountain gateway: an objective he knew was dear to the heart of Lincoln, who was anxious to disenthrall the pro-Union citizens of East Tennessee and gain control of the railroad con-necting Virginia and North Georgia. Accordingly, Halleck gave Buell his in-structions on June 9 for a lateral offensive, the only one of any kind that he intended to launch in the West this summer, simultaneously notifying Wash-ington of the intended movement, and two days later received the expected reply: Lincoln was "greatly delighted."

The extent of the President's delight was shown before the month was out. Alarmed by Lee's assault on McClellan, who was crying for reinforcements as he fell back, the War Department called on the western commander for 25,000 troops to be shifted to the East; but when Halleck replied that to send them would mean that the Chattanooga expedition would have to "be abandoned or at least be diminished," the reaction was immediate and negative, and it came in the form of a telegram from Lincoln himself. This must not be done on any account, he said. "To take and hold the railroad at or east of Cleveland, in East Tennessee, I think fully as important as the taking and holding of Richmond."

By that time Buell was well on his way. He had by no means reached Cleveland — a junction thirty miles beyond his immediate objective, where the railroad, coming down from Knoxville, branched west to Chattanooga and south to Atlanta — but he had advanced his four divisions to Huntsville, having ferried the Tennessee River at Florence, and had repaired the Memphis & Charleston line as far east as Decatur. He had about 35,000 men in his present column, including cavalry and engineers, and Mitchel was waiting up ahead with 11,000 more. Off to the north, ready to coöperate as soon as Knoxville became the goal, George Morgan occupied Cumberland Gap with a division of 9000, which was also a component of Buell's Army of the Ohio. In addition to these 55,000 troops, Thomas was at Iuka, awaiting orders to march east with his own

---

"The long time taken by you to reach Chattanooga will enable the enemy to anticipate you by concentrating a large force to meet you."

— Henry W. Halleck

---

division of 8000, plus two from Grant, which had been promised in case they were required. Just now, however, Buell did not want them. He was having trouble enough feeding the men he had, and the problem got progressively worse as he moved eastward, lengthening his supply line.

The 300 tons of food and forage needed daily — 3¼ pounds for a man, 26 for a horse, 23 for a mule — were more than the guerilla-harried railroads could supply. Besides a shortage of rolling stock, destruction of the Elk River bridge on the Nashville-Decatur line necessitated a forty-mile wagon haul around the break, and sniper fire was so frequent and effective that ironclad boxcars had to be provided for the protection of the train crews. Buell put his men and animals on half rations, much to the discomfort of both. "We are living from day to day on short supplies and our operations are completely crippled," he complained to the Louisville quartermaster. Ahead, he knew, lay additional problems: the river crossing at Bridgeport, for example. Retiring from in front of Chattanooga the month before, Mitchel had burned the milelong span, and Buell had no material with which to build another. In an attempt to fill the shortage and make amends, Mitchel ordered all the sawmills between Huntsville and Stevenson put to work supplying lumber for pontoons and a bridge floor, but this too was an occasion for guerilla interference, causing the workers to run away for fear of being murdered on the job or in their beds.

All in all, the prospect was grim. Buell's chief solace was the knowledge that he was doing the best he could with what he had, and his chief hope was that his industry was appreciated by those above him. The latter was dispelled by an alarming and discouraging message from Halleck, July 8. The alarm came first: Bragg's army was reported to be in motion, either against Grant at Memphis or Corinth, or against Buell at Tuscumbia or Chattanooga. "A few days more may reduce these doubts to a certainty, when our troops will operate accordingly," Halleck reported, unruffled. Then came the discouragement: "The President telegraphs that your progress is not satisfactory and that you should move more rapidly. The long time taken by you to reach Chattanooga will enable the enemy to anticipate you by concentrating a large force to meet you. I communicate his views, hoping that your movements hereafter may be so rapid as to remove all cause of complaint, whether well founded or not."

Buell later declared, "I was so astonished at the message that I made no reply until three days afterward." What jogged him then was a six-word dispatch: "I want to hear from you. H. W. Halleck." In reply, Buell reviewed his difficulties, remarking as he did so: "I regret that it is necessary to explain the circumstances which must make my progress seem so slow." As he saw it, the object was not only to reach his goal quickly, but also to be in condition to fight when he got there. "The advance on Chattanooga must be made with the means of acting in force; otherwise it will either fail" — as Mitchel's had done — or else the city would "prove a profitless and transient prize." His arrangements, made in accordance with this, were "being pushed forward as rapidly as possible," and though he quite understood that "these are matters of fact that cannot be gratifying," he added: "The dissatisfaction of the President pains me exceedingly."

Next day Halleck responded with assurances of personal good will. He could see both sides of the question, and he urged Buell to be more tolerant of the amateurs above them. "I can well understand the difficulties you have to encounter and also the impatience at Washington. In the first place they have no conception of the length of our lines of defense and of operations. In the second place the disasters before Richmond have worked them up to boiling heat." At any rate, he assured him, "I will see that your movements are properly explained to the President."

This was helpful in relieving the pain — lately added to by John Morgan, who had led his gray raiders up through Middle Tennessee and was capturing railroad guards, burning bridges, and smashing culverts in Kentucky — but still more comforting to Buell was the fact that his advance was now past Stevenson, where the Nashville & Chattanooga, coming down through Murfreesboro and Tullahoma, joined the Memphis & Charleston, thus affording him an additional rail supply line. Anticipating this, he had work gangs all along the road, repairing the damage done by retreating Confederates, and to make certain that it was not wrecked again, either by raiders or guerillas, he had stationed a brigade at Murfreesboro — two regiments of infantry, a cavalry detachment, and a four-gun battery — ready to move out in either direction at the first sign of trouble. On July 12, the date of Halleck's sympathetic message, Buell was informed that the repairs had been completed. The first trainload of supplies would leave Nashville tomorrow or the next day; he would be able to take his soldiers off half rations and replace their worn-out shoes as soon as it got there.

What got there tomorrow, however, was not a trainload of supplies, but rather an announcement of disaster. In the gray dawn light, Bedford Forrest struck Murfreesboro with three regiments of cavalry, wrecking the railroad at that point and capturing the Federal commander, Brigadier General T. T. Crittenden, together with all his men, guns, and equipment. Stung, Buell reacted fast by hurrying William Nelson's whole division to the scene; but when it got there, the hard-riding Confederate and his captives had disappeared eastward, in the direction of the mountains. Nor was that all. The work gangs had barely completed their repairs when, eight days later, Forrest struck again — this time up near Nashville, where he celebrated the anniversary of Manassas by firing his captured guns within sight of the capitol tower and wrecking the three bridges across Mill Creek. When Nelson's division marched from Murfreesboro to intercept him, he took a side road, camped for the night within earshot of the bluecoats tramping northward on the pike, then once more made his escape into the mountains beyond McMinnville.

Nettled but not disheartened, Buell put his repair gangs back to work. Within a week, practice having increased their skill, they had the line in operation. July 29, the first train pulled into Stevenson from Nashville with

210,000 rations, followed next day by another with a comparable amount. The troops went back on full allowances of food, and Nelson's infantry replaced the shoes they had worn out chasing Forrest's cavalry. This was a help and was duly appreciated; but something more than footgear had been damaged in the process, and there were pains in other regions than the stomach. Morale and pride were involved here, too. Buell's men began to consider that, with the doubtful exception of Shiloh — which was not really their fight, since they only arrived on the second day and even then were only engaged in part — the Army of the Ohio was the only major Federal command that had never fought a pitched battle on its own. The blame for this, as they saw it, rested with Buell, whose military policy was referred to by one of his colonels as that of a dancing master: "By your leave, my dear sir, we will have a fight; that is, if you are sufficiently fortified. No hurry; take your time."

Distasteful as this was to the men, there was something else about their commander that irked them even more. When Ormsby Mitchel's division came through this region, back in May, one soldier wrote happily in his diary: "Our boys find Alabama hams better than Uncle Sam's side meat, and fresh bread better than hard crackers." Buell, on the other hand, not only put them on half rations, but issued and enforced stern orders against foraging, which he believed would discourage southern civilians from returning to their old allegiance. However true this was or wasn't, it seemed to the men that he

was less concerned with their hunger pangs than he was with the comfort and welfare of the rebels, who after all were to blame for their being down here in the first place. Also, he was denying them the fun and profit enjoyed by comrades who had come this way before them. For example, in reprisal for guerilla activities, one of Mitchel's brigade commanders, Colonel John Basil Turchin — formerly Ivan Vasilevich Turchininov, of the Imperial Russian Army — had turned the town of Athens over to his three

The Federal supply-and-rail depot at Murfreesboro, Tennessee, was destroyed in a raid by Nathan Bedford Forrest's Confederate cavalry on July 13, 1862.

John B. Turchin was the only Russian-born Federal officer to attain general's rank during the Civil War.

regiments, saying, "I shut mine eyes for one hour": whereupon the Illinois, Ohio, and Indiana boys took it completely apart, Cossack-style, raping Negro servant girls and stuffing their pockets and haversacks with $50,000 worth of watches, plate, and jewelry. Grudgingly, Buell's men complained that he would never turn them loose like that, despite the fact that, officially, it would apparently do his career far more good than harm. Turchin was court-martialed and dismissed for the Athens debauch, but before the summer was over he was reinstated and promoted to brigadier. Likewise Mitchel, though he was called to Washington in early July to explain illegal cotton transactions made in his department, was promoted to major general and transferred to the mild, sea-scented atmosphere of coastal South Carolina, where unfortunately he died of yellow fever in October.

Actually, though, the trouble with Buell lay deeper. It was not so much what he did as what he was. Other generals shared his views on the subject of foraging, and enforced them quite as sternly: notably McClellan and, at the present stage of the conflict, Sherman. "This demoralizing and disgraceful practice of pillage must cease," the West Tennessee commander admonished his troops in a general order, "else the country will rise on us and justly shoot us down like dogs or wild beasts." In fact, on the face of it, both were harder on offenders than Buell ever was or tried to be. In Sherman's command, for example, the punishment for molesting civilians or stealing was confinement on bread and water, and he sent out patrols with instructions to shoot if foragers tried to escape arrest. But they gave their men something instead. Better situated, they fed better, and they moved among their soldiers in a way that made the individual feel that, outside battle, his comfort and well-being were his general's main concern. Above all, in their different ways, they had a flair for the dramatic. McClellan's men would turn from their first hot meal in days for a chance to cheer him riding past, and Sherman could make a soldier proud for weeks by asking him for a light for his cigar. It was personal, a matter of personality.

Buell was seldom "personal," and never at all in public. In private, he had a parlor trick which he sometimes performed to amaze his guests with the strength of his rather stubby arms and his stocky, close-knit torso. Grasping his hundred-and-forty-pound wife by the waist, he would lift her straight out before him, hold her there with her feet dangling clear of the carpet, then perch her deftly on the mantelpiece. It was a good trick, and it won him the admiration of those who watched him do it. But the soldiers never saw this side of his nature. He was a headquarters general, anyhow. They saw him only briefly as he made his hurried, sour-mouthed inspections, peering at them with his beady eyes and poking his hawk-beak nose into unexpected corners. The good he took for granted; it was the less-good he was looking for, and he seldom failed to find it. As a result, there was an absence of warmth — and an absence, too, of incidents in which men let their food grow cold while they took time

---

"This demoralizing and disgraceful practice of pillage must cease, else the country will rise on us and justly shoot us down like dogs or wild beasts."

— William T. Sherman

---

out to cheer him riding by or fished in their pockets for a light for his cigar. They were well drilled, beyond question. Three months ago, their professional tone had been such that when Grant's skulkers saw them march ashore at Shiloh they had cried, "Here come the regulars!" Under fire next day, their confident demeanor as they rolled the rebels back had sustained the basic accuracy of this mistake. Since then, however, a great deal had happened, and all of it bad. The inchworm advance on Corinth, with empty earthworks at the end, had been followed by these two belt-tightening months in North Alabama, where they observed with disgust — as if, by a process of unnatural reversion, a butterfly were to have its wings refolded and be stuffed unceremoniously back into its cocoon — their transformation from happy-go-lucky soldiers into ill-fed railroad workers. Out of this had come a loss of former gladness, and a suspicion that they had lost their fighting edge.

This might or might not be the case, but at any rate the signs had been increasing that a test was about to come. Bragg was not only on the move: both Grant and Rosecrans reported him moving eastward, in the direction of Chattanooga. Before Halleck left for Washington in mid-July he released Thomas to Buell's control, bringing his total strength to 46,000, exclusive of the force at Cumberland Gap. Of these, however, 15,000 were needed for guarding

★

Nashville and the railroads, which left him no more than 31,000 for a forward move. For two weeks the advance had been stalled by the lack of a bridge across the Tennessee at Bridgeport; lumber for the pontoons had been cut by now, but there was still a shortage of nails, oakum, and pitch. While waiting for them, Buell was doing his best to build up a forward supply depot from which to feed and equip his men when they crossed the river to close in on the city. He was still at it on the last day of July, when a message reached his Huntsville head-quarters from the commander of his advance division, reporting that Bragg him-self had arrived in Chattanooga two days ago — apparently in advance of his whole army. "On the same evening two trains came in with soldiers. Railroad agent says he has orders to furnish cars for 30,000 as fast as he can."

Informed of this, Halleck replied that Grant would furnish reinforce-ments "if you should find the enemy too strong." Six days later, learning that Bragg's troops had not yet come up, he prodded Buell again: "There is great dis-satisfaction here [in Washington] at the slow movement of your army toward Chat-tanooga. It is feared that the enemy will have time to concentrate his entire army against you." Buell wired back: "It is difficult to satisfy impatience, and when it proceeds from anxiety, as I know it does in this case, I am not disposed to com-plain of it. My advance has not been rapid, but it could not be more rapid under the circumstances. I know I have not been idle nor indifferent." Next day, August 7, he got down to specifics. The Confederate force in East Tennessee was estimated at 60,000 men, he said; "yet I am prepared to find the reports much more exagger-ated than I have supposed, and shall march upon Chattanooga at the earliest possi-ble day, unless I ascertain certainly that the enemy's strength renders it imprudent. If, on the other hand, he should cross the river I shall attack him, and I do not doubt that we shall defeat him." Encouraged, Halleck replied that Grant had been ordered to transfer two divisions to the Army of the Ohio if they were needed; but he cautioned Buell, "Do not ask for them if you can avoid it with safety."

With that, the roof fell in: quite literally. John Morgan had left Kentucky in late July, but now he suddenly reappeared in Middle Tennessee. On August 12 he captured the guard at Gallatin, above Nashville, and wrecked the L & N Railroad by pushing blazing boxcars into the 800-foot tunnel, seven miles north of there, so that the timbers burned and let the dirt cave in. Unplugging it would be a long-term if not an impossible job, and with the Cumberland River too low for shipping, Buell was cut off from his main supply base at Louisville: which meant that his army would have to eat up the rations collected at Stevenson for the intended drive on Chattanooga. Learning next that a Confederate force estimated at 15,000 men had left Knoxville, bound for Nashville and other points in his rear, he called for the two divisions from Grant and on the 16th detached William Nelson to go to Kentucky with a cadre of experienced officers "to organize such troops as

★

could be got together there to reëstablish our communications and operate against Morgan's incursions." Nor was that all; for the pressure came from various directions, including Washington. Two days later, when Halleck threatened to fire him if he did not speed up his operations — "So great is the dissatisfaction here at the apparent want of energy and activity in your district, that I was this morning notified to have you removed. I got the matter delayed till we could hear further of your movements" — Buell replied forthrightly: "I beg that you will not interpose on my behalf. On the contrary, if the dissatisfaction cannot cease on grounds which I think might be supposed if not apparent, I respectfully request that I may be relieved. My position is far too important to be occupied by any officer on sufferance. I have no desire to stand in the way of what may be deemed necessary for the public good."

Either he was past caring or else he recognized a bluff when he saw one. At any rate, whatever satisfaction this gave him, he had only a short time to enjoy it. Next morning, August 19, he learned that Bragg's army was crossing the river in force at Chattanooga. This was the eventuality in which he had said, "I shall attack him"; but now that he was faced with the actual thing, it began to seem to him that his first responsibility was the protection of Nashville, lying exposed in his rear. Accordingly, he shifted his headquarters to Decherd, forty miles northeast on the railroad leading back to the capital. Four days later — by which time Bragg was reported to have crossed the Tennessee with fifty regiments, "well armed and [with] good artillery" — he had made up his mind. Orders went to the commanders of the two divisions on their way from Grant; they were to change direction and "move by forced marches on Nashville." Simultaneously, the officer in charge of the advance depot at Stevenson was told to "expedite the shipment of stores . . . in every possible way, and be ready to evacuate the place at a moment's notice." The work of nailing and caulking the floats for the 1400-yard-long span at Bridgeport had been completed two weeks before, and this too was remembered: "Let engineers quietly prepare the pontoons for burning, and when you leave destroy everything that cannot be brought away."

Presently, like the campaign itself, the unused bridge went up in smoke. "Don Carlos won't do; he won't do," one division commander muttered when he received the order to retire. Others protested likewise, but to no avail. Before the end of August the withdrawal was complete, and the Decherd provost marshal, describing himself as "weak, discouraged, and worn out," recorded in his diary: "The whole army is concentrated here, or near here; but nobody knows anything, except that the water is bad, whiskey scarce, dust abundant, and the air loaded with the scent and melody of a thousand mules."

★   ★   ★

★

Shelby Foote

*White-gloved Federal soldiers
stand guard near a mansion house
in Baton Rouge, Louisiana.
The state capital fell to Union forces
in the spring of 1862.*

SEVEN

Bragg, Kirby Smith, Breckinridge

1862 ★ ★ ★ ★ ★ Having accomplished Buell's repulse without the firing of a shot on either side — except in his rear, when Forrest and Morgan were on the rampage — Bragg now turned his mind to larger prospects, involving nothing less than the upset and reversal of the entire military situation in the enormous theater lying between the Appalachians and the Mississippi, the Ohio and the Gulf of Mexico.

The actual movement which placed him in a position to accomplish this design had been undertaken as the result of a decision reached on the spur of a moment in late July: specifically, the anniversary of Manassas. Before that, he had spent a month reorganizing and refitting the army he inherited when Beauregard left Tupelo for what he thought would be a ten-day convalescence. It had been no easy job. After the long retreat, the troops were badly in need of almost everything, including rest. What they needed most, however, was discipline; or so Bragg told "the brave men of Shiloh and of Elkhorn" in an address issued on June 27, the date of his official appointment to command the Army of the Mississippi.

"I enter hopefully on my duties," he declared. "But, soldiers, to secure the legitimate results of all your heavy sacrifices which have brought this

★

army together, to infuse that unity and cohesion essential for a resolute resistance to the wicked invasion of our country, and to give to serried ranks force, impetus, and direction for driving the invader beyond our borders, be assured discipline at all times and obedience to the orders of your officers on all points, as a sacred duty, an act of patriotism, is an absolute necessity." Great events were impending. "A few more days of needful preparation and organization and I shall give your banners to the breeze . . . with the confident trust that you will gain additional honors to those you have already won on other fields." After much that was turgid, he ended grimly: "But be prepared to undergo privation and labor with cheerfulness and alacrity."

Cheerfulness was by no means a primary characteristic of this sixth among the Confederacy's full generals; dyspepsia and migraine had made him short-tempered and disputatious all his life. In the old army there was a story that in his younger days, as a lieutenant commanding one of several companies at a post where he was also serving as quartermaster, he had submitted a requisition for supplies, then as quartermaster had declined by indorsement to fill it. As company commander he resubmitted the requisition, giving additional reasons for his needs, but as quartermaster he persisted in denial. Having reached this impasse, he referred the matter to the post commandant, who took one look at the correspondence and threw up his hands: "My God, Mr Bragg, you have quarreled with every officer in the army, and now you are quarreling with yourself!" Other stories were less humorous: as for instance that one of his soldiers had attempted to assassinate him not long after the Mexican War by exploding a 12-pound shell under his cot. When the smoke cleared away, the cot was reduced to tatters and kindling, but Bragg himself emerged without a scratch.

He had left the army in 1856 for a civilian career, not in his native North Carolina but as a sugar planter and commissioner of swamp lands in Louisiana. With the coming of the present war — which he believed had been brought on by such ill-advised political measures as the extension of "universal suffrage" — he had sustained his former reputation as a disciplinarian and a fighter by whipping his Gulf Coast command rapidly into a state of efficiency and leading it aggressively at Shiloh. There, he said in his report immediately afterwards, the army had been given "a valuable lesson, by which we should profit — never on a battlefield to lose a moment's time, but leaving the killed, wounded, and spoils to those whose special business it is to care for them, to press on with every available man, giving a panic-stricken and retreating foe no time to rally, and reaping all the benefits of success never complete until every enemy is killed, wounded, or captured."

He was now in a position, with the approval of the authorities in Richmond, to give this precept large-scale application. After informing him on June 29 that his department had been "extended so as to embrace that part of

Louisiana east of the Mississippi, the entire states of Mississippi and Alabama, and the portion of Georgia and Florida west of the Chattahoochee and Apalachicola Rivers," Secretary Randolph not only authorized an offensive, but urged him to "Strike the moment an opportunity offers." That was what Bragg had already told his soldiers he intended to do, as soon as he had completed the reorganization-in-progress. However, this was attended by many difficulties. One problem, beyond the need for restoring (or, Bragg would say, injecting) discipline, was the army's health. The troops had brought their Corinth ailments with them; including the men from the Transmississippi, the July 1 "aggregate present" of 61,561 was re-

duced to 45,393 by deduction of those who were sick or in arrest or on extra duty. Healthier conditions at Tupelo, plus the absence of strain — the nearest bluecoat was two days off — would restore a good part of these 16,000 soldiers to the ranks. More serious, as Bragg saw it, was the shortage of competent high-ranking officers. Van Dorn was gone, transferred to Vicksburg in mid-June when Davis and Farragut threatened the city from above and below; Breckinridge went with him, taking 6000 troops to oppose a landing by the men from Butler, and Hindman was detached at the same time to raise an army in Arkansas. Polk having been relieved of his corps and named second in command of the whole, Hardee and Price

North Carolinian Braxton Bragg
*was the sixth officer appointed a full
general by the Confederacy.*

were the only experienced major generals left in direct charge of troops. The rest, Bragg told Richmond, including most of the brigadiers in the sweeping indictment, were "in my judgment unsuited for their responsible positions"; were, in fact, "only incumbrances, and would be better out of the way."

Despite these shortcomings — and despite the fact that the War Department increased his difficulties by not allowing him to consolidate under-strength regiments bled white at Shiloh, then further reduced to skeletons by pestilence at Corinth — he kept his army hard at work, convinced that this was the sovereign remedy for injured health as well as for injured discipline. In compensation for long hours of drill he issued new uniforms and better rations, both of which had an additional salutary effect. New problems were dealt with as they arose, including an upsurge of desertion. He met it harshly. "Almost every day we would hear a discharge of musketry, and knew that some poor trembling wretch had bid farewell to mortal things here below," one soldier afterwards recalled. The effectiveness of such executions was increased, Bragg believed, by lining up the condemned man's former comrades to watch him pay for his crime. It worked; desertion decreased; but at a price. "We were crushed," the same observer added bitterly. "Bragg, so the soldiers thought, was the machine that did it. . . . He loved to crush the spirit of his men. The more of a hangdog look they had about them the better was General Bragg pleased. Not a single soldier in the whole army ever loved or respected him."

True or false, all this was rather beside the point as far as Bragg was concerned. He was not out after love or respect; he was after results, and he got them. On July 12 he informed the Adjutant General that the time since his last report, forwarded to Richmond when he assumed official command two weeks before, "has been diligently applied to organization, discipline, and instruction, with a very marked improvement. The health and general tone of the troops, too, exhibits results no less gratifying. Our condition for service is good and has reached a culminating point under the defective skeleton organization."

He was ready to strike. The question was, where? In what direction? Grant's army, considerably larger than his own and occupying strong positions under Sherman and Rosecrans at Memphis and Corinth, seemed practically unassailable; besides which, Bragg told Richmond, "A long and disastrous drouth, threatening destruction to the grain crop, continues here and renders any move [into North Mississippi] impracticable for want of water." As for Buell, his lateral advance had been so slow and apparently so uncertain that for a long time the Confederates had found it impossible to determine his objective. It might be Chattanooga — in that case, Bragg had already sent a 3000-man brigade of infantry to reinforce the troops in East Tennessee — or it might be Atlanta, depending on what direction he took after crossing the river at Bridgeport. Whichever it was, Bragg decided in mid-July to give him all the trouble he could by sending two brigades of cavalry, under Colonel Joseph Wheeler and Brigadier General Frank Armstrong, to harass his lines of supply and communication in West Tennessee and North Alabama.

They had excellent models for their work, commanders who had already given cavalry operations — and, indeed the war itself — a new dimension, based on their proof that sizeable bodies of hard-riding men could not only strike and create havoc deep in the enemy's rear, Jeb-Stuart-style, but could stay there to strike again and again, spreading the havoc over hundreds of miles and wearing out their would-be pursuers by causing them to converge repeatedly on thin air. By now the whole Confederate West was ringing with praise for Morgan and Forrest: particularly the former, whose exploits had surrounded him with the aura of a legend. A tall, white-faced, handsome, cold-eyed man, soft-spoken and always neatly dressed in conservative but obviously expensive clothes — fine gray broadcloth, fire-gilt buttons, richly polished boots, and spotless linen — he knew the effectiveness of reticence, yet he could be flamboyant on occasion. "Kentuckians!" he exhorted in a broadside struck off at Glasgow and distributed on his sweep through the Bluegrass, "I have come to liberate you from the hands of your oppressors." Calling for volunteer recruits, "fifty thousand of Kentucky's bravest sons," and implying thereby that he would take only the bravest, he broke into verse:

"Strike — for your altars and your fires;

Strike for the green graves of your sires,

God, and your native land!"

He was seldom flamboyant, however, except for a purpose. For example, he carried with him a telegrapher, a wire-tap expert who, though he would sometimes chat waggishly with enemy operators — once he even went so far as to complain directly to Washington, in Morgan's name, about the inferior grade of mules being furnished Buell's army — not only intercepted messages that kept his chief informed of the Federal efforts to surround him, but also sent out false instructions that turned the converging blue columns off his trail. Such devices yielded profits. Leaving Knoxville on July 4 with fewer than 900 men, he made a

Printed on rough foolscap paper, John Hunt Morgan's ringing broadside called on Kentuckians to rebel against the Federal occupation of their state.

thousand-mile swing through Middle Tennessee and Kentucky, in the course of which he captured seventeen towns, together with tons of Union supplies, paroled nearly 1200 regular army prisoners, and dispersed about 1500 home-guarders, all at a cost of less than 90 casualties, and returned before the end of the month with an additional 300 volunteers picked up along the way. Two weeks later he was back again. Lest it be thought that he was merely a hit-and-run sort of soldier, after wrecking the Gallatin tunnel he turned on his pursuer — Brigadier General R. W. Johnson, a West Pointer and fellow-Kentuckian, whom Buell had assigned the task of intercepting the raiders with an equal force — and whipped him soundly, breaking up his command and capturing the general and his staff.

Forrest was a different sort of man; different in method, that is, if not in results. Recuperating in Memphis from his Fallen Timbers wound — the ball had lodged against his spine and was removed in the field a week later, without the benefit of an anesthetic — he put a recruiting notice in the local paper, calling for "able-bodied men . . . with good horse and gun. I wish none but those who desire to be actively engaged. . . . Come on, boys, if you want a heap of fun and to kill some Yankees." When he returned to Corinth, shortly before the evacuation, Beauregard sent him to Chattanooga with orders to weld the scattered East Tennessee cavalry units into a brigade. He arrived in late June, assembled his men, and, believing active duty the best possible training for a green command, crossed the Tennessee River on July 9 to camp the following night atop Cumberland Mountain, deep in enemy territory. At dawn Sunday, three mornings later and ninety roundabout miles away, civilian hostages held in the Murfreesboro jail — several were under sentence of death, in retaliation for the bushwhacking of Union soldiers on or near their farms — heard what one of them later called "a strange noise like the roar of an approaching storm." It was hoofbeats: Forrest's 1400 troopers were pounding up the turnpike. Two regiments of infantry, one from Michigan, one from Minnesota, each with a section of artillery and cavalry support — their combined strength was about the same as Forrest's, except that he had no guns — were camped on opposite sides of town, with detachments guarding the jail and the courthouse, in which the brigade supplies were stored. Quickly the town was taken, along with the Federal commanding general, and fire-fights broke out on the outskirts, where the blue infantry prepared to defend its camps. Once the hostages had been freed and the captured goods packed for removal along with the prisoners already taken, some of the raiders, believing the alarm had spread to other Union garrisons by now, suggested withdrawal. But Forrest would have none of that. "I didn't come here to make half a job of it," he said, influenced perhaps by the fact that today was his forty-first birthday; "I'm going to have them all."

He got them, too — though he hastened matters somewhat by sending notes to the two commanders in their barricaded camps, demanding "unconditional surrender . . . or I will have every man put to the sword." He added, by way of extenuation and persuasion: "This demand is made to prevent the effusion of blood," and though like Morgan he was still a colonel, in his signature he promoted himself to "Brigadier General of Cavalry, C.S. Army," doubtless to lend additional weight to the threat. It worked. The two blue colonels surrendered in sequence, and Forrest marched his 1200 prisoners back eastward to McMinnville, where he paroled them and forwarded the captured arms and supplies to Chattanooga — all but the guns; he kept them for use around Nashville the following week, where he gave Nelson the slip after re-wrecking Buell's vital railroad supply line.

"I am happy to see that my two lieutenants, Morgan and Forrest, are doing such good service in Kentucky and Tennessee," Beauregard wrote from Bladon Springs, where he was still in exile. "When I appointed them I thought they would leave their mark wherever they passed." This was said in reply to a letter from Bragg, in which the present army commander told his former chief, "Our cavalry is paving the way for me in Middle Tennessee and Kentucky." The letter was dated July 22. By that time Bragg had decided not only on Buell's intentions, but also on his own. After a forty-day Federal head start, it was to be a race for Chattanooga: with further possibilities as the prize.

★ ★ ★ **K**irby Smith, commanding in East Tennessee, had never had much doubt about Buell's intentions from the outset. Promoted to major general after recovering from being shot through the neck at Manassas, Smith had been given the thorny job of restoring order in the area around Knoxville, and in this he had succeeded remarkably well, considering the extent to which the region was torn by conflicting loyalties and ambitions. But since the fall of Corinth the military situation had grown increasingly ominous; George Morgan occupied Cumberland Gap, an immediate threat to Knoxville, and Buell began his eastward advance in the direction of Chattanooga, while Smith himself had less than 15,000 of all arms with which to resist the two-pronged menace. The arrival of the 3000-man brigade from Bragg afforded some relief, but not for long. Learning from northern papers in mid-July that several of Grant's divisions had been released to Buell, he protested to Davis in Richmond: "This brings an overwhelming force that cannot be resisted except by Bragg's coöperation." Four days later, July 19, he reported to the Adjutant General that "Buell with his whole force" had reached Stevenson, thirty miles from Chattanooga, which he was "daily expected to attack." Fortunately, Smith added, Forrest had broken the Union supply line at Murfreesboro. "This may delay General Buell's movement and give General Bragg time to move on Middle Tennessee. The safety of Chattanooga depends upon his coöperation." Next day, not knowing of his opponent's difficulties in procuring pitch and oakum, he made a telegraphic appeal to Bragg: "Buell has completed his preparations, is prepared to cross near Bridgeport, and his passage there may be hourly expected. General Morgan's command moving on Knoxville from Cumberland Gap. Your coöperation is much needed. It is your time to strike at Middle Tennessee."

Bragg's reply, sent from Tupelo that same day, was not encouraging. "Confronted here by a largely superior force strongly intrenched" and threatened on the left by Curtis, who would "now be enabled to unite against us," he found it "impossible . . . to do more than menace and harass the enemy from this quarter." The land was parched; both armies, Grant's and his own, were living out of wells; so that whichever ventured far from its base in search of the other would die of thirst. "The fact is we are fearfully outnumbered in this department, the enemy having at least two to our one in the field, with a comparatively short line upon which he may concentrate." After this recital of obstacles and woes, he made it clear that Smith would have to shift for himself in East Tennessee, without the hope of further reinforcements.

Then overnight he changed his mind. Next day was the anniversary of Manassas, and he saluted it with a telegram as abruptly brief as the discharge of a starting-gun in the race which it announced:

Tupelo, Miss., July 21

President Jefferson Davis,

Richmond, Va.:

Will move immediately to Chattanooga in force and advance from there. Forward movement from here in force is not practicable. Will leave this line well defended.

Braxton Bragg

Next day, in the midst of large-scale preparations for the shift — he was not waiting for specific governmental approval; "Strike the moment an opportunity offers," he had been told three weeks ago — he expanded this somewhat in a second wire to Davis, who he knew must have been startled at being told, without preamble, that the army which was the mainstay of his native Mississippi was being removed forthwith: "Obstacles in front connected with danger to Chattanooga induce a change of base. Fully impressed with great importance of that line, am moving to East Tennessee. Produce rapid offensive from there following the consternation now being produced by our cavalry.

★

Leave this State amply protected by Van Dorn at Vicksburg and Price here."

In a letter to Beauregard that same day — the one in which he wrote, "Our cavalry is paving the way" — he gave a fuller explanation. "As I am changing entirely, under altered circumstances, the plan of operations here," he told his former chief, "I submit to you what I propose and beg your candid criticism, and in view of the cordial and sincere relations we have ever maintained, I trust to your compliance." With Smith "so weak as to give me great uneasiness for the safety of his line," Bragg had had to choose between four alternatives: 1) to remain idle at Tupelo, 2) to attack Grant, 3) to move into Middle Tennessee by crossing the river in Buell's rear and thus disrupt his and Grant's supply lines, or 4) to attack Buell. Of these, the first was unthinkable; the second was impracticable, considering the drouth in North Mississippi and the strength of the fortifications at Memphis and Corinth; the third was unwise and overrisky, since it would invite both Grant and Buell to assault him simultaneously from opposite directions. Therefore he had chosen the fourth, which would not only provide for a combination with Smith, but would also afford possibilities for maneuver and mystification. "By throwing my cavalry forward toward Grand Junction and Tuscumbia" — this referred to Wheeler and Armstrong, who had left three days ago — "the impression is created that I am advancing on both places and [the Federals] are drawing in to meet me. The Memphis & Charleston road has been kept cut, so they have no use of it and have at length given it up. Before they can know my movement I shall be in front of Buell at Chattanooga, and by cutting off his transportation may have him in a tight place. . . . Thus you have my plan."

As might have been expected — for, though it lacked the language, it had nearly the grandeur of one of the Creole's own — Beauregard gave the plan his fervent approval. "Action, action, and action is what we require," he replied, paraphrasing Danton's "De l'audace, encore l'audace, et toujours de l'audace," and added with a paternalistic glow: "I have no doubt that with anything like equal numbers you will meet with success." By the time these encouraging words reached him, however, Bragg was far from Tupelo. He left on July 24, after notifying the Adjutant General: "Major General Van Dorn, with about 16,000 effectives, will hold the line of the Mississippi. Major General Price, with a similar force, will face the enemy on this frontier, and a sufficient garrison will be left for Mobile and the Gulf. With the balance of the forces, some 35,000 effectives, I hope, in conjunction with Major General Smith, to strike an effective blow through Middle Tennessee, gaining the enemy's rear, cutting off his supplies and dividing his forces, so as to encounter him in detail. In any event much will be accomplished in simply preserving our line and preventing a descent into Georgia, than which no greater disaster could befall us."

His confidence that he would win the race, despite the handicap of a six-week lag — not to mention the sobering example of the hare-and-tortoise fable — was based on an appreciation of railroads as a strategic factor in this war. (For one thing, by bringing Joe Johnston's men down from the Valley, through Manassas Gap, to unload within earshot of the Union guns, they had won the battle whose anniversary had now come round.) Ever since his assumption of command Bragg had kept busy, doing not only all he could to wreck Buell's rail facilities, but also all he could to improve his own, especially in urging the completion of a line connecting Meridian and Selma. In the former effort, by grace of Morgan and Forrest, he had been successful, but in the latter he had failed; the Confederacy, it appeared, could afford neither the effort nor the iron. Consequently, with the Memphis & Charleston wrecked and in Federal hands, the only rail connection between Tupelo and Chattanooga was a roundabout, far-south route through Mobile and Atlanta, involving a journey of 776 miles over no less than half a dozen separate railroads, with through trains prohibited by the water gap across Mobile Bay and the narrow gauge of the Montgomery & West Point road. Nevertheless, the sending of the 3000-man brigade to Smith in late June, as a trial run over this route, had opened Bragg's eyes to the possibilities it afforded for a rapid, large-scale movement. The troops had left Tupelo on June 27, and despite congestion all along the line — conflicting orders from Richmond had put other units simultaneously on the rails — reached Chattanooga on July 3, within a week of the day the movement order had been issued.

Now he was out to repeat or better the performance with ten times as many soldiers, the "effective total" of his four divisions being 31,638 of all arms. Horse-drawn elements, including engineers and wagon trains, as well as cavalry and artillery, would move overland — due east to Rome, then north — but the bulk of the command would go by rail, dispatched from Tupelo a division at a time. For this, though they were made on quite short notice, the preparations were extensive, with the emphasis on discipline, as was always the case when Bragg was in charge. Each man was to be handed seven days' cooked rations as he stepped aboard, thus forestalling any excuse for foraging en route, and unit commanders were cautioned to be especially vigilant at junction points to prevent the more adventurous from disrupting the schedule by stealing away for a visit to the fleshpots. The first division left on July 23, the second and third immediately thereafter, and the fourth on July 29: by which time the units forwarded from Mobile and other scattered points to clear the line had been in Chattanooga for two full days. They were followed by a week-long procession of jam-packed cars whose engines came puffing around Missionary Ridge and into the city.

In all the bustle and hurry of preparation and departure, and in spite of the number of wires and letters flying back and forth, Bragg had neglected to mention his sudden volte-face to the one person most immediately concerned: Kirby Smith. While changing trains in Montgomery, however, he was handed an intercepted letter the East Tennessee commander had sent from Knoxville on the

24th — the day Bragg left Tupelo — proposing, with what amounted to clairvoyance if not downright telepathy, the very movement now in progress: "Buell's movements and preparations indicate a speedy attack. . . . Can you not leave a portion of your forces in observation in Mississippi, and, shifting the main body to this department, take command in person? There is yet time for a brilliant summer campaign; you will have a good and secure base, abundant supplies, the Tennessee can be crossed at any point by the aid of steam and ferry boats, and the campaign opened with every prospect of regaining possession of Middle Tennessee and possibly Kentucky." He added: "I will not only coöperate with you, but will cheerfully place my command under you subject to your orders."

Confederate major general Edmund Kirby Smith had been severely wounded at First Manassas.

With this in his pocket, a happy omen as well as an affirmation of his strategic judgment, Bragg continued his journey and reached Chattanooga early on the morning of July 30. Informed of his arrival, Smith came down from Knoxville the following day to confer with him on what Bragg called "measures for material support and effective coöperation." Smith had two divisions, one in front of Cumberland Gap, observing the Federals who occupied that point, the other at Chattanooga; their strength was about 9000 men each, including the brigade that had arrived four weeks ago to thicken the ranks of the slim force confronting Buell. Bragg was reorganizing his still-arriving army into two "wings," one under Polk, the other under Hardee, each with two infantry divisions and a cavalry brigade; their combined strength was 34,000, including the units forwarded in driblets from points along the railroad. His problem was how best to employ these 52,000 men — his and Smith's — against the larger but badly scattered Federal forces to his front and on his flank.

The solution, as communicated to the Adjutant General on August 1, was for Smith to "move at once against General Morgan in front of Cumberland Gap," while Bragg was collecting supplies and awaiting the arrival of his artillery and trains for an advance from Chattanooga. This would require ten days or two weeks, he said. At the end of that time, if Smith had been successful against Morgan, both armies would then combine for a march "into Middle

Tennessee with the fairest prospect of cutting off General Buell, should that commander continue in his present position. Should he be reinforced from the west side of the Tennessee River, so as to cope with us, then Van Dorn and Price can strike and clear West Tennessee of any force that can be left to hold it." Furthermore, once Grant and Buell had been disposed of, either by destruction or by being maneuvered into retreat, he considered the time propitious for an invasion of the region to the north. "The feeling in Middle Tennessee and Kentucky is represented by Forrest and Morgan to have become intensely hostile to the enemy, and nothing is wanted but arms and support to bring the people into our ranks, for they have found that neutrality has afforded them no protection."

Returning to Knoxville much encouraged by these developments, Smith informed his wife that he had found his new partner "a grim old fellow" (he himself was thirty-eight; Bragg was forty-five) "but a true soldier." Presently he was further gladdened by the arrival of two brigades detached by Bragg to reinforce him for the offensive, one from Polk and one from Hardee, and being thus strengthened on the eve of his advance he began to see larger prospects looming out beyond the horizon — prospects based in part on a dispatch from John Morgan, who had reported from northern Kentucky in mid-July: "I am here with a force sufficient to hold all the country outside of Lexington and Frankfort. These places are garrisoned chiefly with Home Guards. The bridges between Cincinnati and Lexington have been destroyed. The whole country can be secured, and 25,000 or 30,000 men will join you at once. I have taken eleven cities and towns with very heavy army stores." If one small brigade of cavalry could accomplish all this, Smith reasoned, what might a whole army do? Accordingly, on August 9 he wrote to Bragg that he "understood" the Federals intrenched at Cumberland Gap had "nearly a month's supply of provisions. If this be true the reduction of the place would be a matter of more time than I presume you are willing I should take. As my move direct to Lexington, Ky. would effectually invest [the Gap] and would be attended with other most brilliant results in my judgment, I suggest my being allowed to take that course, if I find the speedy reduction of the Gap an impractical thing."

Bragg too was nurturing hopes in that direction, though not without reservations. He replied next day: "It will be a week yet before I can commence crossing the river, and information I hope to receive will determine which route I shall take, to Nashville or Lexington. My inclination is now for the latter." All the same, Smith's plan to by-pass Cumberland Gap and head straight for North Central Kentucky was more than his partner had bargained for, even though Smith reinforced his proposal by inclosing a letter from John Morgan's lieutenant-colonel, stressing the opinion that flocks of eager volunteers were waiting to double the size of his army as soon as it reached the Bluegrass. Strategically, Bragg approved, but tactically he urged caution: "It would be unadvisable, I think, for you to move far into Kentucky, leaving [George] Morgan in your rear, until I am able to fully engage Buell and his forces on your left. But I do not credit the amount of Morgan's supplies [at Cumberland Gap] and have confidence in his timidity. When once well on the way to his rear you might safely leave but 5000 to his front, and by a flank movement draw the rest to your assistance. He will never advance to escape."

Smith's ebullience was contagious: as was shown in the final sentence of Bragg's letter. "Van Dorn and Price will advance simultaneously with us from Mississippi on West Tennessee, and I trust we may all unite in Ohio."

———— ⟪⟫ ————

★ ★ ★ Just now, however, Van Dorn was looking south, not north; he had New Orleans on his mind, not Ohio. The grim determination he had brought to embattled Vicksburg in late June — "Let it be borne in mind by all that the army here is defending the place against occupation. This will be done at all hazards, even though this beautiful and devoted city should be laid in ruin and ashes" — gave way to elation in mid-July when the *Arkansas* made her run through the Yankee sloops and gunboats. "Glorious for the navy, and glorious for her heroic commander, officers, and men," he wired Davis. The iron ram changed everything. "Smokestack riddled; otherwise not materially damaged," he exulted. "Soon be repaired and then, Ho! for New Orleans." Both enemy fleets were still on hand, and across the way the bluecoats were still digging their canal; but Van Dorn no longer saw them as much of a threat. A week later, after two all-out attempts to sink the *Arkansas* under the tall red bluff, he pronounced "the failure so complete that it was almost ridiculous." The same went for the engineering project. "Nothing can be accomplished by the enemy," he told Richmond, "unless they bring overwhelming number of troops. This must be anticipated."

His favorite method of anticipation, now as always, was to seize the offensive; to snatch the ball from his opponent and start running. That was what he had done, or tried to do, in Arkansas back in the early spring, and that was what he decided to do now in his native Mississippi in midsummer. When Davis and Farragut gave up the game, turned their backs on each other and went their separate ways — the former to Helena, the latter to New Orleans after dropping the infantry off at Baton Rouge — Van Dorn ordered Breckinridge to pursue southward with 4000 men and knock the bluecoats off balance in the Louisiana capital before they could get set for a return. If possible, he was to take the city: after which, as Van Dorn saw it, would come much else. Five months ago the byword had been "St Louis, then huzza!" Now it was "Ho! for New Orleans."

Breckinridge wasted no time in getting started. On July 27, the day after the Yankee fleets took off in opposite directions, he put his troops aboard railroad cars and proceeded by way of Jackson to Ponchatoula, Louisiana, where they detrained the following afternoon to prepare for the overland advance on Baton Rouge, sixty miles to the west. On the 30th the march began, but was halted the following morning when reports came in "that the effective force of the enemy was not less than 5000 and that the ground was commanded by three gunboats lying in the river." Down to 3400 men as a result of sickness, Breckinridge wired Van Dorn that he would nonetheless "undertake to capture the garrison if the *Arkansas* could be sent down to clear the river or divert the fire of the gunboats." Promptly the reply came back: The ram would be in front of Baton Rouge at dawn, August 5. Breckinridge made his plans accordingly.

Isaac Brown was not in Vicksburg at the time, having left his ship-mates "to sustain without me the lassitude of inaction" while he took a four-day leave in Grenada. If rest and relaxation were what he was after (which was proba-ble; he had had precious little of either in the past two months) he was disap-pointed in more ways than one. For one thing, he had no sooner arrived than he was taken violently ill and put to bed. For another, while he was in this condi-tion, supposedly unable to lift his head off the pillow, he received a wire from his first lieutenant, informing him that the *Arkansas* was under orders to pro-ceed at once to Baton Rouge, despite the fact that her engines were under major repair and much of her rusty plating had still not been

refastened to her battered sides. Brown replied with "a positive order to remain at Vicksburg until I could join him," and had himself carried to the depot, where he boarded the first southbound train. Collapsed on some mail bags, too weak to sit up or even change his position, he rode the 130 miles to Jackson, where he applied for a special train to take him the rest of the way, only to learn that the *Arkansas* had already gone downriver.

She cast off Sunday evening, August 3, barely thirty hours before she was due at her Tuesday-morning ren-dezvous with Breckinridge, 240 wind-ing miles below. This called for her best speed: with the result that there were stoppages from overstrain all along the way, each requiring additional make-up

Confederate general John C. Breckin-ridge had been a congressman and vice president under James Buchanan.

speed thereafter, which produced more frequent breakdowns. Caught up in this vicious cycle, her engines had become so cranky by the time she reached the mouth of the Red, 200 miles out of Vicksburg, that her substitute skipper, Lieutenant Henry Stevens, called a council of war to decide whether to continue or turn back. The decision was to press on. At daybreak, August 5, approaching the final bend above Baton Rouge, the crew heard the boom of guns, which told that the land attack was under way. The *Arkansas* herself appeared to sense this; or, as one of her officers put it, "Like a war horse she seemed to scent the battle from afar, and in point of speed outdid anything we had ever before witnessed." Then, just before rounding the bend, they heard a familiar sound: the crack and jar of naval guns mixed in with the bark of field artillery. The ironclad *Essex* and the two Farragut gunboats were adding the weight of their metal to the attempt to fling back the Confederate attackers. Urged on by the knowledge "that our iron sides should be receiving those missiles which now were mowing down our ranks of infantry," Stevens decided to make an immediate ram attack on the *Essex*, sinking her where she lay, then steam below the city to cut off the retreat of the two wooden gunboats, reducing them to kindling at his leisure. Such was his intention: whereupon the starboard engine suddenly quit, and before the helmsman could port her wheel, the ram ran hard aground. The engineers got to work at once with files and chisels, trying to coax the balky engine into motion, but it would obviously be some hours before they could succeed. Meanwhile, the land attack continued. "There lay the enemy in plain view," one of the *Arkansas* lieutenants afterwards wrote, still mortified years later, "and we as helpless as a shear-hulk."

Breckinridge had marched to within ten miles of the place the night before in order to launch his assault on schedule, although by now he was down to 2600 effectives as a result of sickness brought on by the heat and an irregular diet, the rail movement having been made in such haste that commissary supplies and cooking utensils were left behind. "The day before the battle we had nothing to eat but roasting ears," one Kentucky infantryman afterwards recalled, "and these we ate raw because we had not time to stop long enough to roast them. Our command, with the horses, consumed forty acres of green corn one evening; for we stopped only long enough to gather the corn and feed the horses, [and] we then moved forward to take position to make the attack at daylight." His brigade, which had left Vicksburg with 1800 men, was reduced to 580 within two weeks. "Such were the ravages of sickness, exposure, and battle," he declared.

Of these, the last were the least as the thing turned out, in spite of the fact that they found the enemy waiting to receive them. The Federal commander, Thomas Williams, had formed his line closer to the town than some of his regimental camps, contracting it thus because he was down to about the same effective strength as the attackers: not because of exposure or bad food, but because so many of his men had still not recovered from lowland ailments encountered while plying their shovels opposite Vicksburg. However, he had the advantage in artillery, eighteen pieces to eleven, besides the tremendous added power of the gunboats, plowing the ranks of the charging rebels by arching their big projectiles over the capital, where a naval observer directed their fire by signals from the tower of the statehouse. In the face of this, Breckinridge scored considerable early success, forcing the bluecoats back through the suburbs on the right and capturing two guns; but the warships, unopposed by the missing *Arkansas*, more than tipped the balance. By 10 o'clock, having lost the commanders of one of his two divisions and three of his four brigades, he halted to adjust his line. Williams, observing this, ordered a charge to recover what had been yielded, but then was killed by a bullet through his chest — the first Union general to fall in battle since Nathaniel Lyon died much the same way at Wilson's Creek, a year ago next week. Breckinridge held his ground until late afternoon, hoping to renew the attack as soon as the *Arkansas* arrived. When he learned that the ram was lying helpless four miles above town, he left a small force in observation and pulled the main body back to the Comite River, from which he had marched the night before. The Federals did not follow.

Aboard the grounded ram, the engineers were still at work with their files and chisels. Stevens got her afloat by throwing off some railroad iron lying loose on her deck, and by dusk the black gang had her engines back in operation. She started down the four-mile reach, where the Union boats were standing guard, but had gone no more than a hundred yards when the crankpin in the rocking shaft of the starboard engine snapped. A forge was set up on the gundeck, and one of the engineers, a former blacksmith, hammered out a new one. By the time it was finished, dawn was glimmering through and the lookout spotted the *Essex* coming upstream, making a scant two knots against the current. Hurriedly, the new pin was installed; the rust-red *Arkansas* stood out for battle. Stevens intended to make a short run upstream, then turn and launch a ram attack with the added momentum. Before he could start back, however, the port engine suddenly quit and spun the vessel once more into bank. The *Essex* was coming slowly on, firing as she came, and the *Arkansas* was hard aground, able to bring only one of her guns to bear. The situation spoke for itself. Stevens ordered the crew ashore and fired the vessel, tears streaming down his face as he did so. When the flames reached the gundeck, the loaded guns began to explode: so that the *Arkansas* not only kept the *Essex* at a respectful distance during her death throes, but administered her own *coup de grâce* and fired her own salute as she went down. Thus she made a fitting end to her twenty-three-day career.

Brown almost got there in time to see it. Cured of his fever by the news that his ram had gone downriver without him, he got back onto the southbound train and rode to Ponchatoula, where he transferred to horseback and struck out westward for the river, in hope that he could hail the *Arkansas* from bank and somehow manage to board her or at any rate be near enough to watch and cheer her as she fought. What he saw instead were exultant Union gunboats steaming back and forth across the muddy water where she had exploded and sunk with her colors flying. Sadly — though he was proud, he later wrote, that her deck "had never been pressed by the foot of an enemy" — he rode back the way he had come and returned to Vicksburg.

Breckinridge shared the pride, but not the sadness, at the outcome of the brief campaign. This reaction was based not on the casualty lists — both sides had lost 84 killed, though the Confederate total of wounded and captured was the larger: 372 to 299 — but on his view of the fighting qualities shown. "In one respect the contrast between the opposing forces was very striking," he declared. "The enemy were well clothed, and their encampments showed the presence of every comfort and even luxury. Our men had little transportation, indifferent food, and no shelter. Half of them had no coats, and hundreds were without either shoes or socks; yet no troops ever behaved with greater gallantry and even reckless audacity. What can make this difference unless it be the sublime courage inspired by a just cause?"

Whether right made might, or might made right — or, indeed, whether either was on the former Vice President's side in this case — was a question open to much debate, then and thereafter. Butler, for one, did not agree with his assessment. According to him, the rebels "took advantage of [the garrison's] sickness from the malaria of the marshes of Vicksburg to make a cowardly attack," which was bloodily repulsed with "more than a thousand killed and wounded." But the Southerner's claim to physical as well as moral victory was considerably strengthened two weeks later when Butler, after congratulating his soldiers for their staunchness — "The Spanish conqueror of Mexico won imperishable renown by landing in that country and burning his transport ships, to cut off all hope of retreat. You, more wise and economical, but with equal providence against retreat, sent yours home" — ordered Baton Rouge abandoned, and dispatched those same transports upriver to bring the endangered troops back to New Orleans.

The flow of what Horace Greeley, back in May, had been calling "A Deluge of Victories" was seemingly reversed, and there was corresponding elation in the South. Next to the capture of a northern capital, what could be better than the recovery of a southern one? More important, tactically speaking, the Federal grip on the Mississippi — so close to strangulation a month ago — had been loosened even further, and to make sure that it was not reapplied Breckinridge had already sent most of his troops to occupy and fortify Port Hudson, a left-bank position of great natural strength. Potentially another Vicksburg, its bluff commanded a sharp bend of the river about midway between Baton Rouge and the mouth of the Red, thus assuring a continuation of commerce with the Transmississippi, including the grainlands of Northwest Louisiana and the cattle-rich plains of Texas.

That was but part of the brightening overall picture. In Virginia, McClellan had been repulsed. Grant was stalled in North Mississippi. Buell had lost the race for Chattanooga. And in all these widespread regions Confederate armies were poised to take the offensive: particularly in East Tennessee, as Breckinridge learned from a letter Bragg sent him immediately after the fight at Baton Rouge. Extending an invitation to the former Bluegrass politician, the terrible-tempered North Carolinian was in a strangely rollicking mood: "My army has promised to make me military governor of Ohio in ninety days (Seward's time for crushing the rebellion), and as they cannot do that without passing your home, I have thought you would like to have an escort to visit your family." He added, in a more serious vein, "Your influence in Kentucky would be equal to an extra division in my army. . . . If you desire it, and General Van Dorn will consent, you shall come at once. A command is ready for you, and I shall hope to see your eyes beam again at the command 'Forward,' as they did at Shiloh, in the midst of our greatest success."

This was seconded by Hardee, who telegraphed on August 23, five days before the Chattanooga jump-off: "Come here, if possible. I have a splendid division for you to lead into Kentucky."

Breckinridge wired back: "Reserve the division for me."

★ ★ ★ One prominent Kentuckian already commanded a division under Hardee: Simon Buckner. Exchanged at last, after five months in prison at Fort Warren, he reported in late July to Richmond, where he was promoted to major general and assigned to duty with the army then on its way to Chattanooga. The army commander was glad to have him, not only because of his proved fighting qualities, but also as a recruiting attraction in his native state; spare muskets were being taken along in wagons, ready for transfer to the shoulders of Kentucky volunteers. Bragg was glad, too, to have the approval of the President for the campaign he was about to undertake, though Davis warned him at the outset with a two-edged compliment predicting future strife, off as well as on the field of battle: "You have the misfortune of being regarded as my personal friend, and are pursued, therefore, with malignant censure by men regardless of truth, and whose want of principle to guide their conduct renders them incapable of conceiving that you are trusted because of your known fitness for command and not because of friendly regard. Revolutions develop the high qualities of the good and the great, but they cannot change the nature of the vicious and the selfish."

Kirby Smith — described in the same letter as "one of our ablest and purest officers . . . [whose] promotions, like your own, have come unsought" —

Federal warships support Brigadier General Thomas Williams' hard-pressed troops in this lithograph of the Battle of Baton Rouge.

left Knoxville on August 14 to move against his West Point classmate George Morgan at Cumberland Gap. The two brigades received from Bragg had raised his striking force to 21,000 men, well over twice the number holding the gap; but finding, as he had predicted, that Morgan was better prepared to resist a siege than he himself was prepared to maintain one, he left a 9000-man division in front of the mountain stronghold, as Bragg had advised, and with the rest of his army crossed the Cumberlands thirty miles to the southwest at Big Creek Gap. This was no raid, he told Richmond. "My advance is made in the hope of permanently occupying Kentucky. It is a bold move, offering brilliant results, but will be accomplished only with hard fighting, and must be sustained by constant reinforcements." He marched fast, swinging north for Barbourville, which he occupied on August 18. The "constant reinforcements," of course, would have to be in the form of local volunteers; but none were forthcoming here. Six days later, while preparing to resume the march, he notified Bragg: "Thus far the people are universally hostile to our cause. This sentiment extends through the mountain region of Eastern Kentucky. In the bluegrass region I have better expectations and shall soon test their loyalty."

Bragg's own estimate was rosier and a good deal more specific. "Everything is ripe for success," he informed his co-commander. "The country is aroused and expecting us. Buell's forces are much scattered, and from all accounts much demoralized. By rapid movements and vigorous blows we may beat him in detail, or by gaining his rear very much increase his demoralization and break him up." On August 27, the day before the jump-off, he sent word to Sterling Price, holding the line in North Mississippi: "We move from here immediately, later by some days than expected, but in time we hope for a successful campaign. Buell has certainly fallen back from the Memphis & Charleston Railroad and will probably not make a stand this side of Nashville, if there. He is now fortifying that place. General Smith, reinforced by two brigades from this army, has turned Cumberland Gap, and is now marching on Lexington, Ky. . . . We shall thus have Buell pretty well disposed of. Sherman and Rosecrans we leave to you and Van Dorn, satisfied that you can dispose of them, and we shall confidently expect to meet you on the Ohio and there open the way to Missouri."

Unquestionably — even without the inclusion of Missouri, which was scarcely more than a closing flourish for the benefit of Price — this was an ambitious project. But Bragg was not only ready and willing to undertake its execution; he had already selected a guide, a model. Beauregard and McClellan, along with a cluster of lesser lights, might take Napoleon. Not Bragg. His chosen prototype was a contemporary, a man who in fact was seven years his junior. Back in Tupelo, on the occasion of promising his soldiers to "give your banners to the breeze," he also told them: "Others of your countrymen, under the lead of Jackson and Ewell in the Valley of Virginia, have recently shed imperishable renown on our arms, and shown what a small, obedient, disciplined volunteer army can do." What he intended now, as he stood poised for the jump-off, was a Valley Campaign on a much larger scale, with Smith as Ewell and himself as Stonewall. Like him, he could expect to be badly outnumbered strategically (he had fewer than 30,000 of all arms); yet like him, too, he would translate this disadvantage into "imperishable renown" by means of "rapid movements and vigorous blows." So far, it was true, the only attributes original and copy had in common were dyspepsia and a readiness to stand deserters before a firing squad. However, it was Bragg's intention to extend these similarities into other fields of reaction and endeavor during the trial that lay ahead.

Some measure of this intention, complete with Old Testament overtones, was communicated to his troops in a general order read to them before they left their camps around Chattanooga:

> *The enemy is before us, devastating our fair country, imprisoning our old and venerated men (even the ministers of God), insulting our women, and desecrating our altars. It is our proud lot to be assigned the duty of punishing and driving forth these deluded men, led by desperate adventurers and goaded on by Abolition demagogues and demons. Let us but deserve success and an offended Deity will certainly assure it. Should we be opposed, we must fight at any odds and conquer at any sacrifice. Should the foe retire, we must follow him rapidly to his own territory and make him taste the bitters of invasion.*
>
> *Soldiers, the enemy is before you and your banners are free. It is for you to decide whether our brothers and sisters of Tennessee and Kentucky shall remain bondmen and bondwomen of the Abolition tyrant or be restored to the freedom inherited from their fathers.*

Having heard him out, the long files shouldered their muskets and headed north.

★　★　★

★

Shelby Foote

*R*ebel prisoners taken at Cedar
Mountain dry their laundry in
the tower of Culpeper Court House.
Many were paroled when the
Federals left on August 20, 1862.

EIGHT

Pope Encounters Jackson: Cedar Mountain

1862 ★ ★ ★ ★ ★ ★

In Virginia, though the basis for it was obviously a good deal less substantial — westward, the blue glacier had not only ground to a halt, it had even reversed direction, whereas here in the East no more than a pause, a hesitation of the mass, had seemingly been effected; McClellan, after all, was scarcely a dozen miles farther from Richmond than he had been on the eve of the Seven Days, besides being more securely based on the James than he had been while crouched astride the treacherous Chickahominy, and Pope was hovering northward, a considerably graver threat, both in numbers and position, than McDowell had ever been — the elation mounted higher. One reason was that the result, however far it fell short of expectation, had been obtained by actual fighting, not by maneuver or mere Federal acquiescence. Another was the return of confidence in the government: especially in the President, whose vindication now appeared complete.

Less than a week before the launching of the assault that flung the bluecoats back from the capital gates, Tom Cobb had been declaring that he saw in Davis "the embodiment and concentration of cowardly littleness [which] he garnishes over with pharisaical hypocrisy. How can God smile upon us while we have such a man [to] lead us?" Few were asking that question now: God *had*

★

smiled upon them, and a large part of the credit went to the man who by deed as well as title filled the position of Commander in Chief and triumphed over the adversary who occupied that post in the country to the north. The Hezekiah-Sennacherib analogy still held.

As far as the soldiers themselves were concerned, however, the credit went to the general who had been placed at their head in their darkest hour and in one short month, despite their initial resentment, had welded their four disparate components — Johnston's Manassas army and Magruder's frazzled Yorktown brigades, Jackson's Valley command and Huger's unblooded Norfolk division — into a single striking force, the Army of Northern Virginia, which he hurled with cunning and fury at the blue invaders, massed in their thousands within sight and hearing of Richmond's steeples and public clocks, and sent them reeling backwards or sidling crablike to their present mud-flat sanctuary under the muzzles of their gunboats. Granny Lee, Evacuating Lee, the King of Spades, had become for his troops what he would remain: Mars Robert. They watched him as he rode among them, the high-colored face above and behind the iron-gray beard, the active, dark-brown eyes, the broad forehead whose upper half showed unexpectedly dazzling white when he removed his wide-brimmed hat to acknowledge their cheers. Distrust had yielded to enthusiasm, which in turn was giving way to awe.

On horseback, deep-chested and long-waisted, with his big, leonine head set thick-necked on massive shoulders, he looked gigantic. Partly that was the aura. It must have been; for when he dismounted, as he often did, to rest his horse — he had a tender concern for the welfare of all animals, even combat infantrymen, aside from those times when he flung them into the crackling uproar of battle like chaff into a furnace — you saw the slight legs, the narrow hips, and realized, with something of a shock, that he was no larger than many of the men around him, and not as large as some. The same contrast, above and below, was apparent in his extremities; the hands were oversized and muscular, the feet tiny as a woman's. He was in fact just under six feet tall and weighed less than 170 pounds. Quickly, though, you got over the shock (which after all was only the result of comparing flesh and perfection. However he *was* was how you preferred him) and when you saw him thus in the field your inclination was to remove your hat — not to wave it: just to hold it — and stand there looking at him: Mars Robert.

Not everyone offered such adulation, either in or out of the army. Robert Toombs, for one, who had commanded a brigade under Magruder throughout the Peninsula campaign, considered Lee "far below the occasion." The Charleston *Mercury* for another, while it praised the strategy — "projected, as we hear, by General Johnston" — agreed with Toombs as to the tactics: "The blundering manner in which [McClellan] has been allowed to get away, the desultory manner in which he has been pursued by divisions instead of our whole force, enabling him to repulse our attacks, to carry off his artillery, and, finally, to make a fresh stand with an army reinforced are facts, we fear, not very flattering to the generalship of General Lee."

Lee was rather inclined to agree with the former Georgia statesman, as well as with the South Carolina editor, not only because of his inherent modesty, but also because he knew that what they said was largely true. "His great victory did not elate him, so far as one could see," his cannoneer son later recalled. This was not for lack of material success. The booty had been ample: 52 fine Union guns (by coincidence, one for every battery in the Army of the Potomac), 31,000 rifles (which gave some measure of the Federal panic, since half

---

"Under ordinary circumstances, the Federal army should have been destroyed."

— Robert E. Lee

---

were either dropped by casualties or handed over by captives, while the other half were abandoned by men who preferred to travel light) and 10,000 prisoners, most of them unwounded. All this was duly appreciated, especially the rifled guns and the badly needed small arms, but Lee's essential agreement with Toombs and the *Mercury* was based on a consideration of what had been left undone, as well as of what had been done — on the contrast, in fact, between conception and execution. "Under ordinary circumstances," he said in his report to the Adjutant General, "the Federal army should have been destroyed."

Sound strategy had largely counterbalanced woeful tactics to produce, within limits, a successful campaign. After all, Richmond was no longer even semi-beleaguered. But for the failure, so far as it was a failure beyond those limits, there were three main reasons: 1) poor maps and intelligence, which left the Confederates groping blind, or half blind, all the way from Mechanicsville to Harrison's Landing, inclusively; 2) poor staff work, especially in the transmission of orders, which was the basis for much of the lack of coördination; and 3) the Army of the Potomac, the hard-core staunchness of its infantry and the skill with which its superior artillery was employed. Of these, the last — referred to by one of Lee's own aides as "the character and personality of the men behind the Federal guns" — was clearly the most decisive in preventing the wreckage intended, but it was the first which caused what Harvey Hill summed up in one acid sentence: "Throughout this campaign we attacked just when and where the enemy wished us to attack."

★

Time and effort, self-application on Lee's part, might correct the first two of these drawbacks; the third would be with him from here on out. Yet there was still another problem — one he would always face with reluctance, though it too would remain. This was the task of assessing the character and performance of his lieutenants. Longstreet and the two Hills, whatever their personal eccentricities, whether headstrong or impetuous or caustic, had emerged from the test of combat with brighter laurels than before. The same could not be said of another trio: Magruder, Holmes, and Huger. Their reasons for failure were varied — overexcitability, deafness, chronic bad luck — but now that Lee had faced the problem, no matter with what reluctance, he was quick to act. He got rid of them. In Magruder's case it was simple; for he had been offered, and had accepted, command of a department in the Transmississippi. Lee wished him Godspeed along with Holmes, who went out there too, being placed in charge of the whole far-western theater. That left Huger; but not for long. He was kicked upstairs to the War Department, as chief inspector of artillery and ordnance.

In the course of replacing these departed leaders and redistributing their twelve brigades — which meant, in effect, a drastic reorganization for the work that lay ahead — Lee dealt with another problem of command: the question of what to do about Jackson, whose poor showing throughout the Seven Days was now the subject of much talk. He was reported to have said that he did not intend for his men to do all the fighting, and when he overheard some of his staff discussing his strange delay above White Oak Swamp while Longstreet was struggling desperately at Glendale, he remarked coldly: "If General Lee had wanted me, he could have sent for me." Lee of course did not join the chorus of critics, nor did he consider shunting Stonewall off to the Transmississippi; but in his regrouping of the army's nine divisions into two "wings" under its two ranking generals, Longstreet and Jackson, the former was assigned twenty-eight brigades, the latter seven. Stonewall thus had only half as many as had been under him during the late campaign, while Old Pete had nearly five times as many as the half dozen with which he had crossed the Chickahominy.

All through this period of refitting and reorganization, of distributing the captured arms and replacing his veterans' flop-soled shoes and tattered jackets, Lee had also kept busy trying to determine the enemy's intentions. It was a complicated problem, involving no less than four Federal armies of various strengths, all unknown. First there was the main force, under McClellan at Harrison's Landing. Then there was Pope's newly consolidated Army of Virginia, assumed to be in the vicinity of Manassas. Either or both might take the offensive at any time. The third was at Fredericksburg, threatening Richmond from the north, much as McDowell had done for months. The fourth was Burnside's, brought up from North Carolina in the emergency, but still kept aboard its transports, anchored mysteriously off Fort Monroe. Both

★

of these last two forces were in positions from which they could move rapidly to combine and join either of the other two: Pope, for an advance against the vital Virginia Central Railroad: or McClellan, for a renewal of his drive on the capital itself. For the present, though both of course were possible, Lee could find out nothing that would indicate which was probable. All he knew for certain was that delay was not to the advantage of the South. Northern determination had stiffened after this defeat, just as it had done the year before, and

*A Federal work crew repairs a wagon
bridge over the Rappahannock River
in the summer of 1862.*

★

Lincoln's call for 300,000 volunteers had gone out on the day of Malvern Hill.

In chess terms, Lee's immediate problem was whether to keep his pieces where they were, concentrated to checkmate the king — McClellan — or to disperse them in order to meet an advance by the knights and bishops, off on another quarter of the board. While awaiting developments he withdrew his infantry from the malarial swamps and left the observation of Harrison's Landing to the cavalry, newly gathered into a two-brigade division under Stuart, who was promoted to major general. Simultaneously, by way of discouraging an attack from that direction, he put his engineers to work constructing permanent fortifications. Anchored to the James at Drewry's Bluff and extending north along an arc shielding Richmond, these installations would also permit his present lines to be more thinly held if alternate pressure required dispersion. Once they were completed he would be much better prepared for whatever came.

What came, on July 12, was startling news from the north: Pope had occupied Culpeper that morning. What made this startling was that Culpeper was on the Orange & Alexandria, less than thirty miles above Gordonsville. And Gordonsville was on the Virginia Central, at the northern apex of an exposed bend known as "the Gordonsville loop," which led on westward to Charlottesville and Staunton. This was alternate pressure indeed; for if Pope took Gordonsville he would cut the Confederate supply line connecting Richmond and the Shenandoah Valley, where a bumper crop of corn and wheat was ripening for the harvest. Lee was obliged to meet this threat, and he did so the following day by sending Jackson with his own and Ewell's divisions — the old Army of the Valley — by rail to Louisa Court House, fifteen miles this side of Gordonsville, which he was instructed to occupy if Pope had not already got there in too great strength to be dislodged. The movement was made rapidly by way of Hanover Junction, using eighteen trains of fifteen cars each to transport Stonewall's 10,000 infantry and artillery, while his cavalry and wagons moved by road.

Strategically, this riposte was as sound as it was necessary, but Lee had other compelling reasons for ordering the movement: one being that he had developed a scathing contempt for the leader of the force at which it was aimed. After issuing the bombastic address to his soldiers ("Let us understand each other. . . . Disaster and shame lurk in the rear") Pope had joined them in the field and had proceeded at once, in a series of formal orders, to give his attention to the civilians in his prospective theater of operations. One directed his army to live off the country and to reimburse only those persons who could prove devotion to the flag he represented. Another prescribed stern measures to be taken in retaliation for guerilla activities. A third provided for the arrest of all male noncombatants within his lines, the expulsion of those who refused to take a loyalty oath, and their prosecution as spies if they returned. Furthermore, any man or woman who remained would be liable to the death penalty for attempting to

★

communicate with the enemy — presumably including a mother who wrote to a son in the southern army. These mandates were not in accordance with Lee's notion of civilized warfare; he was downright contemptuous of the man who ordered their adoption. "The miscreant Pope," he called him, and he said of him: "He ought to be suppressed if possible."

Just now it was not possible, Jackson reported. He had beaten Pope to Gordonsville, arriving there from Louisa on July 19, but the bluecoats around Culpeper were too numerous to be attacked at present. Reinforce him, Stonewall added, and he would gladly undertake all the suppression Lee could ask for. That was what Lee was considering, though the risk was admittedly great. Left with just under 70,000 men — including Holmes' former command, shifted south of the James to cover Petersburg and placed under D. H. Hill with an eye toward possible future operations in his native North Carolina — he knew he was badly outnumbered by McClellan, who moreover was beginning to show signs of activity. Besides, there were those other two armies, at Fredericksburg and off Fort Monroe: Lee still did not know in which direction they might move. Much as he wanted Pope whipped and driven back across the Rappahannock, the odds were long against weakening the capital defenses for that purpose. Nevertheless he decided to take the gamble. On July 27 he ordered A. P. Hill to Gordonsville, where the Light Division would join the Valley Army for a strike at Pope.

Alexander Boteler, one of Stonewall Jackson's aides, sketched his chief lost in thought near Louisa Court House, Virginia, in July 1862.

His hope was that this combined force would deliver its blow quickly, disposing of Pope with a knockout punch, then return to Richmond in time to help block any assault McClellan might attempt when he learned of its detachment. This would call for rapid, well-coördinated movements and a style of fighting characterized by a minimum of confusion and hesitation: quite the opposite, in fact, of the style Jackson had demonstrated throughout the Seven Days. One reason for his poor showing on the Peninsula, Lee suspected, was his known reluctance to take subordinate commanders into his military confidence. Also, in consideration of Little Powell's sensitive and highly volatile nature — he had already clashed with Longstreet over what he considered a slight to his division in the distribution of honors, and Longstreet had promptly put him in arrest, from which Lee had released him for the present expedition — there was the danger of an explosion when he came into contact with the stern and taciturn Stonewall. Accordingly, Lee wrote Jackson a letter in which he alluded tactfully to the problem. After repeating the injunction, "I want Pope to be suppressed," he concluded: "A. P. Hill you will, I think, find a good officer, with whom you can consult, and by advising with your division commanders as to your movements much trouble will be saved you in arranging details, as they can act more intelligently. . . . Cache your troops as much as possible till you can strike your blow, and be prepared to return to me when done, if necessary. I will endeavor to keep General McClellan quiet till it is over, if rapidly executed."

Keeping McClellan quiet might well turn out to be a good deal easier said than done. With one third of his army off after Pope, Lee was down to 56,000 men, including two brigades that arrived next day from South Carolina: whereas McClellan was not only half again larger now, he would have twice as many troops as Lee if he were reinforced by Burnside and the brigades at Fredericksburg, which Lee could do absolutely nothing to prevent. Besides, the Young Napoleon had considerable freedom of action. He could stay where he was, a hovering threat; he could steam back up the Potomac to join Pope and the others; he could advance from his present camp against the southern capital, less than twenty air-line miles away. In the latter case, two routes were available to him. He could move up the left bank of the James, more or less as before, except that he would be securely based; or he could cross the river, under cover of his gunboats, capture Petersburg, and swarm into Richmond by the back door. All were possibilities to fret the mind of Lee, who so far had been able to find no clew as to which course his adversary favored. "In the prospect before me," he wrote his wife, "I cannot see a single ray of pleasure during this war."

One way to keep McClellan quiet, Lee reasoned paradoxically, or at any rate make him hug his camp while the southern army was divided, might be to stir him up; that is, make him think he was about to be attacked. An infantry feint being impractical, Lee decided on an artillery demonstration. Under cover of darkness, forty-three guns of various calibers were concentrated on the south side of the James at Coggin's Point, opposite Harrison's Landing, and on the last night of July they opened fire on the Federal camp. The result, as in the case of Stuart's popgun bombardment four weeks back, was more spectacular than effective. After some original confusion, the Union artillerists and sailors brought their heavier guns to bear and smothered the Confederate batteries. On August 3, threatened with capture by an amphibious countermovement, they had to be withdrawn. Except for the effect it might have had on McClellan himself, enlarging his natural caution, the demonstration was a failure.

Two days later, by way of recompense, Lee got his first real hint as to the Federal overall strategy. A young Confederate cavalry officer, Captain John S. Mosby, had been captured two weeks before while on his way upstate to find recruits for a partisan command, and had been taken to Fort Monroe to await exchange. As soon as he was released he came to Lee with information he had picked up while imprisoned: Burnside was under orders to take his transports up the Potomac, debark his troops at Aquia Creek, and march them overland to Fredericksburg. If true, this meant considerable danger to Jackson, who was already badly outnumbered by the enemy north of Gordonsville, as well as to the Virginia Central, which led westward to the Valley granary. What was more, it was a strong indication that the enemy's next major effort would be in northern Virginia, where Lee was weakest, not here on the James. He would have moved at least a portion of his force to meet this threat at once, except that on the same day his cavalry reported a heavy force advancing from Harrison's, up the left bank of the river, against Richmond. Apparently it was not McClellan's caution which had been enlarged by the abortive Coggin's Point demonstration, but rather his self-confidence.

Lee marched three divisions out to meet him the following day, August 6, and approaching Malvern Hill near sundown found the Federals drawn up menacingly on the crest. Intending no repetition of last month's headlong, blind attack up the rolling slope, he extended his left, skirmished briskly on the right, and braced his troops for the downhill assault. At nightfall there was every indication that the armies would be locked in battle tomorrow. Instead — as had been more or less the case five weeks ago — dawn showed the hill empty of all but a handful of blue vedettes, who at the first sign of a Confederate advance scampered down the reverse slope to join the main body, already well on its way back to its camp on the James.

This was strange indeed: passing strange. Lee decided that the only explanation for McClellan's sudden advance-and-retreat was that it was intended to cover the movement Mosby had discerned at Fort Monroe. If this was so, and Burnside was headed for Fredericksburg, there still remained the question of what he would do when he got there. He could join Pope directly; he could operate against Richmond from the north; or he could attempt to cut the Virginia Central in Jackson's rear, between Gordonsville and Hanover Junction. The best way to forestall this last — the most immediately dangerous of the three — would be for Jackson to strike Pope, who would then be likely to call on Burnside for support. Until Lee knew whether McClellan intended to renew his advance on Richmond, however, he did not feel that he could further weaken the capital defenses in order to reinforce Jackson; nor did he feel that he should give him peremptory orders to attack, unsupported, without himself knowing the tactical situation at first hand. Accordingly, before the day was over, he did the next best thing. He sat down and wrote Stonewall a long letter in which he made it clear that he relied on his discretion.

After warning him not to count on reinforcements — "If I can send them I will; if I cannot, and you think it proper and advantageous, act without them" — he outlined the dilemma as he saw it and suggested what he believed was the best solution, an immediate thrust at Pope, though he cautioned against rashness: "I would rather you should have easy fighting and heavy victories." It was a warning addressed more to the erstwhile hard-driving hero of the Valley, who smote the enemy hip and thigh, wherever found, than to the sluggard of the Seven Days, who dawdled and withheld his hand from bloodshed. Apparently Lee had put the latter out of his mind. "I must now leave the matter to your reflection and good judgment," he concluded. "Make up your mind what is best to be done under all the circumstances which surround us, and let me hear the result at which you arrive. I will inform you if any change takes place here that bears on the subject."

★ ★ ★ *M*osby was right: Burnside had been ordered to Fredericksburg a week ago, on August 1, nine days after Halleck's arrival in Washington from the West. Having scattered the armies there for an assimilation of what had been won, Old Brains now proposed to unite those of the East for a new beginning. In both cases, however — since the concentration was not to be on the Peninsula, where defeat was recent, but in northern Virginia, where defeat was a full year old — the effect was the same: to shift the Union juggernaut into reverse. McClellan, too, was about to be withdrawn.

Nothing less than a new beginning would put the derailed engine back on track; or so it seemed to the newly appointed general-in-chief, who had reached the capital in a time of gloom. Flags drooped at half-mast under the press of heat and crape festooned the public buildings in observance of the death of Martin Van Buren, a used-up man. No such honors had marked the passing of the Virginian John Tyler the month before; but that was in a sunnier time, and even in the present instance the crape seemed more an expression of the general mood than grief for a particular man, ex-President or not; Van Buren was already part of ancient history. Halleck, at any rate, wasted little time in speculation on such matters. Instead, after spending a day in Washington, he got aboard a steamer and went straight to what he believed was the source of discontent: the Army of the Potomac, camped now on the mud flats of the James.

In spite of the pride he took in having executed the movement under pressure, and in spite of the fact that Lincoln had been congratulatory and Stanton even fawning, McClellan had been expecting trouble ever since his change of base. The President had wired him "a thousand thanks" after Malvern Hill. "Be assured," he added, "the heroism and skill of yourself and officers and men is, and forever will be, appreciated. If you can hold your present position [at Harrison's] we shall hive the enemy yet." Stanton put it stronger, or anyhow longer. "Be assured," he wrote, "that you shall have the support of this Department as cordially and faithfully as was ever rendered by man to man, and if we should ever live to see each other face to face you will be satisfied that you have never had from me anything but the most confiding integrity." That was larding it pretty thick, but he larded it even thicker in conversation with McClellan's father-in-law, who went to Washington to see him. "General Marcy," he told the chief of staff, with a sudden rush of feeling, "I have from the commencement of our acquaintance up to the present moment been General McClellan's warmest friend. I feel so kind toward him that I would get down on my knees to him if that would serve him. Yes sir," he continued, warming as he spoke. "If it would do him any service I would be willing to lay down naked in the gutter and allow him to stand upon my body for hours."

Stanton lying naked in the gutter was a prospect McClellan could contemplate with pleasure, but he was not deluded into thinking such a scene would ever be staged — except in his mind's eye. He knew well enough that Stanton was working against him, tooth and nail. Nor did Lincoln's assurances carry their former weight: especially after the arrival of John Pope and the Administration's tacit approval of the mandates he issued regarding noncombatants in his theater of operations. That was what really tore it, McClellan wrote his wife. "When you contrast the policy I urged in my letter to the President with that of Congress and of Mr Pope, you can readily agree with me that there can be little natural confidence between the government and myself. We are the antipodes of each other; and it is more than probable that they will take the earliest opportunity to relieve me from command and get me out of sight."

Now here came Halleck, slack-fleshed and goggle-eyed, formerly his subordinate, now his chief, holding the office he himself had lost. It was bitter. Presently, however, after a hasty review of the troops, Halleck calmed McClellan's apprehensions by informing him that he had not come to undermine him or relieve him of command, but to find out what he required in the way of additional

*General-in-Chief Henry Halleck (right) informs a pensive
General McClellan that portions of his army will be detached
for service with Pope's army in northern Virginia.*

men in order to renew the drive on the rebel capital. McClellan brightened and
unfolded a map on which he began to indicate, with pride and enthusiasm, a new
plan of attack. He would cross the James and capture Petersburg, outflanking the
enemy fortifications and severing the southside supply lines, then swing north
and enter Richmond by the back door. Halleck shook his head. Too risky, he said,
and vetoed the proposal then and there. McClellan, his enthusiasm dampened,
proceeded to an estimate of the situation. His effective strength, he said, was
88,665; Lee's was 200,000. Nevertheless, if the government would give him
30,000 reinforcements he would assault the northside intrenchments with "a
good chance of success." Halleck frowned. No more than 20,000 were available,
and if these would not suffice, he said, the army would have to be withdrawn
from the Peninsula to unite with Pope in the vicinity of Washington. Horrified at
the notion, McClellan excused himself in order to confer with his corps commanders. Next morning he reported, somewhat gloomily, that he was "willing to
try it" with that number. Halleck nodded and got back aboard the steamboat to
return to Washington. McClellan's genial spirits rose again. "I think that Halleck
will support me and give me the means to take Richmond," he wrote his wife.

Whatever Halleck intended when he left, his final decision was considerably affected by a telegram he found waiting for him when he docked. It was from McClellan; apparently it had been sent almost as soon as Halleck's steamer passed from sight. Confederate reinforcements, he said, were "pouring into Richmond from the South." To meet this new development, and to enable him to deliver "a rapid and heavy blow," he wanted more troops than the 20,000 just agreed on. "Can you not possibly draw 15,000 or 20,000 men from the West to reinforce me temporarily?" he pleaded. "They can return the moment we gain Richmond. Please give weight to this suggestion; I am sure it merits it."

Halleck was amazed, and went to Lincoln with the problem. Lincoln was not amazed at all. In fact, he found the telegram very much in character. If by some magic he could reinforce McClellan with 100,000 troops today, he said, Little Mac would be delighted and would promise to capture Richmond tomorrow; but when tomorrow came he would report the enemy strength at 400,000 and announce that he could not advance until he got another 100,000 reinforcements. Halleck turned this over in his mind, together with another consideration. If Lee was as strong as McClellan said he was — stronger than Pope and McClellan combined — it was folly to keep the Federal armies exposed to destruction in detail. It was in fact imperative to unite them without delay. At last he made his decision, agreeing with Lincoln that McClellan's army would have to be withdrawn. On July 29 he ordered every available steamer in Baltimore harbor to proceed at once to the James, and next day he instructed McClellan to prepare to evacuate his sick and wounded. He did not tell him why; he merely remarked ambiguously that this was being done "in order to enable you to move in any direction." Two days later, Burnside was told to take his transports up the Potomac to Aquia Creek, where the troops would debark for a twelve-mile march to Fredericksburg. McClellan's own orders were sent on August 3: "It is determined to withdraw your army from the Peninsula to Aquia Creek. You will take immediate measures to effect this, covering the movement as best you can."

McClellan was thunderstruck. The order for the removal of his sick had aroused his suspicions five days ago, despite — or perhaps because of — the disclaimer that it would leave him free "to move in any direction," and he had been prompt to register his protest: "Our true policy is to reinforce [this] army by every available means and throw it again upon Richmond. Should it be determined to withdraw it, I shall look upon our cause as lost." Perhaps he thought the weight of this opinion would forestall any such calamity. If so, he now saw how useless it had been. Yet he did not abandon hope; or anyhow he did not stop trying to ward off the blow. At noon on August 4 he knelt figuratively at the feet of Halleck and made a final anguished plea. "Your telegram of last evening is received. I must confess that it has caused me the greatest pain I ever experienced, for I am convinced that the order to withdraw this army to Aquia

Creek will prove disastrous to our cause." First he pointed out that it was tactical folly to make "a march of 145 miles to reach a point now only 25 miles distant, and to deprive ourselves entirely of the powerful aid of the gunboats and water transportation. Add to this the certain demoralization of this army which would ensue, and these appear to me sufficient reasons to make it my imperative duty to urge in the strongest terms afforded by our language that this order may be rescinded." Then came the impassioned words to which the rest had served as prologue: "Here, directly in front of this army, is the heart of the rebellion. It is here that all our resources should be collected to strike the blow which will determine the fate of the nation. . . . It matters not what partial reverses we may meet with elsewhere. Here is the true defense of Washington. It is here, on the banks of the James, that the fate of the Union should be decided."

Halleck replied by wire and by mail. "I must take things as I find them," he said in the letter. "I find the forces divided, and I wish to unite them. Only one feasible plan has been presented for doing this. If you or anyone else had presented a better plan I certainly should have adopted it. But all of your plans require reinforcements, which it is impossible to give you. It is very easy to ask for reinforcements, but it is not so easy to give them when you have no disposable troops at your command." The telegram, being briefer, was more to the point. After saying, "You cannot regret the order of withdrawal more than I did the necessity of giving it," Halleck put an end to the discussion: "It will not be rescinded and you will be expected to execute it with all possible promptness." Next day, August 7 — the date of Lee's letter urging Jackson to consider a strike at Pope — the need for haste was emphasized in a second wire received by the harassed commander at Harrison's Landing. "I must beg of you, General, to hurry along this movement," Halleck told him. "Your reputation as well as mine may be involved in its rapid execution."

Left with neither voice nor choice in the matter, McClellan worked hard to speed the evacuation. But he wrote his wife: "They are committing a fatal error in withdrawing me from here, and the future will show it. I think the result of their machination will be that Pope will be badly thrashed within ten days, and that they will be very glad to turn over the redemption of their affairs to me."

★ ★ ★   *T*he danger, the crying need for haste as Halleck saw it, was that Lee might take advantage of his interior lines and attack one or the other of the two main Federal forces before the northward shift began, or, worse still, while the movement was in progress. Of the two — Pope on the Rappahannock and McClellan on the James — Old Brains was most concerned about the former. As he put it to McClellan, who was struggling to extract his troops from the malarial Peninsula bottoms, "This delay might not only be fatal to the health of your army, but in the meantime General Pope's forces would be exposed to the heavy blows of the enemy without the slightest hope of assistance from you."

Pope was worried too, although he did not let it show in his manner. Privately he was complaining to Halleck about "the supineness of the Army of the Potomac," which he said "renders it easy for the enemy to reinforce Jackson heavily," and he urged: "Please make McClellan do something." Publicly, however, he showed no symptoms of doubt or trepidation. On August 8, when he transferred his headquarters southward to Culpeper, Halleck wired him uneasily: "Do not advance, so as to expose yourself to any disaster, unless you can better your line of defense, until we can get more troops upon the Rappahannock. . . . You must be very cautious." Pope seemed unalarmed; he appeared, in fact, not to have a single cautious bone in his whole body. He intended to hold where he was, despite the risk involved in the knowledge that Stonewall Jackson was before him with a force he estimated at 30,000 men.

Numerically, as of early August, his confidence was well founded. Exclusive of Burnside, whose 12,000 had debarked at Aquia and were now at Falmouth, he had 77,779 soldiers in the Army of Virginia. Even after deducting the troops in the Washington fortifications, along with those in the Shenandoah Valley and beyond, he was left with just over 56,000 in the eight divisions of infantry and two brigades of cavalry comprising the three corps under McDowell, Banks, and Sigel. This was the field force proper, and it seemed ample for the execution of the project he had conceived at the outset. His intention had been to operate southward down the Orange & Alexandria to Gordonsville and beyond, thereby menacing the Virginia Central so that Lee would weaken the Richmond defenses to the point where McClellan could make a successful assault. McClellan's pending withdrawal would alter at least a part of this, of course, but Pope still thought the plan a good one: not the least of its advantages being that it had the approval and support of the Administration, since it simultaneously covered Washington. What was more, his assignment — formerly minor, or anyhow secondary — now became major. Instead of setting Richmond up for capture by McClellan, he would take the place himself and be known thereafter as the man who broke the back of the rebellion. That was a thought to warm the heart. He would consolidate his gains, then proceed with his advance, reinforced by such numbers as reached him from the Army of the Potomac.

At present, it was true, his striking force was rather scattered. More than a third of McDowell's corps — 11,000 infantry, with 30 guns and about 500 cavalry — was still at Fredericksburg, under Brigadier General Rufus King, blocking the direct approach to Washington. Now that Burnside had arrived, Pope might have summoned King to join him, but just now he preferred to keep him where he was, menacing Jackson's supply line and playing on Lee's fears for the safety of his capital. Besides, he felt strong enough without him.

★

Banks and Sigel had come eastward through the passes of the Blue Ridge, and though their five divisions had not been consolidated, either with each other or with McDowell's two, Pope still had better than 44,000 troops with which to oppose the estimated 30,000 rebels in his immediate front. The situation was not without its dangers: Halleck kept saying so, at any rate, and old General Wool, transferred from Fort Monroe to Maryland, had warned him at the outset: "Jackson is an enterprising officer. Delays are dangerous." But Pope was not alarmed. If the highly touted Stonewall wanted a fight, at those odds, he would gladly accommodate him.

Banks felt the same way about it, only more so; for while Pope intended to earn a reputation here in the East, Banks was determined to retrieve one. On August 8, therefore, he was pleased to receive at Culpeper an order directing him to march his two divisions south: Jackson had crossed the Rapidan, moving north, and Pope wanted Banks to delay him while the rest of the army was being assembled to give him the battle he seemed to be seeking. Banks did not hesitate. McDowell and Sigel were behind him; King was on the way from Fredericksburg. Next morning, eight hot and dusty miles out of Culpeper, he came under long-range artillery fire from the slopes of a lone peak called Cedar Mountain, and pressing on found rebel infantry disposed in strength about its northern base and in the woods and fields off to the right. After more than two months of brooding over the shocks of May, he was face to face with the old Valley adversary whose soldiers had added insult to injury by giving him the nickname "Commissary" Banks.

He was itching to attack, then and there, but in the face of the known odds — he was down to about 8000 men as a result of multiple detachments, while Jackson was reported to have at least three times that many — he did not feel free to do so on his own responsibility. Then a courier arrived from Culpeper, a staff colonel sent by Pope with a verbal message which seemed to authorize an immediate all-out attack. (The officer's name was Louis Marshall, a Union-loyal Virginian and a nephew of R. E. Lee, who had said of him: "I could forgive [his] fighting against us, but not his joining Pope.") Welcome as the message was, Banks could scarcely believe his ears. In fact, he had it written down and then read back for verification:

> *General Banks will move to the front immediately,*
>
> *assume command of all the forces in the front,*
>
> *deploy his skirmishers if the enemy approaches, and*
>
> *attack him immediately as soon as he approaches,*
>
> *and be reinforced from here.*

This ambiguous farrago, dictated by Lee's nephew in the name of Pope, was open to conflicting interpretations. It might mean that the attack was to be made with skirmishers only, holding the main body on the defensive until McDowell arrived to even the odds and Sigel came up to stretch them in favor of the Union. On the other hand, it might mean what it said in the words that were quickest to catch the eye: "Attack him immediately as soon as he approaches." That sounded like the army commander who three weeks ago had admonished his generals "to seek the adversary and to beat him when he was found." At any rate, whatever the odds, Banks took him at his word. He put his men in attack formation and sent them forward, on the left and on the right.

★ ★ ★   **Lee's letter of August 7, recommending a swipe at Pope, had not been needed;** for while he was writing it Jackson was already putting his 25,000 soldiers in motion to carry out the strategy it suggested. His cavalry having reported the superior enemy forces badly scattered beyond the Rapidan, he hoped to make a rapid march across that stream, pounce on one of the isolated segments, and withdraw Valley-style before Pope could concentrate against him. So far, it had not worked at all that way, however — primarily because another letter of Lee's, while needed, had not been heeded. A. P. Hill was kept as much in the dark as to his chief's intentions as Winder and Ewell had ever been. "I pledge you my word, Doctor," the latter told an inquiring chaplain before the movement got under way, "I do not know whether we march north, south, east or west, or whether we will march at all. General Jackson has simply ordered me to have the division ready to move at dawn. I have been ready ever since, and have no further indication of his plans. That is almost all I ever know of his designs."

Stonewall was still Stonewall, especially when secrecy was involved, and no one — not even Robert E. Lee, of whom he said: "I am willing to follow him blindfolded" — was going to change him. The result, as Lee had feared, was mutual resentment and mistrust. Not only did Jackson not "consult" with his red-haired lieutenant, whose so-called Light Division was as large as the other two combined; he rode him unmercifully for every slight infraction of the rules long since established for the Army of the Valley. Consequently, glad as he had been to get away from Longstreet, Hill began to suspect that he had leaped from the frying pan into the fire. Resentment bred confusion, and confusion mounted quickly toward a climax in the course of the march northward against Pope. Having reached Orange in good order the first day, August 7, Jackson issued instructions for the advance across the Rapidan tomorrow, which would place his army in position for a strike at Culpeper the following day. The order of march would be Ewell, Hill, Winder; so he said; but during the night he changed his mind and told Ewell to take an alternate road. Unin-

Captain Joseph M. Knapp's Pennsylvania
Battery duels with Rebel batteries on
the slope of Cedar Mountain.

formed of the change, Hill had his men lined up next morning on the outskirts of town, waiting for Ewell to take the lead. That was where Jackson found him. Angry at the delay, he rebuked him and passed Winder to the front. The result was further delay and a miserable showing, complicated by Federal cavalry probing at his wagon train. Ewell made barely eight miles before sundown, Winder about half that, and Hill was less than two miles out of Orange when the army halted for the night. Jackson was furious. So was Hill. Ewell fretted. Winder was down with fever, riding in an ambulance despite his doctor's orders that he leave the field entirely. Several men had died of sunstroke, and the rest took their cue from their commanders, grumbling at the way they had been shuffled about in the dust and heat.

Overnight, Jackson's wrath turned to gloom. The fast-stepping Army of the Valley, formerly such a close-stitched organization, seemed to be coming apart at the seams. Rising next morning to resume the march, he informed Lee: "I am not making much progress. . . . Today I do not expect much more than to close up [the column] and clear the country around the train of the enemy's cavalry. I fear that the expedition will, in consequence of my tardy movements, be productive of but little good."

Ewell had the lead; Winder was in close support; Hill was marching hard to close the gap. The morning wore on, hot as yesterday. Noon came and went. Presently, up ahead, there was the boom of guns, and word came back to Jackson that the Federals were making a stand, apparently with horse artillery. He rode forward and made a brief reconnaissance. This was piedmont country, rolling, heavily wooded except for scattered fields of grain. The bluecoats did not appear to be present in strength, but there was no real telling: Jackson decided to wait for Hill before advancing. Off to the right was Cedar Mountain, obviously the key to the position. Ewell was told to put his batteries there and his infantry below them, along the northern base; Winder would take position on the left in order to overlap the Yankee line when the signal was given to go forward. There was no hurry. It was now past 2 o'clock and Culpeper was eight miles away: too far, in any event, for an attack to be made on it today. Jackson went onto the porch of a nearby farmhouse and lay down to take a nap.

Meanwhile the artillery duel continued, the Union guns firing accurately and fast. This was clearly something more than a mere delaying action staged by cavalry; there was infantry out there beyond the woods, though in what strength could not be told. Manifestly weak, pale as his shirt — he was in fact in his shirt sleeves — Winder had left his ambulance, ignoring the doctor's protests, put his troops in line, extending the left as instructed, and then had joined his batteries, observing their fire with binoculars and calling out corrections for the gunners. It was now about 4 o'clock. An officer went down alongside him, clipped on the head by a fragment of shell; another was eviscerated by a jagged splinter; a third was struck in the rump by an unexploded ricochet and hurled ten feet, though he suffered only bruises as a result. Then came Winder's turn. Tall and wavy-haired, he kept his post, and as he continued to direct the counter-battery fire, calm and cool-looking in his shirt sleeves, with the binoculars held to his eyes, a shell came screaming at him, crashing through his left arm and tearing off most of the ribs on that side of his chest. He fell straight back and lay full length on the ground, quivering spasmodically.

"General, do you know me?" a staff lieutenant asked, bending over the sufferer in order to be heard above the thunder of the guns.

Stern and aristocratic, Stonewall Brigade commander Charles S. Winder never gained his men's affection.

"Oh yes," Winder said vaguely, and his mind began to wander. The guns were bucking and banging all around him, but he was back at home again in Maryland. In shock, he spoke disconnectedly of his wife and children until a chaplain came and knelt beside him, seeking to turn his thoughts from worldly things.

"General, lift up your head to God."

"I do," Winder said calmly. "I do lift it up to him."

Carried to the rear, he died just at sundown, asking after the welfare of his men, and those who were with him were hard put for a comforting answer. By then the fury of the Union assault had crashed against his lines, which had broken in several places. Jackson's plan for outflanking the enemy on the left had miscarried; it was he who was outflanked in that direction. The sudden crash of musketry, following close on the news that Winder had been mangled by a shell, brought him off the farmhouse porch and into the saddle. He rode hard toward the left, entering a moil of fugitives who had given way in panic when the bluecoats emerged roaring from the cover of the woods. Drawing his sword — a thing no one had ever seen him do before in battle — he brandished it above his head and called out hoarsely: "Rally, brave men, and press forward! Your general will lead you; Jackson will lead you! Follow me!"

This had an immediate effect, for the sight was as startling in its way as the unexpected appearance of the Federals had been. The men halted in their tracks, staring open-mouthed, and then began to rally in response to the cries of their officers, echoing Stonewall, who was finally persuaded to retire out of range of the bullets twittering round him. "Good, good," he said as he turned back, Winder's successor having assured him that the Yankees would be stopped. Whether this promise could have been kept in the face of another assault was another matter, but fortunately by now the battle was moving in the opposite direction: A. P. Hill had arrived with the Light Division. Opening ranks to let the fugitives through, Little Powell's veterans swamped the blue attackers, flung them back on their reserves, and pursued them northward through the gathering twilight. So quickly, after the manner of light fiction, had victory been snatched from the flames of defeat, if not disaster.

Thankful as Jackson was for this deliverance, he was by no means satisfied. Banks had escaped him once before; he did not intend to let him get away again. A full moon was rising, and he ordered the chase continued by its light. Whenever resistance was encountered he passed his guns to the front, shelled the woods, and then resumed the pursuit, gathering shell-dazed prisoners as he went. Four hundred bluecoats were captured in all, bringing the total Federal losses to 2381; Jackson himself had lost 1276. At last, however, receiving word from his cavalry that the enemy had been heavily reinforced, he called a halt within half a dozen miles of Culpeper and passed the word for his men to sleep on their arms in line of battle. He himself rode back toward Cedar Mountain,

★

seeking shelter at roadside houses along the way. At each he was told that he was welcome but that the wounded filled the rooms. Finally he drew rein beside a grassy plot, dismounted stiffly, and lay face down on the turf, wrapped in a borrowed cloak. When a staff officer asked if he wanted something to eat: "No," he groaned, "I want rest: nothing but rest," and was soon asleep.

Sunday, August 10, dawned hot and humid, the quiet broken only by the moans and shrieks of the injured, blue and gray, presently augmented by their piteous cries for water as the sun rose burning, stiffening their wounds. Surgeons and aid men passed among them, and burial details came along behind. The scavengers were active, too, gleaning the field of arms and equipment; as usual, Old Blue Light wanted all he could lay hands on. Thus the morning wore away, and not a shot was fired. Aware that Sigel and McDowell had arrived to give Pope two whole corps and half of a third — King was still on the way from Fredericksburg, where Burnside was on call — Jackson would not deliver a Sabbath attack; but he was prepared to receive one, whatever the odds, so long as there were wounded men to be cared for and spoils to be loaded into his wagons. That afternoon, as always seemed to be the

A mounted Union officer chides Confederates for gathering arms under a flag of truce after the Battle of Cedar Mountain.

case on the morrow of a battle, the weather broke. There were long peals of thunder, followed by rain. Jackson held his ground, and the various details continued their work into the night.

Next morning a deputation of Federal horsemen came forward under a flag of truce, proposing an armistice for the removal of the wounded. Jackson gladly agreed; for King's arrival that night would give Pope better than twice as many troops as he himself had, and this would afford him additional time in which to prepare for the withdrawal he now knew was necessary. While the soldiers of both armies mingled on the field

5ᵗʰ REGT. C. V.

This flag of the 5th Connecticut was among several colors captured by the Confederates at Cedar Mountain.

where they had fought, he finished packing his wagons and got off a message to Lee: "God blessed our arms with another victory." When darkness came he lighted campfires all along his front, stole away southward under cover of their burning, and recrossed the Rapidan, unmolested, unpursued.

Another victory, he called it: not without justification. He had inflicted a thousand more casualties than he suffered, and for two days after the battle he had remained in control of the field. Yet there were other aspects he ignored. Banks had done to him what he had tried to do to Shields at Kernstown, and what was more had done it with considerably greater success, even apart from the initial rout; for in the end it was Stonewall who retreated. But now that the roles were reversed he applied a different set of standards. Privately, according to his chief of staff, he went so far as to refer to Cedar Mountain as "the most successful of his exploits." Few would agree with him in this, however, even among the men in his own army. They had been mishandled and they knew it. Outnumbering the enemy three to one on the field of fight, he had been careless in reconnaissance, allowing his troops to be outflanked while he drowsed on a farmhouse veranda, and had swung into vigorous action only after his left wing had been shattered. Following as it did his sorry performance throughout the Seven Days, the recrossing of the Rapidan gave point to a question now being asked: Had Stonewall lost his touch? "Arrogant" was the word applied by some. Others remarked that his former triumphs had been scored against second-raters out in the Valley, "but when pitted against the best of the Federal commanders he did not appear so well." Then too, there had always been those who considered him crazy — crazy and, so far, lucky. Give him "a month uncontrolled," one correspondent declared, "and he would destroy himself and all under him."

★

Time perhaps would show who was right, the general or his critics, but for the present at least two other men derived particular satisfaction from the battle and its outcome, despite the fact that they viewed it from opposite directions. One of the two was A. P. Hill. Still fuming because of the undeserved rebuke he had received on the outskirts of Orange the day before, he had marched toward the sound of firing and reached the field to find his tormentor face to face with disaster. After opening his ranks to let the fugitives through — including hundreds from the Stonewall Brigade itself — he had launched the counterattack that saved the day and provided whatever factual basis there was for Jackson's claim to "another victory." Revenge was seldom sweeter; Hill enjoyed it to the full.

The other satisfied observer was John Pope, who celebrated his eastern debut as a fighting man by publishing, for the encouragement of his army, Halleck's personal congratulations "on your hard earned but brilliant success against vastly superior numbers. Your troops have covered themselves with glory." Pope thought so too, now, although at first he had experienced definite twinges of anxiety and doubt. Alarmed by what had happened to Banks as a result of misinterpreting the verbal message garbled by Lee's nephew, he had hastened to assemble his eight divisions (including King's, which arrived Monday evening to give him well over 50,000 men) for a renewal of the contest on the morning after the armistice expired. While Jackson was stealing away in the darkness behind a curtain of blazing campfires, Pope was wiring Halleck: "The enemy has been receiving reinforcements all day. . . . I think it almost certain that we shall be attacked in the morning, and we shall make the best fight we can." This did not sound much like the belligerent commander who had urged his subordinates to "discard such ideas" as the one of " 'taking strong positions and holding them.' " However, when he found Stonewall gone with the dawn he recovered his former tone and notified Halleck: "The enemy has retreated under cover of the night. . . . Our cavalry and artillery are in pursuit. I shall follow with the infantry as far as the Rapidan." Now it was Halleck's turn to be alarmed. "Beware of a snare," he quickly replied. "Feigned retreats are secesh tactics."

But he need not have worried; not just yet. Pope was content to follow at a distance, and when he reached the near bank of the Rapidan he stopped as he had said he would do. Presently he fell back toward Culpeper, pausing along the way to publish Halleck's congratulations. He was "delighted and astonished," he told his soldiers, at their "gallant and intrepid conduct." Whatever their reaction to this astonishment might be, he went on to venture a prophecy: "Success and glory are sure to accompany such conduct, and it is safe to predict that Cedar Mountain is only the first in a series of victories which shall make the Army of Virginia famous in the land."

★ ★ ★

Epilogue

───── ⌒ ─────

The sun indeed seemed to be shining on the South. Although the North still held the extremes of the Mississippi River, the ill-fated C.S.S. *Arkansas* had reclaimed a section of the river's central stretch. Withdrawn southward through western Kentucky and Tennessee and into Mississippi, the Confederates had managed to consolidate their forces, use their shorter interior lines, and move into the heartland around Chattanooga, where they could and did threaten Federal holdings. Lightning cavalry raids by Forrest and Morgan devastated vital Union communications lines between Corinth, Mississippi, and Cumberland Gap. Jackson's "foot cavalry" in the Shenandoah Valley marched circles around three separate Federal commands, outmaneuvering, bewildering, and beating them at every turn. Stonewall's Valley campaign had hampered McClellan's march up the York-James peninsula by threatening the Federal capital and causing Lincoln and Halleck to withhold troops and supplies from McClellan's drive. "Prince John" Magruder's theatrics, coupled with a few stubborn rear-guard actions, slowed McClellan's advance while allowing the rebels to withdraw into a concentrated defensive line astride the Chickahominy River, a few miles outside Richmond. There the two sides slugged it out to an inconclusive draw, during which Confederate commander Joe Johnston was wounded and Robert E. Lee was pulled from behind his desk as Davis's military adviser and given command of the army in the field. Over the next Seven Days, McClellan would attempt side step after side step toward the south, effecting what he defined as a "change of base" to the James River. Lee, supported by Jackson's recently arrived units, countered McClellan's every move. Neither side fought very well in this running string of bloody clashes. On the Seventh Day, with their backs against the James, Federal artillery atop Malvern Hill mangled Confederate attackers struggling to finish the retreaters off. No great victory had been won by either side, and both were exhausted and disorganized. McClellan went into camp at Harrison's Landing and Lee regrouped, considering his options.

Lee, however, was given little time to plan. Federal forces under John Pope were moving southward against Richmond. Jackson headed north to counter the threat, and he countered it well at Cedar Mountain, sending Pope's army scurrying back toward Washington. Lee, eventually convinced that McClellan was withdrawing, moved north to join Jackson in an attack on the Union bases near Centreville and Manassas before McClellan could bring his forces to bear up northward. The result was a blistering Confederate victory on, and a chaotic Federal skedaddle from, the plains of Manassas — a Second Bull Run.

The gray-clad forces were victorious, the nearest blue-clads were in disarray, and most of McClellan's troops were still en route. Facing a disorganized and dispersed enemy, the rebels could go almost anywhere they wished. By early September the crops in the Valley and the rest of Virginia were nearly ready for harvest. Pressure on northern soil would allow that harvest to go unmolested and assure much-needed foodstuffs for the Confederate cause. Europeans still refused to declare for the South; an attack on Washington, Baltimore, or perhaps even Philadelphia might convince them to recognize the Confederacy. Then Lee and Davis decided to abandon their defensive strategy and invade the North.

Lee moved quickly. He crossed the Potomac into Maryland and reinforced Jackson to seize the Federal garrison at Harpers Ferry while the rest of his army, split in two for faster travel, used the Appalachians of northwestern Maryland as a screen for their movements. But the Union moved quickly too. Surprisingly, McClellan took little time reorganizing his army and setting off in pursuit of the invaders. He met tough resistance at South Mountain, which slowed him enough to give Lee time to reunite his forces on high ground along Antietam Creek near Sharpsburg. There, on September 17, the two armies clashed in what would become the single bloodiest day in American history. Throughout the following day the two exhausted sides watched each other across the Antietam, each expecting the other to attack. But neither did. That night, Lee withdrew across the Potomac back into Virginia, his invasion over. McClellan failed to pursue.

The Federal West was being invaded as well. In mid-August Kirby Smith moved out of Knoxville into central Kentucky and toward Cincinnati but was stopped at Frankfort in early October. Meanwhile, Bragg left Chattanooga and drove his forces toward Louisville. He was stopped at Perryville, and then followed Kirby Smith's line of retreat southward.

Confederate invasions East and West had been stymied, but the gray armies had not been destroyed. The South would fight on, but the very nature of the war had changed. After Antietam, Lincoln's highly symbolic yet somewhat hollow emancipation of slaves in territories over which he held no control changed the perceived reason for the war from being purely political — national power versus states' rights — to a moral imperative: freedom for the slaves.

★   ★   ★

Picture Credits

The sources for the illustrations are listed below. Credits from left to right are separated by semicolons, from top to bottom by dashes.

Dust jacket: Front, Library of Congress, Neg. No. USZ 262-47759; rear, Library of Congress, Neg. No. B8184-10006; flap, Larry Shirkey. 8-10: Library of Congress. 14: Library of Congress, Neg. No. 25302. 17: Map by Peter McGinn. 19: Civil War Photograph Album, Louisiana and Lower Mississippi Valley Collections, LSU Libraries, Louisiana State University, Baton Rouge. 21: Courtesy Vermont Historical Society, Montpelier. 26: Library of Congress, Neg. No. B8171-656. 29: Massachusetts Commandery Military Order of the Loyal Legion and the U.S. Army Military History Institute, Carlisle Barracks, Pa. (MASS-MOLLUS/USAMHI), copied by Robert Walch. 32, 33: Library of Congress, Waud #760D. 39: Department of the Navy/Naval Historical Center, Washington, D.C. 43: Private collection, copied by Evan H. Sheppard. 46-48: MASS-MOLLUS/USAMHI, copied by A. Pierce Bounds. 51: Map by R. R. Donnelley & Sons Co., Cartographic Services. 54: MASS-MOLLUS/USAMHI, copied by Robert Walch. 58: Courtesy Frank and Marie-Thérèse Wood Print Collections, Alexandria, Va. 63: The Valentine Museum, Richmond, photographed by Larry Sherer. 66: Map by Walter W. Roberts. 72: Library of Congress, Waud #180. 76: MASS-MOLLUS/USAMHI, copied by A. Pierce Bounds. 78: The Valentine Museum, Richmond. 80: The Valentine Museum, Richmond—The Museum of the Confederacy, Richmond, photographed by Larry Sherer. 84, 85: Library of Congress, Forbes #027A. 90: National Archives, Neg. No. 111-BA-1568. 93: Map by Walter W. Roberts. 96, 97: Library of Congress, Forbes #026a. 100-102: Library of Congress, Neg. No. B8171 7383. 107, 110: The Gilder Lehrman Collection at the Pierpont Morgan Library, New York. 113: Courtesy Frank and Marie-Thérèse Wood Print Collections, Alexandria, Va. 116: MASS-MOLLUS/USAMHI, copied by A. Pierce Bounds. 118: Library of Congress, Waud #407. 120-122: National Archives, Neg. No. 90.CM.497. 125: Old Court House Museum, Vicksburg, Miss. 127: Library of Congress, Waud #652. 130: Map by Walter W.

Roberts. 135: From The Photographic History of the Civil War, Vol. 10, The Review of Reviews Co., New York, 1912. 136: Courtesy Commonwealth of Massachusetts, Bureau of State Office Buildings, photograph by Douglas Christian (#1987.378). 140: Library of Congress, Waud Collection. 144: MASS-MOLLUS/USAMHI, copied by A. Pierce Bounds. 150: From *The Photographic History of the Civil War*, Vol. 10, The Review of Reviews Co., New York, 1912. 155: The Museum of the Confederacy, Richmond, photographed by Larry Sherer. 156, 157: Library of Congress, Waud #746 (B). 161: M. and M. Karolik Collection, courtesy of Museum of Fine Arts, Boston. 168: Library of Congress, Waud #116. 170-172: Library of Congress, Neg. No. BS171 622. 178: Library of Congress, Neg. No. B8172 2136. 183: Library of Congress, Neg. No. 262-32540. 186: Rosemonde E. and Emile Kuntz Collection, Manuscripts Department, Tulane University Library, New Orleans. 189: Courtesy James Mellon Collection. 191: From *The Photographic History of the Civil War*, Vol. 10, The Review of Reviews Co., New York, 1912. 192, 193: G. H. Suydam Collection, Louisiana and Lower Mississippi Valley Collections, LSU Libraries, Louisiana State University, Baton Rouge. 196-198: The Western Reserve Historical Society, Cleveland. 201: Map by Peter McGinn. 204, 205: From *The Photographic History of The Civil War*, Vol. 2, The Review of Reviews Co., New York, 1911. 207: From The Photographic History of the Civil War, Vol. 6, The Review of Reviews Co., New York, 1911. 211: From *Battles and Leaders of the Civil War*, Vol. 3, edited by Robert Underwood Johnson and Clarence Clough Buel, The Century Company, New York, 1887. 216: Civil War Times Illustrated Collection. 219: Painting by A. O. Revenought, Tennessee State Museum, photographed by Bill LaFevor. 224, 225: Courtesy Frank & Marie-Thérèse Wood Print Collections, Alexandria, Va. 226: From *The Photographic History of the Civil War*, Vol. 10, The Review of Reviews Co., New York, 1912. 230-232: Andrew D. Lytle Collection, Louisiana and Lower Mississippi Valley Collections, LSU Libraries, Louisiana State University, Baton Rouge. 235: Confederate Memorial Hall, photographed by Bill van Calsem. 237: Kentucky

Military History Museum, photographed by Mary S. Rezny. 243: Library of Congress, Neg. No. B8172-2013. 246: The Valentine Museum, Richmond. 250, 251: Courtesy The Historic New Orleans Collection, Acc. No. 19479. 254-256: Library of Congress, Neg. No. B8171 523K. 261: Library of Congress, Neg. No. 3217 B871. 263: Alderman Library/University of Virginia, photo by Henry Mintz. 268: Courtesy Frank & Marie-

Thérèse Wood Print Collections, Alexandria, Va. 274: Library of Congress. 275: From *The Photographic History of the Civil War,* Vol. 10, The Review of Reviews Co., New York, 1912. 277: M. and M. Karolik Collection, courtesy Museum of Fine Arts, Boston. 278: Courtesy of State of Connecticut General Assembly, Joint Committee on Legislative Management, photographed by Gus Johnson.

Index

SHELBY FOOTE, THE CIVIL WAR,
A NARRATIVE
VOLUME 3 YORKTOWN TO
CEDAR MOUNTAIN

Library of Congress Cataloging-in-Publication Data
Foote, Shelby.
  [Civil War, a narrative]
  Shelby Foote, the Civil War, a narrative/ by Shelby
Foote and the editors of Time-Life Books.— 40th
Anniversary ed.
    p. cm.
    Originally published: The Civil War, a narrative.
New York: Random House. 1958-1974. in 3 v.
    Includes bibliographical references and indexes.
    Contents: v. 3 Yorktown to Cedar Mountain
    1.United States—History—Civil War, 1861-1865.
I. Time-Life Books. II. Title.
E468.F7   1999   99-13486
973.7—dc21   CIP
ISBN 0-7835-0102-1

R 10 9 8 7 6 5 4 3 2 1

For information on and a full description of any
of the Time-Life Books series listed at right, please
call 1-800-621-7026 or write:

Reader Information
Time-Life Customer Service
P.O. Box C-32068
Richmond, Virginia 23261-2068

 Time-Life Books is a
division of Time Life Inc.

TIME LIFE INC.
PRESIDENT and CEO: George Artandi

TIME-LIFE BOOKS
PUBLISHER/MANAGING EDITOR: Neil Kagan
SENIOR VICE PRESIDENT, MARKETING:
Joseph A. Kuna
VICE PRESIDENT, NEW PRODUCT
DEVELOPMENT: Amy Golden

PROJECT EDITOR: Philip Brandt George
DIRECTOR, NEW PRODUCT
DEVELOPMENT: Elizabeth D. Ward
DIRECTOR OF MARKETING: Pamela R. Farrell
Deputy Editor: Harris J. Andrews
Design Director: Barbara M. Sheppard
Marketing Manager: Peter Tardif
Copyeditor: Christine Stephenson
Photo Coordinator: Susan L. Finken
Editorial Assistant: Patricia D. Whiteford

Special Contributors: Matt Baumgardner, John
Drummond, Kimberly Grandcolas, Janet Dell Russell
Johnson, Monika Lynde (design and production);
Anne Farr (copyediting); Christine Higgins
(administration); Roy Nanovic (index).

Correspondent: Christina Lieberman (New York).

Director of Finance: Christopher Hearing
Directors of Book Production: Marjann Caldwell,
Patricia Pascale
Director of Publishing Technology: Betsi McGrath
Director of Photography and Research:
John Conrad Weiser
Director of Editorial Administration: Barbara Levitt
Manager, Technical Services: Anne Topp
Senior Production Manager: Ken Sabol
Quality Assurance Manager: James King
Chief Librarian: Louise D. Forstall

Separations by the Time-Life Imaging Department

OTHER TIME-LIFE HISTORY PUBLICATIONS

★